Tears of laughter

MANCHESTER
1824

Manchester University Press

Tears of laughter

Comedy-drama in 1990s British cinema

Nigel Mather

Manchester University Press

Manchester and New York

distributed exclusively in the USA by Palgrave

Published by Manchester University Press
Oxford Road, Manchester M13 9NR, UK
and Room 400, 175 Fifth Avenue, New York, NY 10010, USA
www.manchesteruniversitypress.co.uk

Distributed exclusively in the USA by
Palgrave, 175 Fifth Avenue, New York,
NY 10010, USA

Distributed exclusively in Canada by
UBC Press, University of British Columbia, 2029 West Mall,
Vancouver, BC, Canada V6T 1Z2

British Library Cataloguing-in-Publication Data
A catalogue record for this book is available from the British Library

Library of Congress Cataloging-in-Publication Data applied for

ISBN   0 7190 7076 7   *hardback*
EAN   978 0 7190 7076 1
ISBN   0 7190 7077 5   *paperback*
EAN   978 0 7190 7077 8

First published 2006

14 13 12 11 10 09 08 07 06   10 9 8 7 6 5 4 3 2 1

Typeset
by Northern Phototypesetting Co Ltd, Bolton
Printed in Great Britain
by Bell & Bain Ltd, Glasgow

Contents

Illustrations

Acknowledgements

The University of Kent in Canterbury has provided a friendly and stimulating environment for the writing of this book. The Kent University Templeman library, and the British Film Institute library in London have provided excellent help with research facilities and materials. Sincere thanks are due to members of the Film Studies Faculty at Kent, and to friends and colleagues such as Barnaby Taylor, Gary Bettinson and William Collier. I have benefited enormously from attending a yearly Film Summer School at Oxford University since 1992, and being taught by Dr Anthony Aldgate, Jim Hillier and Brian Spittles. Brian has proved to be an inspirational figure, and his courses are always immensely stimulating and enjoyable.

Special thanks to Dr Catherine Grant, Director of Film Studies at Kent University, for the invaluable insights and observations offered on earlier drafts of my research into developments within British cinema, and for allowing me to attend her excellent course on 1990s romantic comedy. Dr Sarah Cardwell, Senior Lecturer in Film and Television Studies at Kent University, and Robert Murphy, Professor of Film Studies at De Montfort University in Leicester, also made many helpful suggestions. I am grateful to Sara Peacock for her diligent copy-editing, and to Matthew Frost and everyone at Manchester University Press for their support.

For the use of stills provided by the British Film Institute Stills Department, I would like to thank the following for permission: Canal + Image UK Ltd for *Till Death Us Do Part* and *Love Thy Neighbour*, MGM for *Four Weddings and a Funeral*, Channel Four for *Brassed Off* and *East is East*, Twentieth Century Fox for *The Full Monty* and Universal *for Notting Hill* and *Love Actually*. Every effort has been made to obtain permission to reproduce the images in this book. If any proper acknowledgement has not been made, copyright holders are invited to contact the publisher.

The book is dedicated to my family, and to the memory of my mother, Thelma Mather (1924–2004), and the happy times we spent watching films together.

Introduction
'Tears of laughter':
comedy-drama in 1990s British cinema

This study of British cinema will explore the interactions of comedy *and* drama within a group of significant and influential films released during the decade of the 1990s. The opening chapter, '"Things can only get better . . . ": comedies of class, culture and community', will examine a group of British films from this period which engage with economic and social issues in unusual and compelling ways. The chapter concludes with case studies of *Brassed Off* (Mark Herman, 1996) and *The Full Monty* (Peter Cattaneo, 1997), two films invoking very different cultural traditions as possible activities for unemployed males and troubled communities in modern British society.

Chapter 2 discusses a number of contemporary British films focusing upon the experiences of British-Asian and African-Caribbean characters and their efforts to feel 'at home' in Western and British society. This section of the book features an extensive analysis of *East is East* (Damien O'Donnell, 1999), a comedy-drama about the cultural and ideological tensions surfacing between members of a British-Asian family living in Salford, circa 1971. The differences of opinion between mother and father and their children lead to situations which are both funny and unsettling.

Chapter 3 explores the emergence of romantic comedy as a popular genre in 1990s British cinema, and includes case studies of *Four Weddings and a Funeral* (Mike Newell, 1994), *Notting Hill* (Roger Michell, 1999) and *Love Actually* (Richard Curtis, 2003). These films are indicative of attempts by British film producers during the decade to forge closer working relationships between British and American film production companies, and to demonstrate that British cinema was capable of producing films with wide international appeal. The comic aspects of both *Four Weddings* and *Notting Hill* emerge, however, from a sense that the English male (as personified by Hugh Grant) is not necessarily emotionally compatible with the modern American woman (as represented by Andie MacDowell and Julia Roberts, respectively), implying, perhaps, that a rapprochement between the creative tendencies and more typical features of Hollywood and British national cinemas would not be easily achieved, or seamlessly maintained.

Love Actually (although it is a post-1990s film) will be considered as a narrative which appears to offer a sort of 'ultimate' treatment and summation of themes and motifs explored in the previous two highly successful films. *Love Actually* is also fascinating for the manner in which Hugh Grant's character is elevated to the position of a British Prime Minister, who is revealed to be more concerned with the state of his love life than the 'state of the nation': an interesting situation given the criticisms voiced in films such as *Brassed Off* about the uncaring and irresponsible nature of recent British governments.

The book will investigate the ways in which humour is deployed for dramatic and emotional effect in the context of scenarios dealing with such seemingly non-comic subjects as mass unemployment, failed or uneasy relationships, bitter family disputes, or instances of racial tension and conflict in British society. I will seek to demonstrate that the interaction of comic and dramatic modes of narration within the films discussed proved to be a dynamic creative mechanism in 1990s British cinema, facilitating and enabling the construction of innovative and genuinely exploratory narratives about characters who are striving to realise particular aspirations and hopes within a complex culture.

In the entry on comedy in *Key Concepts in Cinema Studies* (1996), Susan Hayward writes that 'Britain has a strong tradition with its Ealing comedies and Carry-On movies. But these are past history (1940s–50s and 1958–78 respectively) – as indeed is the British film industry itself'.[1] My study will contest the latter claims of this statement, and argue that native comic traditions did play a significant role in the considerable achievements of British cinema during the 1990s.

Although the British film industry lacked a studio-based, centrally organised system of production and distribution during this period, filmmakers were influenced by movements and cycles associated with earlier traditions of British film production, such as the Ealing Studios comedy-dramas produced in the 1940s and 1950s, the British 'new wave' films of the early 1960s set in the north of England, and 1970s films based upon popular television situation comedies of the time.

Each of the three main chapters includes a discussion of earlier British films dealing with themes of industrial relations and the importance of regional communities in British society, issues of ethnicity and cultural allegiance, and the difficulties encountered in searching for a suitable long-term or short-term lover and partner.

Chapter 1 considers key examples of community-based comedies and social dramas in British cinema, and proceeds to an examination of their relationship to current-day exemplars of these traditions of British film-making.

The second chapter explores three 1970s British film comedies which treat issues of race and ethnic identity in British society as inherently comical subjects, and from ideological viewpoints which might now be considered racist and objectionable. The influence of such 'disreputable' traditions of humour on 1990s British comedy-dramas dealing with such themes will subsequently be scrutinised. Chapter 3, focusing upon romantic comedy, considers how far such a type of narrative format might be deemed to have played an important role in British film culture prior to the 1990s.

In his book *Dracula* (2003), Peter Hutchings claims that 'despite all the new work being done on British film, evaluative claims are not being made nearly enough'.[2] One way he suggests of countering this short-coming is to examine 'individual films in detail', and to identify how particular films deploy 'the resources of cinema in an imaginative, intelligent and distinctive manner'.[3]

The detailed case studies of *Brassed Off*, *The Full Monty*, *East is East*, *Four Weddings and a Funeral*, *Notting Hill* and *Love Actually* will seek to examine these films within such parameters and guidelines. These films, alongside many others discussed in individual chapters, strike me as major achievements in their own right, and evidence that British cinema underwent a number of exciting transformations during the 1990s, developments which I believe are especially worthy of in-depth study, interpretation and evaluation.

Notes

1 Susan Hayward, *Key Concepts in Cinema Studies* (Routledge, London, 1996), p. 56.
2 Peter Hutchings, *Dracula* (I.B. Tauris, London/New York, 2003), p. 4.
3 *Ibid.*

1

'Things can only get better ...': comedies of class, culture and community[1]

In the *Daily Telegraph* review of *Up 'n' Under* (John Godber, 1998), a belated cinematic adaptation of a play about amateur rugby players first performed in 1984, Chris Peachment noted that 'We have had a minor renaissance of British regional comedies lately . . . in which a team of blokes from some chronically depressed area regain their pride through a healthy burst of team spirit'.[2]

This formulation neatly encapsulates several of the features which distinguish the two most significant movies of this particular cycle of British films: *Brassed Off* (Mark Herman, 1996) and *The Full Monty* (Peter Cattaneo, 1997). Both of these films draw creative inspiration from their northern settings as they follow the tragi-comic fortunes of a group of characters endeavouring to make a success of a specific venture.

Approaching the subject of unemployment in Britain from an ironical or farcical perspective did run the risk of appearing glib, uncaring or facile. Film critic Tom Charity observed in *Time Out* that when he initially heard about the narrative form, style and tone of *Brassed Off*, it sounded to him 'like a bad joke, the kind of thing Ian Carmichael and Terry Thomas churned out with the Boulting Brothers 30 years ago'.[3] The writer and director of *Brassed Off*, Mark Herman, admitted in an interview in the *Weekly Alibi* that a treatment of mass redundancy, conceived and filtered through a comic outlook, could be regarded as socially tactless and ideologically dubious: 'As a writer you get worried that you've done too much caricature. That you've made a comedy about pit closures.'[4]

An interview with Simon Beaufoy, screenwriter of *The Full Monty*, in *Story and Character: Interviews With British Screenwriters* (2003) revealed that the humorous elements pervading *The Full Monty* were part of a calculated attempt to make the film more appealing to a wider audience:

we did sit down and say, 'Let's see if we can make a film about working-class people which working-class people will actually want to watch'. Uberto Pasolini . . . saw that the way to do this was to make it funny. Ken Loach's work has got funnier and funnier over the years, because I think he's realised that comedy is a way of pulling in audiences . . . It's a way of sugaring the pill – and sadly you now have to use more and more sugar.[5]

In the case studies of *Brassed Off* and *The Full Monty*, I will explore some of the important critical and commercial issues raised by the obser-vations of Mark Herman and Simon Beaufoy, in relation to the willing-ness of both films to create humorous and comically absurd moments within the serious subject material – the effects of unemployment on a group of male characters – explored in each film.

In an essay entitled 'The Social Art Cinema: a Moment in the History of British Film and Television Culture' (1996), Christopher Williams identified a strand of prominent filmmaking in British cinema which interrogated and explored conceptions of what he termed 'the social', and involved the construction of narratives dramatising the experiences of 'groups of characters', whose 'emotions, motives and ideas' unfold within 'a version of a social context, which the film usually takes some pains to establish'.[6] Williams concludes that British cinema's interest in notions of community and society constitutes what our national cinema 'has been and is good at doing'.[7]

Brassed Off and *The Full Monty* are both concerned with the rela-tionships between individuals and communities, and the social and eco-nomic state of a particular regional setting. Important examples of native films exploring the nature of industrial and community relations in British society (whilst drawing upon comic and dramatic modes of narration) would include two 1930s films starring Gracie Fields, *Sing As We Go* (Basil Dean, 1934) and *Shipyard Sally* (Monty Banks, 1939), and post-war Ealing comedies such as *Passport to Pimlico* (Henry Cornelius, 1949), *Whisky Galore* (Alexander Mackendrick, 1949) and *The Titfield Thunderbolt* (Charles Crichton, 1953).

Two seminal comedy-dramas, *The Man in the White Suit* (Alexander Mackendrick, 1951) and *I'm All Right Jack* (John Boulting, 1959) were also influential for the ways in which they probed the 'state of the nation' by satirising relationships between management and labour in British society at the beginning and end of the 1950s. The two films explored how notions of community might come into conflict with philosophies concerned to promote the importance of competition in a free-market economy. Laughter amongst viewers of each film can be generated by the 'comical' clashes between idealistic points of view and more cynically held perspectives. *I'm All Right Jack*, as the title indicates, takes place within a largely cynical and opportunistic environment, and *The Man in the White Suit* implies that the excessively idealistic scientist may pose something of a threat to communities, so that the laughter caused by both narratives is not necessarily comforting or celebratory.

As noted by Chris Peachment at the beginning of this chapter, a number of regional comedy-dramas were produced in the 1990s that seemed particularly to have been conceived in the spirit of modern-day Ealing narratives. *The Englishman Who Went Up a Hill But Came Down a Mountain* (Chris Monger, 1995), for instance, was described by Philip French in the *Observer* as a film containing 'a classic Ealing plot – a tight little community making common cause against threats from officious outsiders representing remote, powerful forces'.[8] Tom Hutchinson in the *Hampstead and Highgate Express* summed up *Waking Ned* (Kirk Jones, 1999) as 'A relish of human behaviour which reminded me of nothing so much as an Ealing comedy'.[9] These films (along with *Up 'n' Under*) will be considered in relation to the earlier examples of communal comedy-dramas outlined above, and *Brassed Off* and *The Full Monty*.

Concepts of community, 'comical' cultural clashes and British cinema

In his study *The Country and the City* (1973), Raymond Williams noted that, in pre-industrial Britain, the notion of the country town or village had seemed to offer the prospect of becoming what he described as a 'knowable community'.[10] This term referred to the opportunities for inhabitants of particular settlements to become well acquainted with their fellow neighbours, so that even if the wider world may have been something of a mystery, the immediate 'community' was perceived as a comprehensible and meaningful entity. Social stability, regular interactions between members of a village, and a level of continuity between past and present traditions of community life were, consequently, conceivable features of such societies.

Williams records that the Industrial Revolution went on to change the landscape of Britain both literally and metaphorically. Society became increasingly organised around distinctions between those workers who sold their labour for wages, and those who actually owned the means of production. A corresponding broad division between town and country, and north and south, subsequently emerged in British culture. Raymond Williams suggests that the English novel of the nineteenth century formed a creative outlet for writers to document and respond to these social and economic changes, and to affirm the value of human relationships within a system that could appear in certain respects to be beyond immediate human control and intervention.

All novels in Williams' view involved the construction of micro-communities, based around the interactions and inter-connections between a group of characters – 'the novelist offers to show people and their relationships in essentially knowable and communicable ways'[11] – so that art and fiction now seemed to offer the possibility of 'knowing' and understanding individuals in ways which actual industrialised communities possibly denied. Nonetheless, Williams goes on to record in *The Country and the City* that many English novelists of the nineteenth century found the experience of industrialism and capitalism to be fundamentally tragic in nature and effect. In the novels of Emily Brontë and George Eliot, Raymond Williams detects the presence of what he terms a 'tragic separation between human intensity and any available social settlement', a state of affairs which produces a sense of 'sad resignation' by the close of the narratives.[12]

James F. English in *Comic Transactions: Literature, Humour, and the Politics of Community in Twentieth Century Britain* (1994) explored a similar series of themes within a group of novels inflected by differing strands of British humour. English claims that humour is generated in particular examples of the English novel by what he terms the inherent conflict between the 'inescapable heterogeneity of society' and the 'ceaseless conflict of social life'.[13] English concludes from his studies that 'Comic practice is always on some level . . . an assertion of group against group',[14] leading to the formulation of narrative situations which may be amusing and disturbing in equal proportions.

Simon Critchley in *On Humour* (2002) suggested that 'A sense of humour is often what connects us most strongly to a specific place and leads us to predicate characteristics of that place, assigning certain dispositions and customs to its inhabitants'.[15] Such an observation raises questions about the significance of cultural stereotypes and caricatures within British society. Martin Green in *A Mirror for Anglo-Saxons*, for instance, conjured up a picture of 'The northerner' as 'tougher, blunter, dowdier, warmer than the southerner . . . strongly rooted in himself and his own fireside'.[16] Writing in 1957, Green also claimed that the 'northerner' was capable of being patronised by his southern counterparts: 'The northerner is only a comic, one-dimensional figure; in a film a local accent signalises humorous relief – only characters speaking BBC English are to be taken seriously'.[17]

Charles Barr in an article 'Opening the drama archives' (1976), went so far as to claim that British culture possessed a genre which could be specifically categorised under the heading of the 'northern': 'where America has the western, we have the "northern", featuring a north as mythical . . . as the west . . . an area whose life and values conflict with metropolitan and middle-class culture'.[18] The north of England clearly lacked the epic dimensions or spatial vastness of the American West, but films set in northern Britain did offer the possibility of a fresh perspective on British society at particular historical moments.

The much vaunted 'Angry young man' literary and cinematic movement of the late 1950s and early 1960s was, in part, a regional challenge to a London-based critical and cultural establishment capable of being perceived as distant, elitist and complacent. The films and novels of the 'new wave' movement did not, however, romanticise or sentimentalise their northern, regional settings, and many of the stories revolved around men and women who longed to escape from their surroundings, but were unable to do so because of various social constraints and personal responsibilities.

Prior to the 'new wave' phenomenon of the late 1950s, the northern areas of the United Kingdom had often been represented in a comic manner within British film culture. David Sutton in his study *A Chorus of Raspberries: British Film Comedy 1929–1939* (2000), associates 1930s regional comedies with what he defines as 'working-class' comedy, a type of narrative which he reads as 'dominated' by comic performers, and composed of 'loose organisational structures'[19] and tenuously connected sequences.

Films starring such northern performers as George Formby and Gracie Fields tended to be episodic in form due to the regular insertion of scenes featuring the stars singing directly to the camera. This created the sense of an intimate, direct relationship existing between such stars and British cinema audiences, promoting an impression that Britain was fundamentally a happy and hopeful place to live, despite the problems caused by an uncertain economy, and the differences between working-, middle- and upper-class lifestyles in 1930s British society.

In *Sing As We Go* (Basil Dean, 1934), for example, Gracie Fields appears as a redundant textile weaver who maintains her good spirits throughout an enforced stay in Blackpool. When the textile works' revue team is disbanded because of the closing of the factory (which makes the entire workforce redundant), Gracie's character declares that 'We'll be able to practise while we're all queuing up for the dole. It'll be very funny.'

In *Sing As We Go*, the good-natured resilience of the workers is finally rewarded by the discovery of a more economical means of weaving which enables the factory to reopen at the close of the film, making the intervening period of unemployment depicted in the film seem as if it were merely an extended holiday for the workers in which they were able to enjoy a state of freedom and mobility normally denied to them.

Marcia Landy in *British Genres: Cinema and Society 1930–1960*
(1991), however, warned against too easily assuming that 1930s audiences would necessarily have assumed that this concluding segment represented anything more significant than the propensity of film comedies
to end happily, rather than sadly: 'The implication that the comic ending
resolves the film's conflict lies in the face of the insoluble problems posed
by the film, namely ... the unlikelihood of magical "cures" for the
depression ... Moreover, the assumption that audiences confused conventional comic closure with "reality" is ... untenable'.[20]

Shipyard Sally, which concluded Gracie Fields' career in British
cinema, also dealt with the subject of unemployment in the form of a
topical musical-comedy. The film begins with newsreel footage of a ship
being launched in Clydebank on a rainy day, watched over by members
of the Royal Family and enthusiastic crowds. The narrative then takes
up the fictional story of Sally Fitzgerald (Gracie Fields), who laments the
fact that her matinee performance at a local theatre has been largely
unattended because of the ship launch. A few scenes later, when Sally is
now running a public house in the centre of the town, the prospect of
mass unemployment once again casts a shadow over the proceedings of
a Gracie Fields film narrative.

Newspaper headlines are glimpsed announcing that work has been
suspended at the local shipyard, resulting in massive job losses. Sally is
encouraged by the redundant shipbuilders to travel to London to present a petition to Lord Randall (Morten Setten), who is heading an
enquiry into whether public money should be used to reopen the shipyard. 'With national finance in its present condition ... a favourable
report cannot be anticipated', predict the newspaper analysts. The film
will proceed to disprove such pessimistic views, but only by removing
Sally from the film's initial working-class Scottish setting, and trans-
planting her to a series of upper-class locations based in the south of
England, such as an exclusive gentlemen's club, a London apartment,
and a luxurious country house. The pretext for this radical change in
social setting is that these are the very places where Sally might be able
to meet Lord Randall, and thus try to persuade him to reopen the ship-
yards. (This does mean that the film can also evince a commitment to
working-class struggles, without having to produce sustained images of
working-class life.)

Sally reveals an uncanny ability to adapt to the privileged social circles
in which she now moves, before she is eventually exposed as someone
who does not really belong in such locations. In the gentlemen's club,
Sally disguises herself as a man, and engages in bizarre and banal conversations about colonial life in Africa with a well-meaning but scatter-

brained upper-class male. She then infiltrates Lord Randall's London home by impersonating an American singer who is too ill to perform at a function and performs a 'Jitterbug' song. When Lord Randall expresses disdain, however, at what he feels is an excessively raucous example of contemporary music, she undertakes a public rendition of 'Danny Boy' (and adopts an Irish accent) to try to pave the way for asking him to reopen the shipyard. (Lord Randall later admits that he had anticipated that the American singer would turn out to be 'loud and artificial'.)

A later scene set in Lord Randall's country retreat begins with house-guests and staff emerging from a makeshift underground shelter wearing newly issued gas masks. This has the comic effect of making the characters resemble grotesque mutant-like figures, while hinting at the more sombre fact that another world war was imminent. The film's quest to attain a form of social justice for the beleaguered Scottish workforce also appears to end bleakly when Lord Randall's initial conclusion is that there should be 'no resumption' of work at the shipyard. On finding out that Sally is, in fact, an impostor and an interloper, he banishes her from his home, declaring, 'I should appreciate it if you leave, young lady'.

When Sally and her father (Sydney Howard) return on foot to Scotland, it emerges, however, that the men's petition – and Sally's sincerity – have belatedly persuaded Lord Randall to change his mind and call for the shipyard to resume work! The film closes with images of men back at work and the launching of a newly built ship. Graham Greene noted in his bemused review of the film in the *Spectator* that 'a large close-up of Miss Fields singing "Land of Hope and Glory" is transposed over the launching of a new liner by the Queen'.[21] Greene concluded that 'values are confused' at this point and that it seemed odd that the 'liner' should be used as 'background to the face'.[22] Greene was equally sceptical about developments within the narrative which implied that 'unemployment' could 'be wiped out by a sentimental song', or 'industrial unrest . . . calmed by a Victorian ballad'.[23]

The closing images of Gracie Fields in the film present her as a performer on the verge of becoming a mythical figure in British culture at a historical moment when a time of regional economic recession for particular regions will culminate in a period of total war for the whole nation. Despite the proletarian connotations of its title, *Shipyard Sally* actually spends most of its running-time in the upper-class homes of members of London high society, suggesting that the filmmakers are more interested in parodying (and perhaps pandering to?) the 'idle rich', rather than representing the 'deserving poor' in any detail or depth.

The film does not question the desirability or logic of one man having the power to open or close a shipyard, and, interestingly, we never observe Lord Randall actually changing his mind. Nonetheless, however much these concluding images of Fields' singing, and the men back at work, might appear both contrived and naive to a modern-day audience, the scene still conveys a moving sense of how things might be in a British society not riddled with unemployment, as well as hinting at the importance of shipping as Britain prepares for war.

It could be argued that films such as *Brassed Off* and *The Full Monty* are in their own idiosyncratic fashion paying homage to such films as *Shipyard Sally* and *Sing As We Go*, works which seek to integrate music and comedy, regional specificity and social observation, all within a single narrative structure. Equally, I would suggest that these two 1990s narratives rework the themes of closing factories and turbulent times, central to the Gracie Fields films, for a more cynical, modern era in which filmmakers do not necessarily feel compelled to affirm existing political and economic infrastructures in British society.

Brassed Off does, though, feature moving renditions of 'Danny Boy' and 'Land of Hope and Glory' in its own tribute to the efforts of a down-trodden workforce to hang onto their jobs during another cataclysmic economic downturn, and, as in *Shipyard Sally*, the film's chief spokesperson for the workers emphasises the importance of work for men's self-belief and the good of society.

During the Second World War, the qualities of endurance and perseverance displayed by figures such as Formby and Fields were applied to the national war effort, and the British nation, as it struggled to survive a terrible ordeal, came to be increasingly conceived of as a total community-in-itself, rather than as a collection of disparate (if linked) series of regions. Internal conflicts and divisions, and cultural and economic distinctions between the north and south of England temporarily declined in importance, as a potentially overwhelming external threat was posed to the countryside, city, town and village alike.

After victory was finally achieved by the Allied Forces in 1945, the nature of British film comedy and of drama-based representations of British communal life were both gradually re-imagined for a new era. Gracie Fields and George Formby now seemed less cinematically and socially vital and ceased making feature films after 1946. The immediate post-war years were concerned with processes of reconstruction, and the aftermath of the war, with its ensuing 'period of austerity', did not initially appear to be a promising time for film comedy.

The most significant post-war development in British cinema was the production of a new series of comedy-dramas (often set in the south of England, but occasionally venturing out to more far-flung areas) which were released by Ealing studios between 1949 and 1955. The most effective Ealing comedies combined the propensity of Hollywood comedies to indulge in moments of heightened characterisation, accentuated narrative tension and knockabout farce, alongside a 'neo-realist-type' desire to formulate stories about 'ordinary' people, which had some kind of sociological basis and emotional investment in the post-1945 concerns of reconstruction and rebuilding.

Films such as *Passport to Pimlico* and *Whisky Galore* contemplated the nature of post-war Britain, and considered how the relationship between a small segment of society and the larger governing body might be made more dynamic and imaginative. David Bordwell and Kristin Thompson in *Film History: An Introduction* (1994) noted that 'While many Hollywood-style comedies depended on slapstick or on sophisticated screwball situations, Ealing's humour was built on injecting a single premise into an ordinary situation'.[24] The speculative and imaginative scenarios explored in three seminal Ealing comedies included such unusual situations as a London borough becoming an independent and self-sufficient nation, a rural community working together to preserve a feature of economic life deemed to be no longer viable in a modern world, and a small, self-contained society unexpectedly acquiring enough free whisky to sustain itself through the long winter nights ahead.

In his *Screen* article 'Projecting Britain and the British Character: Ealing Studios' (1974), Charles Barr constructed a table denoting the main settings and collective aspirations of the central characters in Alexander Mackendrick's Ealing comedies.[25] I have extended the table to include three Ealing comedies made by other directors, to be discussed, briefly, in the section which follows:

Table 1

Title	Location	Aims of community
Whisky Galore (1949)	Todday, Hebridean island	Salvage shipwrecked whisky
Passport to Pimlico (1949)	Pimlico, London borough	Achieve 'home rule' and become an independent country
The Man in the White Suit (1951)	Textile factory, Lancashire	Develop an everlasting cloth; maintain economic 'status quo'
The Lavender Hill Mob (1951)	London	Convert gold bullion into Eiffel Tower souvenirs
The Titfield Thunderbolt (1953)	Titfield village	Maintain a local railway service

In *Passport to Pimlico*, the attempts of shopkeeper Arthur Pemberton (Stanley Holloway) to persuade the local council to convert a bomb-site into a swimming and play area for children, during the period of an intense heat wave, are dismissed by a committee as impractical 'day-dreams'. As this meeting proceeds, however, a bomb due to be detonated suddenly explodes on the site under discussion, and a situation is created in which it appears that out of the disruption and fragmentation which follows, even greater 'daydreams' than Pemberton's might prove to be realisable. The bomb blast unearths a charter stating that Pimlico really belongs to the French state of Burgundy, and therefore stands outside the rule of English law.

Following the revelation of Pimlico's 'alternative' status, a French descendant of the Duke of Burgundy emerges as a possible new head of State for the would-be independent borough of Pimlico: 'Show me my Dukedom', he declares to the local citizens. But as the narrative progresses his character is overshadowed by the emergence of an anarchical society in which people are reluctant to accept any kind of limits as to how they should behave or operate within the community.

In his study of the English novel, James English pointed out that sustaining a cohesive community is a difficult task: 'For under the least scrutiny the discourse of community begins to break apart, shattering into a thousand microdiscourses, each with its own declared aims and affiliations'.[26] This is precisely what occurs in *Passport to Pimlico*, where no smooth transition to a new form of self-government is managed by the community, and the dream of home rule quickly descends into a social nightmare, as Pimlico is disowned by Britain, and a siege situation develops in which the inhabitants are dependent on food supplies dropped in by sympathetic nations from around the world.

At the height of this morally turbulent and comically chaotic section of the narrative, however, the film suddenly draws back from depicting the repercussions of the Pimlico inhabitants' stand against the British state any further, and the narrative is swiftly brought to a close by a final scene in which the community is re-admitted to Britain as a London suburb, and their independent status suddenly becomes a distant memory. The final image in the film is of a ceremony to celebrate the opening of a newly built swimming pool constructed out of the local bomb-site (suggesting that some lasting improvements and adjustments to community life did prove to be possible). In a moment of comic and poetic 'realism', however, even this modest celebration party is abandoned because of the onset of torrential rain. The heat wave, which has pervaded the rest of the film (alongside the deluded 'dreams' of the citizens of Pimlico), evaporates, and 'ordinary' British life is resumed. By the close, even the British weather has returned to a more typical and less demanding state of being.

Passport to Pimlico appears to both comment on and vindicate certain conceptualisations of Englishness at a particular historical conjuncture in British society. In the form of a controlled experiment, the Pimlico community are allowed a fleeting moment of liberation and freedom as they experience the joys of local autonomy (no policeman can demand a cessation of after-hours drinking, for example), and are presented with the opportunity to form a society conceived along utopian lines. Conflicts between individuals, though, soon destroy the notion of a coherent, self-governing 'mini-society'. Much of the dry wit and ironic humour in this situation comes from the fact that the people of Pimlico begin by regarding their separation from Britain as a form of liberation, but end up viewing their situation as a state of exile from which they are grateful to be rescued.

Whisky Galore similarly revolved around a concerted revolt against English authority, on this occasion as personified by Captain Waggett (Basil Radford) of the British Home Guard, who seeks to stop Scottish islanders from taking crates of whisky from on board a sinking ship, and keeping them for their own pleasure. Unlike in *Passport to Pimlico*, the community here succeeds in achieving its (admittedly more limited) aims of outwitting the British state. Captain Waggett is ultimately framed into appearing to be pilfering whisky himself, so that the 'joke' of the narrative is ultimately on him, and the somewhat puritan, officious manner in which he seeks to enforce the law of the land. Some of the 'liberated' whisky is used to celebrate the marriage of an English army officer (Bruce Seton) to a Scottish woman (Joan Greenwood), suggesting that in the right circumstances England and Scotland might not exist in a state of opposition.

The narrative proper, in fact, concludes with a curious coda undercutting the previous events, and claiming that the happiness gained by the successful seizure of the whisky turned out to be short-lived. The film's voice-over narrator (Finlay Currie) relates how eventually the supply of whisky ran out, the drink became too expensive for the local inhabitants to purchase, and depressed times returned to the island: 'No one in Todday could afford even a dram', he laments. The final image in the narrative is of the English soldier and the Scottish woman, strolling contentedly along the beach, as Currie's voice-over narration informs the audience that 'They all lived unhappily ever after. Except for Peggy and her sergeant. They weren't whisky drinkers. And if that isn't a moral story, what is?'

The unexpected tone of the conclusion (and its stark contrast to the earlier scenes detailing the comic energy of the islanders in outwitting the

English officials) signals a new mood and attitude in British film comedy, indicating that an unambiguously affirmative ending was no longer seen as a prerequisite of films falling within this category of native cinema.

While the central situations of *Passport to Pimlico* and *Whisky Galore* contain the potential for a radical critique of the British state, both films, in their final moments, back away from completely endorsing the actions of their central figures. The Pimlico citizens are grateful to be allowed back into society, and the Todday islanders (it is claimed) do not find lasting happiness from the illicit whisky. The narratives thus parody and satirise the pitfalls of trying to find a 'short cut' to success in British society, and offer a cautionary note about the dangers of over-reaching ambition.

Duncan Petrie, in *Creativity and Constraint in the British Film Industry* (1991), claims that 'Ealing comedy concerned itself with the idealisation of community', a trait which he sees as emanating from intense 'nostalgia for the war years in a period of post-war austerity'.[27] Jeffrey Richards, in his study *Films and British National Identity: From Dickens to Dad's Army* (1997), suggests that 'Interestingly, the early Ealing comedies were more or less remade in the Conservative era (1951–58) and show . . . instructive changes'.[28]

To test these claims and observations in relation to particular examples of late Ealing comedy, it can be noted that *The Lavender Hill Mob* (Charles Crichton, 1951) explores the possibility of moving up the social ladder through drastic and illicit means, while illustrating that ultimately crime does not pay; *The Man in the White Suit* (1951) examines conflicts of interest and social tensions within the British industry, and finds no real solution to the problems unearthed; and *The Titfield Thunderbolt* (1953) combines a rural setting with a celebration of steam technology, and seeks to prove that the old and the new in post-war Britain can co-exist if nourished and sustained by a supportive local community.

While *The Lavender Hill Mob* evinces a wry sense of regret that it is not really possible to produce a British crime picture capable of imitating and matching its Hollywood counterparts, and one which doesn't (in the end) lapse into farce or improbability, *The Man in the White Suit* is a more sombre and troubled film, concerned with the relationship between working communities and technological developments. The title refers to Sidney Stratton (Alec Guinness), a scientist, who accidentally stumbles upon a formula for producing a fabric that never wears out or needs replacing, out of which he has a suit made. Such an innovation is understandably seen as a threat to the future of workers and capitalists alike, and Stratton is faced with the problem of being a would-be innovator in a society suspicious and wary of change.

Stratton may innocently enquire about whether the invention of the mechanical loom turned out to be 'a disaster', implying that in the long run technological improvements will always prove to be beneficial, but his new invention denotes him in the eyes of his detractors as a dangerous idealist, who ultimately has to be forced into hiding. Stratton's invention leads to scenes of comic farce in which representatives of management and labour, anxious to destroy his formula and safeguard their employment, chase him frantically through the mill-town streets by night. (Despite the intellectual and ingenious nature of the central conceits of the key Ealing comedies, the films still tended to build towards concluding scenes featuring frenzied physical action and extended chase scenes.)

Stratton maintains a commitment to the noble sanctity of the scientific pursuit, and believes in pursuing experiments to their logical conclusion, but he only finally escapes being torn apart by an angry crowd when his infamous 'white suit' disintegrates as he is prodded and pushed by his pursuers, proving that the experiment was not in fact an infallible success. This penultimate scene in the film balances farce, suspense and irony, as the textile industry is saved at the cost of Stratton's dignity, pride and 'white suit'. The film ends with Sidney, in abeyance, amidst a sense that whilst he may be banished, the future with which he is associated cannot necessarily be held back indefinitely.

The Titfield Thunderbolt also plays upon fears of redundancy, and the film, in fact, begins with notice of a closure – a close-up shot of a poster announcing that the local Titfield railway service will be permanently withdrawn after 14 June, 1952, to be replaced by a bus service. The Vicar (George Relph), along with the Squire (John Gregson), determine to keep 'the oldest surviving branch line in the world' going by running it themselves as a private, non-nationalised enterprise. On being informed that 'the old Canterbury to Whitstable line' was closed down by rationalising forces, the Vicar replies, 'Perhaps there were not men of sufficient faith in Canterbury!' In a variation of the legal loophole which allowed the citizens of Pimlico their brief moment of self-government, the railway supporters learn that their venture will not come under the terms of the 1947 Railway Nationalisation Act. A rich local resident (Stanley Holloway), whose main interest in life is drinking, provides the group with the necessary £10,000 to press ahead with their plans, despite being informed that the line has been losing money for years.

The Titfield Thunderbolt was the first Ealing comedy to be shot in colour, and the lovingly composed photography of the green southern English countryside adds a sense of enchantment to the film's representation of an enclosed community resisting the onset of modernity and social conformism. Much of the film's humour is of a visual nature, evoking the era of silent film comedy, and involving the locals rallying around to allow the ancient train to pass an examination by an official from the Ministry of Transport. Through the community's ingenuity and cunning (as in *Whisky Galore*), the civil servant is fooled into thinking that there are not, in fact, major problems of carriage coupling, refuelling and safety as the journey progresses.

The actual ineptitude of their 'test run' performance is concealed from the transport official, and in the film's vision of a happy conclusion, the line is leased out to a private company. (Ken Loach, nearly fifty years later in his film *The Navigators* (2001), would dramatise what he saw as the ruinous and dangerous consequences of de-nationalising the railways in the 1990s, and, in particular, of placing rail safety in the hands of private companies.)

Ealing directors and screenwriters did not have to consider such future aspects of modern culture as the possibility of nuclear war, or the existence of mass unemployment in British society, and the Ealing comedies discussed above would have been conceived with memories of the Second World War still fresh in the filmmakers' minds. Conceivably, as a result, several of the films stressed the importance of Britons ultimately displaying a loyalty to the nation-state, whatever internal dissensions and tensions might exist within particular localised communities.

As David Bordwell and Kristin Thompson note in their *Film History: An Introduction*, the Ealing comedies make great play with notions of 'English eccentricity',[29] as a means both of generating narrative complications, and of promoting the international appeal of the films abroad. Several of the filmmakers who, during the 1990s, produced what one might term 'neo-Ealing' comedy-dramas would interestingly revive this characterisation trait and marketing strategy.

As John Ellis points out in his essay, 'Made in Ealing' (1975), the Ealing comedies tend to privilege the concerns, ambitions and frustrations of male characters, often downplaying or reducing women characters to the level of spectators. Ellis suggests that in the case of Ealing, 'Since comedy involves the infringement of ideals and accepted structures, it is possible for men to be involved, but not women'.[30] The communities depicted, therefore, tend to be male-oriented and defined in somewhat masculine terms. The Lavender Hill mob is all-male, and it is the men who most enjoy consuming the whisky in *Whisky Galore*. The films still tend to value social groupings that include both men and women, whilst implying that male figures within the narrative landscapes may be more likely to harbour private fantasies and ambitions than the female members of the communities depicted. This particular feature of the narratives can also be found to pervade a number of the 1990s British comedy-communal-dramas, particularly *Brassed Off* and *The Full Monty*.

Ealing comedies (although comparatively small in number) have acquired an important position in world cinema, and are regarded fondly and regularly revived. The films clearly benefited from having been produced within a studio system which allowed directors, writers and producers to exchange ideas, and to feel that they were contributing to the formation of a body of work, rather than simply working towards the production of a single film, which might have no immediate or recognisable successor.

A more satirical and topical kind of humour than that associated with Ealing Studios was produced by the Boulting brothers (Roy and John) in a group of late 1950s and early 1960s films which dared to go beyond Ealing's stringent but fundamentally benign studies of the 'moral state of the nation'. Their most commercially successful and critically contentious film was *I'm All Right Jack*, a film presenting industrial relations in Britain as synonymous with industrial conflict, with greed and laziness seen as affecting both management and workers during a period of full employment and job security. The narrative follows the fortunes of Stanley Windrush (Ian Carmichael), who expresses a desire to go into industry, albeit a form of 'light industry', rather than 'a thumping great business like iron and steel'. His Aunt Dolly (Margaret Rutherford) hopes that this course of action will not result in him having to join a union: 'I do so hate violence', she observes sardonically.

Workers in the film are presented as intending to do as little as possible for the maximum amount of pay, and, whereas in *Sing As We Go* and *Shipyard Sally* the workers downed tools only when made redundant, in *I'm All Right Jack* there are constant stoppages at every possible opportunity (a strike is welcomed as a 'nice little break'). Management is characterised by an equal type of virulent self-interest. Characters on both the shop-floor and executive-office levels of business are shown making racist remarks. Major Hitchcock (Terry-Thomas) announces that the 'Deputy chairman is bringing those group of darkies we're doing that contract for' on a visit to the factory. Shop steward Fred Kite (Peter Sellers) worries about 'coloured labour' being brought into the factory, with 'blacks doing our jobs here, like they do on the buses in Birmingham' (the television series *Love Thy Neighbour*, 1972–76, to be discussed in the next chapter, had its origins in these kind of 'comically held' viewpoints).

I'm All Right Jack concludes with a television discussion programme, 'Argument: the programme that puts you in the picture', in which the various sides involved in a labour dispute are allowed an opportunity to state their side of the story. Stanley claims that 'we've all been betrayed', and denounces the 'phoney patriotic claptrack' of the employers *and* the 'bilge and talk of workers' rights'. To his uncle, Bertram Tracepurcel (Dennis Price), he declares that the only reason 'You're always waving such a ruddy great Union Jack' is so 'nobody can see what you're up to behind it'. A judge, acting on behalf of 'British society', however, eventually designates Stanley as mentally and emotionally unstable after watching him make such observations on television. The final image of Stanley in the film is of him being chased by a group of naked women from a nudist colony, implying (in a surreal and somewhat bewildering conclusion) that he may never find a stable and non-threatening community.

The sheer level of cynicism, intransigence and self-interest displayed by so many of the characters in *I'm All Right Jack* continues to be both amusing and disturbing. The film as a whole suggests that if representatives of capital and labour continue to 'carry on' in this fashion, then the future of British industry will indeed be grim. Characters within the story are depicted as being essentially trapped within their respective social and ideological positions – a situation which Anthony Carthew, reviewing the film in the *Daily Herald*, described as 'both funny and sad', with the 'pathos' of the film contributing to a sustained critique of what he called the 'false values that have stained the 1950s'.[31]

I'm All Right Jack does not make suggestions as to how these class-based conflicts might be alleviated or avoided, and the distanced tone in which the disputes are recorded heralds the emergence of a new kind of mood and tone in British film comedy, and an attitude which refuses (as in the Gracie Fields films discussed earlier) to imply that better times and more positive responses to situations may lie around the corner.

The cycle of films known as the British 'new wave' (or as examples of northern-based social realist narratives) also explored the effects of relatively full employment on a group of male characters at a particular moment in British social history. These films were fundamentally dramas rather than comedies (although *Billy Liar* (John Schlesinger, 1963), fuses the two modes), but there was a kind of 'Bakhtinian' humour to be found in many of the main characters' iconoclastic attitudes and lack of regard for established traditions and notions of social decorum.

Several of the male figures in these films do seek alternative opportunities for personal expression and fulfilment to those generally offered by their place of work: accountant Joe Lampton (Laurence Harvey) takes up amateur dramatics in *Room at the Top* (Jack Clayton, 1958), miner Frank Machin (Richard Harris) plays rugby in *This Sporting*

Life (Lindsay Anderson, 1963), and 'daydreamer' Billy Fisher (Tom Courtney) in *Billy Liar* writes pop songs and jokes for comic performers, while using most of the material to turn his own life into a work of fiction. (*Brassed Off* and *The Full Monty* also depict male figures searching for a creative outlet for energies not otherwise tapped by society but, crucially, characters in these films lack the stability of a regular job and wage as a material basis for their cultural pursuits.)

In *A Kind of Loving* (John Schlesinger, 1962), the subject of the position of brass band music within popular British culture (a key topic in *Brassed Off*) is specifically addressed. In the film, Vic (Alan Bates) has been forced to settle down with Ingrid (June Ritchie) after she becomes pregnant, and live in the house belonging to her mother (Thora Hird). A key scene set around the kitchen table has Vic trying to persuade Ingrid to accompany him to watch his father playing in a brass band performance. Ingrid claims that the music is old-fashioned, and indicative of a pastime for elderly folk. The scene concludes with Vic stating firmly that they will be going.

The film then cuts to the performance of the brass band, and the camera pans along a section of the audience before focusing on two empty seats, which turn out to be signifiers of Vic and Ingrid's absence from the musical event. There then follows a sudden cut to the image of a quiz show on television. The picture on the set keeps going out of focus, the quiz show host cannot get the details of the contestant correct, and the contestant somewhat bizarrely lists 'watching people' as one of his hobbies. The camera then pulls back to reveal that Vic, Ingrid and her mother are viewing the quiz show ('watching people', like the contestant), rather than the brass band recital in which Vic's father is an active participant, much to Vic's annoyance and disgust. The humour and irony of the transition from the musical performance to the inanities of television entertainment carries a clear suggestion that the filmmakers value the cultural efforts of localised communities over the commercialised products of the modern media.

The scenes imply that 1960s British television is somewhat mindless and trivial, particularly when compared to active participation in a brass band orchestra, and John Hill in *Sex, Class and Realism: British Cinema 1956–1963* (1986) notes that in such instances as this sequence from *A Kind Of Loving*, 'modern mass culture is being . . . defined negatively in relation to traditional working-class culture'.[32]

One can see from the images of communal and regional (particularly northern) life examined so far that filmmakers did not find it easy to present comic or dramatic images of community life in Britain which were not also images of conflict, dissatisfaction or restlessness. Equally, however, the directors, performers and writers of the films cited appeared to have been stimulated by the challenge of producing narratives which engaged with the specific, the regional and complex 'mini-societies' of Britain.

One of the possible inspirational motivations behind the production of the Ealing comedies considered was a sense that the British government was assuming an excessive level of control over the typical post-war citizen through the processes of nationalisation and increasing state intervention in matters of education, health and social welfare. Films from a later period in British social history such as *The Man in the White Suit* and *I'm All Right Jack* implied that class conflict in a free-market economy was both comically absurd and potentially tragic. *A Kind of Loving* and *Billy Liar*, in turn, concentrated on depictions of frustrated protagonists who longed for a more exciting and authentic existence within their northern-based communities, without knowing exactly how this could be achieved.

The narrative and ideological paradigms associated with Ealing comedies and British 'new wave' cinema did not necessarily correspond with the aesthetic aims of a certain strand of auteur-oriented, art-house cinema produced in Britain during the 1980s. I would suggest, however, that a defining feature of several of the communal/regional narratives produced during the 1990s was a concern to resurrect an earlier tradition of British filmmaking which was topical, provocative and entertaining, and through which writers and directors could draw attention to what was perceived to be a lack of government and collective intervention, aimed at ensuring a reasonable and tolerable standard of living for current-day citizens.

As a result, the comic edge of several of these 1990s community-oriented narratives has, arguably, more in common with the tone and mood of the British social realist films of the 1960s than with some of the 'classic' Ealing comedies. However, a group of regional-based comedy-dramas from the 1990s did specifically appear to emulate and aspire to Ealing tropes and traits, and I will examine these films briefly, before embarking on a case study of the two major communal comedy-dramas of the 1990s, *Brassed Off* and *The Full Monty*.

The 'Ealing spirit' and 1990s regional comedies

A number of key films within this category of recent British cinema were not set in the north, and did not specifically deal with the problems of unemployment. *Up 'n' Under* (1998) was set in Yorkshire, but lacked a specifically social perspective, and had its origins in regional theatre and television situation comedy. *The Englishman Who Went Up a Hill But Came Down a Mountain* (1995) concerned the ideological conflict between two English cartographers and a small Welsh community over the legal and geographical definition of a prominent feature of the local landscape. *Waking Ned* (1999) portrayed the wily efforts of a Southern Irish community to outwit representatives of the national lottery. *In the Bleak Midwinter* (Kenneth Branagh, 1995) focused upon a group of 'resting' actors encouraged by a passionate theatre director to stage a production of *Hamlet* in a church hall on Christmas Eve. The 'Ealingesque' collective aims of the regional groups in these films are outlined in the table below:

Table 2

Title	Location	Aims of community
In the Bleak Midwinter (1995)	Hope village, South of England	Stage an amateur production of *Hamlet*
The Englishman Who Went Up a Hill. . . (1995)	Ffynnon Garw, South Wales (1917)	Have a local hill designated as a mountain by English cartographers
Up 'n' Under (1998)	Yorkshire	Demonstrate that a rugby team can beat difficult local opponents
Waking Ned (1999)	Tullymore, Southern Ireland	Keep £7 million lottery winnings of deceased local resident

From a consideration of this table, we can discern certain similarities in themes and plot structures between these films and certain Ealing comedies discussed earlier. Both *Whisky Galore* and *The Englishman Who Went Up a Hill. . .* , for instance, revolve around communities seeking to outwit the representatives of an English establishment attempting to impose a kind of colonial rule over the local inhabitants. *Waking Ned*, similarly, features a group of individuals desperately striving to hang onto an unexpected financial windfall which chance has placed in their vicinity. *Waking Ned*, despite some striking instances of black humour, is able to depict a community gradually working together to achieve a shared objective, and so, as in *Whisky Galore*, this extended group is eventually rewarded with an unexpected victory.

The Englishman Who Went Up a Hill. . . is the only film within the table to be set in the past, and the story of the film is relayed by a grand-father to his grandson, a narrative device alluding to the ways in which social myths and legends are constructed, elaborated and passed down to younger generations. This narrative device also, implicitly, warns audiences that the events subsequently to be conveyed may be the result of a highly romanticised and comically inflated account of past incidents.

The narrative is set within a tragic period of history, namely, the First World War, an era in which the Reverend Jones (Kenneth Griffith) describes the small Welsh community at the centre of the tale as 'exhausted by loss'. (The Reverend, himself, dies during the final stages of the narrative, but he, at least, passes away in the midst of the community to which he belongs, and which he believes in so fervently.)

In working together on the practical task of trying to turn a hill into a mountain, the local inhabitants find a common sense of purpose in the sheer physical effort and native guile needed to accomplish their intention. Scenes depicting the villagers moving strips of earth from nearby fields to extend the size of the hill can, thus, be read as images of noble labour, in contrast with the futile fighting taking place in the blood-soaked trenches of nearby France, which are evoked in the film's narrative in the form of flashbacks experienced by the character known as Johnny 'Shellshocked' (Ian Hart).

From a distanced perspective, both the 'mountain-building' and the conflict of the war could be considered equally futile and meaningless. The desire to restore local pride by remaking the hill as a mountain denotes an attempt by the villagers to restore some kind of positive relationship between human beings and the natural world, a relationship that is simultaneously being sundered on the battlefields of World War One. In an ironical twist, Reginald Anson (Hugh Grant), the upper-class English surveyor at the centre of the tale, is also revealed to be recovering from shell shock, and so he too is psychologically damaged and socially vulnerable. Being an Englishman in 1917, the film implies, leaves him without the emotional assurance of a vibrant and supportive community.

The Englishman Who Went Up a Hill. . ., despite its period setting, shares with contemporary-set films such as *Brassed Off* and *The Full Monty* a sense that the comedy of its narrative is unfolding against a background of evolving social tragedy and distress, meaning that the film's comic elements are always qualified and defined in relation to the moral seriousness of the overall situation. Of these three films, *The Englishman*, despite its wartime setting, is somewhat ironically the most light-hearted (perhaps, in part, because the community at the centre of the story appears to be economically self-sufficient).

As the story progresses, Grant's character in the film is helped to recuperate emotionally from his disturbing memories of the war (which unlike Johnny's are not conjured up in the form of flashbacks), by forming a cultural and romantic alliance with Tara Fitzgerald's Welsh maidservant, 'Betty of Cardiff', a relationship which serves to symbolise, by the close, a possible rapprochement between the nations of Wales and England (the wedding between an English soldier and a Scottish woman in *Whisky Galore* served a similar purpose).

In *Waking Ned*, the local villagers set out to trick and bamboozle representatives of the national lottery into handing over a cheque for £7 million after a local citizen of Tullymore has dropped dead at the shock of possessing a winning ticket. Two particularly wily characters played by Ian Bannen and David Kelly are forced to include the local community in their plans to fool the authorities when it is necessary for the recently deceased Ned to be brought back from the dead. This deception has to be supported by the other 52 inhabitants of the village who, in return for their co-operation (and, crucially, their silence), become eligible for a share of the winnings.

Only an elderly woman in a wheelchair, Lizzy Quinn (Eileen Dromey), opposes the masquerade, although this response is more due to her cantankerous and contrary personality than any inherent moral scruples. (She is also aware that the lottery might offer a reward for information about the fraud.) At the crucial moment when she seeks to inform the 'Lotto' about the deception, via a public telephone, a car accidentally swerves into the phone booth from which she is calling, and knocks her to a watery death in the sea, serving to remove the threat she posed to the community. This incident is the narrative's supreme moment of black comedy, bad taste and high-farce, and represents a kind of divine intervention on the part of the film's writer, which enables the islanders to inherit the lottery money, rather than go to jail.

In a *Screen* article, 'Directions to Ealing' (1977), Philip Simpson noted the prevalence of scenes featuring 'sing-songs, scenes in pubs, offers and acceptance of tea'[33] as emblematic signifiers of communal life in many of the Ealing comedies. In *Waking Ned*, the scenes revealing Lizzy Quinn's failed and fatal attempt to inform on the locals are intercut with images of the rest of the community enjoying a celebration, complete with flowing Irish music and drink in the village's public house.

The harsher side of the comic frameworks structuring *Whisky Galore* and *Waking Ned* can be witnessed in the fates of those characters who oppose the community at large, and suffer disparagement, disappointment and (in extreme cases) death, as a result. The comedic impulses of this tradition of British communal-comedy are, thus, not necessarily benign or blameless, and may work towards a diminishing of characters who exhibit an overly individualistic or independent streak in their character. (The treatment of Tara Fitzgerald's character in *Brassed Off* will prove to be especially telling in this respect.)

In *Waking Ned*, the villagers are seemingly allowed to succeed in illicitly claiming the money because the proceeds will be used for the good of the whole community (thereby subverting the individualist ethics of the lottery system, whereby only separate and unrelated individuals are arbitrarily rewarded). In keeping Ned's winnings, the villagers are also, in a way, avenging his fate as a victim of the lottery – Ned dies clutching his lottery ticket with an incredulous look on his face, the surprise having proved too much for his heart to bear.

A number of the community-centred films produced within British cinema during the 1990s dramatised the attempts by a group of individuals to realise a particular cultural, dramatic or sporting ambition. Much of the humour, and the accompanying dramatic tension within the respective narratives of such films, emerged from the discrepancy between the collective aims of the group, and the actual levels of ability, patience and discipline displayed by the individuals concerned.

Up 'n' Under (1998), a comedy about ageing rugby players, was directed by John Godber, who had written the original treatment as a play which had first been performed in 1984. The popularity of *Brassed Off* (1996) and *The Full Monty* (1997) had created favourable conditions for *Up 'n' Under* to be adapted into a feature film in 1998, and the presence in the cast of three actors associated with popular BBC television situation comedies of the 1990s, Gary Olsen (*2 Point 4 Children*, 1991–99), Neil Morrissey (*Men Behaving Badly*, 1992–98) and Samantha Janus (*Game On*, 1995–98), resulted in the film being modestly successful at the UK cinema box office.[34]

The narrative revolves around a declaration by Arthur Hoyle (Gary Olsen), a self-employed painter and decorator, and banned rugby league player, that he can train any group of players to defeat a local pub team of rugby 'sevens' regulars. In an introduction to the play in 1985, Godber stated that he had been inspired by the irony of trying to recreate the mood and tone of a Hollywood 'underdog' story in a starkly English regional setting: 'at the time of 'writing the most popular videos available on the mass market are the *Rocky* videos. This is an attempt to stage *Rocky* . . . and where else? In Yorkshire, of course'.[35]

The film version of *Up 'n' Under* rewrites the original ending of the play (in which Arthur fails to convert a try at the last moment to ensure victory), so that something of the kind of triumphant ethos associated with the Hollywood *Rocky* (1976–90) films can prevail during the closing moments of the narrative. Arthur and his team manage to defeat their awesome rivals after he succeeds in gaining a vital point in the last second of the game. Despite this wish-fulfilment ending, a slightly melancholy and resigned tone can be detected within the film as a whole (a feeling which was accentuated by the subsequent death of the film's main stars: Gary Olsen passed away from cancer in 2000, at the age of only 42, and Brian Glover had died of a brain tumour before the film was even released).[36]

In the Bleak Midwinter plays out a similar scenario to *Up 'n' Under*, but replaces the latter's economically depressed northern setting with a southern location (a village named Hope). Joe Harper (Michael Maloney), an unemployed actor, gathers a group of similarly 'resting' actors, and seeks to stage a production of *Hamlet* on Christmas Eve in a local church threatened with closure. Joe's sister, Molly (Hetta Charnley), in a keynote speech, complains that 'There is nowhere for people to go apart from the pub . . . There's no village hall, there's no art centre. We need this place to give people a focus, and prove to the council that there is a community worth maintaining'. Molly's lament echoes an observation made by Roger Scruton in his study *England: An Elegy* (2000) that 'Gone are the institutions – the village shop, the market . . . the bandstand in the park – through which local communities renewed themselves'.[37]

Molly expresses surprise, however, at the choice of play for a village Christmas Eve performance: 'Why not do a comedy?' she enquires, rather than a story about 'a depressed aristocrat in a 400-year-old play?' If the selected piece is a tragedy, the backstage events leading up to the play are nonetheless farcical, and enshrouded in chaotic mistakes and ridiculous disputes. As the performers fail to remember their lines, or agree on how the play should be staged, the 'miserable, tormented life' of Hamlet (as Joe sums up the life of the protagonist) also seems to become an appropriate description of the mood of the company.

Declaring that 'Churches and theatres close every week, because . . . people don't come to them', Joe appears set to leave the play and Britain by accepting a role in a Hollywood picture. Nina (Julia Sawalha), a young widowed woman, and comically short-sighted actress, begs him not to go, but the group is adamant that he should take the opportunity, knowing that the prospects for an actor in British theatre and cinema are inevitably somewhat limited.

Joe, subsequently, does leave, and his sister, Molly, plays the lead part of Hamlet (in an unusual piece of casting). Once the figurehead of the community has gone, however, much of the resilience and underlying sense of purpose that he generated tends to depart with him. (The role of an enthusiastic leader is also central to the narratives of *Brassed Off* and *The Full Monty*.) In an ending which evokes the sense of hopefulness associated with traditional comedy (as opposed to tragic drama), rehearsals of the play resume, and Joe returns with a Hollywood film producer, Nancy Crawford, who agrees to watch the first perform-ance of the play before flying out with him to Los Angeles. (The fact that she is played by British comedienne Jennifer Saunders identifies the film's links with television situation comedy traditions, and its concern to somewhat caricature the appeal of Hollywood.)

Joe turns down the opportunity of relocating to America (another member of the cast will go in his place) and acknowledges that he and the widowed Nina are in love. The film ends with an image of the pair, looking forward to the prospect of getting 'depressed together' as actor-managers in British theatre. As in *Whisky Galore*, the film closes with a couple representing a wider community, and symbolising many of its values of cohesiveness, warmth and pride.

Local landscapes are an important feature of these particular comedy-dramas, but the designated setting does not always correspond with the area in which the filming was actually undertaken. *Up 'n' Under*, for instance, makes a good deal of the authentic, low budget 'grittiness' of its rugby league, Yorkshire setting, but those who wait for the very end of the credits will learn that the film was shot entirely on location in Cardiff, whilst *Waking Ned*, despite being set in Ireland, was filmed on location in the Isle of Man.[38]

Even though this group of films placed a great deal of emphasis on notions of 'Britishness', and stressed the importance of regional differ-ences within their respective narratives, financial backing outside Britain still had to be sought on occasions. In an article on the making of *The Englishman Who Went up a Hill But Came Down a Mountain*, Tristan Davies reported in the *Daily Telegraph* that even though the film had 'a British cast, British director, and British script, no British money could be found'.[39] (Two American companies, Parallax and Miramax pictures, eventually financed the film.[40])

The 1990s films discussed in this section of the chapter represented honourable attempts to celebrate concepts of community, loyalty and ambition in British society, and did so by privileging a comic mode over more drama-based modes of expression. *Brassed Off* and *The Full Monty* made an even greater impact in British and world culture, how-ever, by combining comic and dramatic modes of expression within a single narrative. I will now examine the antecedents and achievements of these two seminal 1990s films.

Case studies: *Brassed Off* (1996) and *The Full Monty* (1997)

> This is a comedy in the Ealing mode, but with explicitly anti-Tory bias. The two intentions . . . don't go any too well together . . . The film wins its case by sentiment, not argument.[41]

> *The Full Monty* was made in the traditions of Ealing . . . with a clear sense of identity and with a moral certainty about its audience.[42]

The above quotations suggest that *Brassed Off* and *The Full Monty* both continue and extend traditions of Ealing comedy, although Alexander Walker criticises the former narrative for what he sees as its special pleading on behalf of the miners. Each film emerged within the context of a political period notable for the ending of eighteen years of Conservative government, and the election of a Labour government in May 1997. Perry Anderson in his political study *English Questions* (1992) summarised the effects of such a sustained period of one-party rule in the following terms:

> income taxes reduced, public industries privatised, municipal housing sold off, trade union power broken, local government checked. The momentum of this programme never flagged . . . if the economic cure has failed to take, the social body has nevertheless been notably altered. Mass unemployment became a normal part of the landscape . . . In Britain, social polarisation went further than anywhere else.[43]

David N. Ashton, in an essay studying 'Unemployment' in *Beyond Thatcherism* (1989) similarly claimed that 'Over the period 1979–88, the Government steadfastly refused to raise the importance of unemployment in its hierarchy of values', and observed that 'we now face a situation of second-generation unemployment, and there is evidence that unemployment is being inherited'.[44]

If the ethnic comedy-dramas to be discussed in the next chapter take as their subject the lives and experiences of second- and third-generation immigrant communities, *Brassed Off* and *The Full Monty*, by way of a contrast, focus on the lives and experiences of first- and second-generation unemployed white males. Danny (Pete Postlethwaite) in *Brassed Off* will bemoan the fact that the fates of 'seals and whales' appear to exert more fascination in the public sphere than the fortunes of such men and the communities from which they originate. The films themselves, through a mixture of pathos, social outrage and irrepressible comic energy, will seek to redress the balance and suggest that, perhaps, a reconsideration of the social and economic priorities of modern British society needs to be undertaken.

I would suggest that a decisive creative and political influence on *Brassed Off* and *The Full Monty* in this respect was the re-emergence of Ken Loach as a major British director following his early 1990s films, *Riff-Raff* (1991) and *Raining Stones* (1993). In *British Cinema in the 1980s (1999)*, John Hill notes that the scenario of *Riff-Raff* is focused 'firmly upon . . . the experiences of the male working-class (rather than the female working-class)',[45] a narrative feature which it shares with *Brassed Off* and *The Full Monty*.

In *Riff-Raff*, Robert Carlyle plays Stevie, a Scottish labourer, working with a group of men to convert a former hospital into luxury homes for the rich. Loach has admitted that he was especially keen to imbue the drama with a pervasive comic element, which could (in part) reflect the men's determination not to let their difficult and increasingly dangerous working conditions, and vulnerability in the job market destroy their self-belief or hope.

In a 1994 interview in the American journal *Film Comment*, Loach stated that 'Humour's very subversive; it's a way of maintaining your own bit of territory in your mind'.[46] Loach also argued that the presence of a great deal of comic banter in the narrative served as a realist device aimed at evoking the ways in which men interact in such communal working situations: 'It'd be quite unrealistic to make an earnest film where everybody looks very solemn, because life isn't like that'.[47] Equally, he felt that the integrity of the characterisations should take precedence over a desire to create comic moments, suggesting that 'In getting the laughs you can't undermine the truth of the characters'.[48]

Much of the humour in *Riff-Raff*, however, is of a bitter and ironic nature. When a new worker offers his P45 tax form to the foreman, the latter replies, 'I don't want to know about your private life', illustrating that the builders will work at their own risk and without insurance. This becomes a central issue as safety procedures are ignored by an impatient management team, who simply want the job to be finished as quickly and cheaply as possible. The building team, which includes workers from Liverpool and Scotland, gradually disintegrates as men who speak out about the dangerous conditions are sacked. Communities in this film are subsequently of a fragmentary nature, and the men's jovial banter cannot hide the unsatisfactory and insecure nature of their lives.

Stevie and another builder eventually burn down the apartments they are building, following the death of a fellow worker on the site as a direct result of the negligent safety conditions. The men's good humour, thus, appears finally helpless in the face of the stark economic conditions experienced by certain sections of society as a Conservative government entered a new decade in office. *Riff-Raff* ends bleakly with the two disillusioned builders (and arsonists) staring into a flaming abyss. Loach denied that this ending was nihilistic, claiming that 'there's got to be an anger before you can start to organise or do anything more conscious'.[49]

Riff-Raff was financed by Channel 4 on a production budget of £0.75m, but despite being critically well reviewed the film received only a short cinematic release in London, taking just £61,069 at the UK box office.[50] The film had, however, subtly rekindled an interest amongst British filmmakers in the workings of ordinary lives and tight-knit local communities, and *Brassed Off* and *The Full Monty* would draw upon *Riff-Raff*'s representations of group activity and individual resilience in the context of modern capitalist ethics operating within British society.

Raining Stones depicted a world in which characters struggle to find any kind of continuous or meaningful work, leading to farcical situations such as those glimpsed at the beginning of the narrative where two unemployed middle-aged men, Bob (Bruce Jones) and Tommy (Ricky Tomlinson), kidnap a lone sheep from a farmer's field with a view to killing it and selling its produce in local public houses. The tragic, traumatic and rather sordid elements inherent in this scenario (not least for the sheep) soon rise to the surface. The men prove incapable of murdering the sheep, and have to pass that job over to a local butcher (who has no such qualms), only for him to inform them that the sheep constitutes mutton, rather than lamb, and is hence of little financial value.

This sorry escapade is followed by the theft of Bob's van, setting in motion a sequence of events in which he will unsuccessfully take a job as a security guard in a drug-ridden local nightclub, and borrow money from a dangerous 'loan shark' which will result in his wife and daughter being viciously threatened.

Bob will somewhat miraculously survive these threatening scenarios (and a possible charge of manslaughter) through his religious faith, and help from figures such as his father-in-law (Ronnie Ravey), local priest Father Barry (Tom Hickey), and his good-natured friend Tommy (who, nonetheless, precipitates Bob's descent into debt by failing to lock the van). The sometimes difficult situations generated by work as a security guard, the dangers associated with borrowing money from local individuals, rather than from banks or official organisations, and the piecemeal, fragmented nature of the employment opportunities available to many men in 1990s northern towns and cities were all themes within the film which would be explored further in both *Brassed Off* and *The Full Monty*, as I shall attempt to demonstrate in my subsequent analyses of these two films.

Table 3

Title	Location	Aims of the community
Brassed Off (1996)	Grimley, Yorkshire	Win a national brass band competition and keep local coal mine open
The Full Monty (1997)	Sheffield	Stage a successful male strip show and regain pride

Brassed Off

Brassed Off, significantly, for a film based around a coal mine on the verge of extinction, begins in darkness, with a series of lights gradually moving towards the centre of a black background, accompanied by the sound of jaunty brass band music on the soundtrack. These images gradually become identifiable as lamps worn by miners to guide their way from the murkiness of the pit towards daylight, safety and society. The film will conclude with these same men having become ex-miners, and close with them evocatively travelling through the darkness of a London evening, towards an unclear and unpromising future. The narrative, thus, conveys the story of men catching up with a future in which coal mining as a way of life in Britain turns out to be 'history'.

A synopsis of the plot of *Brassed Off* in *Sight and Sound*[51] locates the events of the narrative as taking place in 1992, and the pit-closure scenario does seem to be based upon the real-life mine closures initiated by the Conservative government during this period. The film text itself, however, does not identify a particular year or date for its setting, and, in a dispute amongst a group of miners about attitudes towards the 1984–85 miners strike, one miner declares that 'was ten years ago, pal', putting the date of the film's events nearer to 1994 or 1995 (the film was released in October 1996). *Brassed Off*, in certain respects, possesses a kind of 'timeless' allegorical quality, as the film develops its particular moral fable about the harsh consequences of unemployment and the fading away of cultural traditions.

The narrative is generated out of a series of journeys undertaken by the members (and supporters) of the Grimley Colliery brass band. These journeys increasingly acquire a portentous and metaphorical significance, culminating in a prestigious trip to the Royal Albert Hall in London, where the band succeed in winning the national brass band competition, having failed in their efforts to keep the local coal mine in operation. The men, thus, meet with triumph and disaster, simultaneously.

The dominant force behind the band is Danny (Pete Postlethwaite), an ex-miner, who, as conductor, possesses an overwhelming ambition to witness the band's talents being displayed on a national (rather than just a local) platform. This aspiration to succeed at the highest possible level is accentuated by the fact that Danny appears to be dying from an illness brought on by his previous work down the mine (Danny's poor state of health can be read as a symbol of what the film perceives to be the precarious – and unfeeling – state of British industry). By the close of the narrative, his physical state is in a critical condition, and, significantly, the final shot in the film is a close-up of Danny's face, a lifetime of striving and suffering engrained in his proud features.

Danny's commitment to the importance of music, and striving for excellence, is rooted in a respect for northern working-class traditions of self-education, and of communities who refuse to be ground down by external pressures. Danny delivers a number of speeches during the film in which the camera pans towards a close-up of his expressive face, the camera movement serving to underline the dignity and validity of his view of the colliery band as a reminder of what he terms a 'hundred bloody years of hard graft'. 'They can shut up the unions, they can shut up the workers', declares Danny, in his position as a conductor, desperately trying to maintain a link with previous generations of musicians and miners, before claiming that 'They'll never shut us up. We'll play on, loud as ever'. Danny's words recall Karl Marx's observations in *The Eighteenth Brumaire of Louis Bonaparte* (1869) that 'Men make their own history . . . under circumstances directly encountered from the past', and that honouring the past is no straightforward matter: 'The tradition of all the dead generations weighs like a nightmare on the brain of the living'.[52]

The film is seemingly aware that its real subject is, perhaps, what comes after the end of the story, when a particular social and economic history has drawn to a close (*The Full Monty* begins at a point in the 1990s when work in the steel industry has become a distant memory for citizens of Sheffield). A sequence early in the film depicts the wives of two of the band members, Vera (Sue Johnston) and Rita (Lili Roughley), chatting over a backyard fence in the style of a 'time-honoured' tradition of British comedy and television soap operas. Rita is shown drinking a mug of tea, and talking with a cigarette in hand, against a backdrop of bras hanging on a washing line. The women state that if the pit shuts down, and the band follows suit, 'We'll all have bugger all to do'. At this point, the film cuts to a previously unseen character, a grey-haired man, reading a popular and sensationalist newspaper in his backyard (we catch a glimpse of a naked woman on the front cover of his paper, as he changes pages). 'You get used to it' is his laconic summation of the social changes wrought by unemployment.

The 'joke' of this scene turns out to be that the women are actually separated by the length of the man's backyard, and are talking across his living space, as if he doesn't really exist or matter: what appears as an intimate, unmediated conversation would in reality have involved the women shouting to be heard. This short scene, with its almost sublimi- nal, ironically delivered 'message' about the dangers of getting 'used to' having no compelling reason to leave the house, ends in a brief shot, framing all three characters in a momentarily frozen tableau, accompa- nied by the sound of wistful brass band music on the soundtrack.

This character (referred to as 'elderly man' in the credits, although he does not appear to be that old) does not re-appear in the film. This could be simply that he is a figure needed for a punchline to the scene. Equally, it could be that his resigned and apathetic attitude is so alien to the ideological and emotional impulses determining the shape of the rest of the narrative that the film deliberately banishes him from the rest of the story. The implication of this sequence is that the blackness of the pit is preferable to the grey emptiness connoted by the unemployed man's backyard.

The film then compares passive and active responses to the modern world by cutting to a shot of Danny, pumping up his bike tyres, and preparing to make his way to the band's rehearsal room. The contrast between having a purpose and a goal, and having nothing very much to do is subtly indicated. This juxtaposition is emblematic of a pattern to emerge in the narrative in which the 'comic' elements have a serious point to make, and cannot be abstracted from the meanings generated by the narrative as a whole.

The opening scenes of *Brassed Off* economically introduce the major characters, and maintain a steady level of exposition, reflecting the steady determination of the male characters to achieve their joint objec- tives regarding the coal mine and the national brass band competition. Once the former aspiration is consigned to history, however, the pace of the film itself slows down, as if the characters themselves feel excessively weighed down by the burdens and disappointments placed upon their shoulders.

An early scene in the narrative introduces Danny's son, Phil (Stephen Tomkinson), and his family, watching a television news item about a proposed redundancy offer to be placed before the Grimley coal miners. The film will set out to personalise and dramatise the details of the prob- lematical redundancy situation, which the television coverage contrast- ingly presents in a distanced, impassive tone in the form of localised events happening to other people, somewhere else. Sandra (Melanie Hill) urges her husband to accept the redundancy money while it is on offer, before they are 'out on bloody street', highlighting the differences of opinion which will emerge between the male and female characters as to how to respond to the events unfolding.

'There's always Mr Chuckles', observes Phil, in an allusion to his alter ego and alternative form of employment as a children's entertainer. Ironically enough, it is in his guise as a clown that Phil will subsequently launch his fiercest denunciation of the political and economic state of the nation, and reach his most profound sense of personal despair.

The reference to 'Mr Chuckles' has the effect of driving Sandra to a form of 'comic' violence, and she hurls a plate at Phil when he is climbing onto the back of his father's bike, as he collects him for the band practice. The plate lands on the fence, as if at this early stage of the narrative events are moving too quickly for characters to be pinned-down or laid-low. Phil will later be attacked by moneylenders outside his home, and lose everything that is most dear to him. The 'comic' violence of this opening scene will, thus, escalate into a tragic and painful form of violence, leaving physical and mental scars which no clown's make-up can quite hide.

In *Brassed Off*, music serves to bind a disparate group of individuals together, and provide a common aim for an increasingly beleaguered and divided community. At the band's first practice session, two of the men, Jim (Philip Jackson) and Ernie (Peter Martin), had declared an intention in 'the present climate' to quit. Persuaded to 'carry on' (and the term seems appropriate in this context) by the unexpected presence and participation of the sexually desirable flugelhorn player, Gloria (Tara Fitzgerald), Jim, Ernie and the other band members accompany her in her chosen audition piece, the second movement from *Concierto de Aranjuez*.

This piece of music was written in 1939 by a blind Spanish composer, Joaquin Rodrigo, while exiled in Paris, during the Spanish Civil War (1936–39). The work was premiered in 1940 upon his return to Spain, and has been described as almost 'a second national anthem, with its haunting melody evoking distinctly Spanish moods and colours'.[53] Its prominent position within a text about British social tragedy and economic turmoil suggests a desire by the makers of *Brassed Off* to imply a link between the struggles of the Republicans in the Spanish conflict (who were supported by thousands of British men sympathetic to their plight and who travelled to Spain to fight for their cause[54]), and British miners made redundant since the 1970s.

The sequence juxtaposes Gloria's audition (representing the beginning of her association with the band) with night-time scenes of union representatives and coal board officials meeting to discuss the future of Grimley colliery (a meeting which will herald the end of the pit as an ongoing concern). The elegiac Spanish music performed by the band is played over the sounds of the men's voices in the crucial discussion, so that we never hear what is actually said. Alexander Walker in his *Evening Standard* review of *Brassed Off* suggested that 'Loach wouldn't have missed this class-confrontation opportunity'.[55] In *Brassed Off*, the implication of the sequence appears to be that nothing that is said by the union officials can deflect the moves afoot to close down the mine.

Father–son relationships, a major structural element and emotional force within the narrative as a whole, are prominent in the subsequent scene of Phil's son, Shane (Luke McGann), watching his father speak to two 'loan sharks' who have come to collect money owed. The effect of watching the scene through a window, and from the perspective of a child struggling to comprehend what is transpiring, encourages an audience to share the child's feelings of helplessness in the face of external threats to the safety and sanctity of the family. Phil tries to laugh off his son's concern by claiming that the men are from the pleasure department, and are only there to exhort the family to have fun. 'I'm not a child, dad', is the boy's telling response.

The film then moves to Gloria's lodgings, and in a medium close-up shot depicts her looking into a mirror as she tries on her new band uniform, whilst simultaneously watching her employer (Stephen Moore) through the mirror proclaiming on a television screen that 'No one wants Grimley to close'. This representation of an authority figure mediated twice over (through the television screen, and the full-length mirror), contrasts with the more direct viewing experience of the boy in the previous sequence. The scene also implies that management, through its distance from the messy business of actually digging for coal, draws upon a form and use of language which is inevitably less rooted in a tangible, material reality than the earthier, far-less mediated discourses of the miners.

The subsequent competition scenes set in various Yorkshire villages present cinema audiences with a sense of a thriving local brass band culture. As we observe the Grimley band marching proudly down a neighbouring high street, their distinctive purple outfits are intermingled with the uniforms of other bands, such as the Yorkshire Building Society and Uppermill village, creating a sense of the Grimley band as one amongst many (real life) enthusiastic regional competitors. As the defeats mount up for Danny's band, an increasingly relaxed and casual attitude, however, becomes evident in the performances of the group. As the effects of several pints of beer begin to lessen their skills of co-ordination, Phil's trumpet disintegrates, and the band itself seems to fragment before our very eyes. The film assumes a kind of 'fly-on-the-wall' documentary approach at this stage, downplaying narrative development in favour of recording the 'carnivalesque' behaviour of the band.

In the inquest which follows, 'conducted' by Danny, Ernie will describe this casual approach to the music as the band's way of going 'out on a high note', a view which does not find favour with Danny, who is horrified that audiences were 'Laughing . . . bloody laughing at us'. For Danny, the band's disintegration is tantamount to artistic blasphemy, and indicative of a lack of respect shown for both the noble beauty of the music, and the memory of their working-class predecessors in the band. Danny's viewpoint is, thus, capable of making audiences re-assess their own responses to the band's performances in the local villages, making the film more self-reflexive and self-interrogating in places than it may have been given credit for.

A subsequent scene relocates to a local fish and chip shop, whose motto 'In Cod We Trust' is noted in an establishing shot. Gloria and Andy (Ewan McGregor) have reconvened here for a meal, and the sparseness and lack of sophistication in the setting is highlighted by the amplified sound of the waitress artlessly dropping cutlery noisily onto their table. Gloria wryly comments that if she'd realised they were 'going this posh', she'd have got 'dolled up'. The table is adorned with tomato ketchup and vinegar bottles and both characters are smoking. These features anchor the film in a kind of implicit form of protest against antiseptic 'new worlds' in which coal fires, unhealthy eating and smoking have all been banished.

The unglamorous and mundane nature of the setting appears to militate against the romantic possibilities inherent in having the film's youngest and most attractive characters alone together in a restaurant. The sequence suggests that the characters hold differing political views regarding the future of the mine, but (at the same time) are attracted to each other, a fact which allows a romantic sub-plot to be introduced. (The following scene will suggest that they do, indeed, pair off, and have sex together before the night is over.)

The fundamentally repetitive and circular structure of the narrative is evident in the next scene, which begins with Danny (once again) checking names against a list of participants in a local brass band competition. This particular event is of more significance than the previous event because it constitutes the semi-final of a national brass band competition (taking place in Halifax), the winners of which will go through to the final at the Albert Hall in London. This contest takes place in what appears to be a former textile mill (evoking distant memories of the 'comic' struggles to ensure that the textile industry has a viable future in *The Man in the White Suit*). The Grimley band performance on this occasion is composed and confident, but, nonetheless, as in Gloria's audition scene, an underlying impression of crisis and despair permeates the sequence.

Scenes of the band's performance in the contest are interwoven with the results of the coal pit ballot about whether the miners themselves want to keep the mine open. The result is announced as 'four to one' in favour of redundancy. Shots of the managing director being informed of the result of the ballot on his mobile phone, and subsequently smiling at the result, imply that his professed desire to keep the pit open was always false. Grimley colliery band emerge as winners of the semi-final competition with 198 points, but the montage sequence (composed of sublime musical moments and disturbing narrative developments) make it clear that the latter statistic counts for little besides the 'four to one' result of the ballot.

The hollowness of their musical success is starkly illustrated by a shot of the band returning home, and being greeted by a town in an apparent state of mourning. Miners and town-folk are portrayed walking in slow motion, as if time itself has stopped still. Danny walks away from the town, setting off on his journey home, with the now immobile pithead clearly visible in the background. His sudden collapse to the ground interrupts this particular journey within the narrative, however, and as the band, led by Phil, rush to his aid the camera is positioned amidst the group of concerned onlookers in order to convey a vivid sense of the urgency and despair of this particular moment. Personal crises and social tragedies are inextricably linked by this stage of the proceedings, with the more comic elements of the narrative seemingly banished to the margins.

Danny is hospitalised and seemingly no longer in a position to criticise either the band's performances or the attitudes of individual members. Phil is unable to inform Danny that the men no longer wish to play on now that the pit is to close, and so the band survives in a kind of limbo. A number of suspenseful questions now emerge – will Danny live or die? If Gloria's position as a 'viability assessor' is discovered by the men she has befriended, how will they respond? Can Gloria and Andy enter into a lasting relationship? Will the members of the band relent and agree to play in the final?

The film will reveal a degree of ambiguity and complexity in detailing the resolutions to these particular dramatic situations, suggesting that the narrative's commitment to its working-class characters works against the formation of a wholly tragic tone, while equally rejecting the possibility of a happy ending in which the town's main source of employment is saved (as it ultimately is in *Sing As We Go* and *Shipyard Sally*). Danny's condition is serious and probably terminal, but he does live on to see the band's excellence affirmed by a national audience after the men and Gloria perform in the final.

Gloria (having been largely responsible for the initial continuance of the band) *is* publicly vilified and rejected, once it is revealed that she has a 'management logo on her key ring'. Having been subjected to a male gaze that desired to know her sexually, she is now objectified as an enemy of the male working class. It seems as if she has to be punished for the erotic desire she has provoked, and can now only be viewed as a destructive intruder within the community.

The film goes on to suggest that once things turn bad, situations can only deteriorate. A subsequent scene presents the 'loan sharks' taking away the remaining contents of Phil and Sandra's home. A medium close-up shot reveals Phil, dressed in his clown's outfit, rushing to remonstrate with the men emptying the contents of his house, but being held-up by his huge clown's feet. The incongruity of his cheerful appearance and made-up smiling face, given the seriousness and menacing nature of the scene, creates a sense of a tragi-farcical situation being played out to its logical conclusion.

The scene ends not with a comic punchline that might dissipate the tension and allow spectators to appreciate the potential of wit and humour to overcome a difficult situation. Instead, the dramatic 'social realist' elements of the film are foregrounded, as Phil is knocked to the ground by a punch in the face from one of the 'removal men', and the sequence ends with the sound of a crying baby, and a shot of the distraught family.

In a makeshift job-finding club (aptly or ironically named the 'rescue room'), erected on the former pit-site, Phil is consequently revealed to be suffering from an increasingly disturbed state of mind. There is no work of any substance on offer for the men. Phil reappears in the next scene, seated alone in an empty home, bereft of both family and furniture. By some strange oversight, the phone has not been cut off, and he receives a call summoning him for another performance as 'Mr Chuckles'. This 'alter ego' persona allows him to go on and berate 'Margaret, bloody, Thatcher' to a group of six-year-olds in a church celebration of the harvest festival, and to ponder why God lets her live when people such as John Lennon and two young miners are allowed to die.

The incongruities of the situation mean that the attack on Mrs Thatcher is partly qualified, and moderated, by the way in which it is presented to an audience of children who do not fully understand what

Phil is talking about, and by the fact that the speech is delivered by a character in the throes of a nervous breakdown. The scene does imply, however, that the children's essential innocence and faith in the world will be shattered as they grow older, and become more aware of the cynical and harsh nature of the society in which they live.

Having been harried out of the church hall by appalled mothers, aghast at his conduct, we next witness Phil hanging from the top of the pithead in a failed attempt to kill himself. Ironically, this time his huge clown's feet prove to be his salvation, as they draw attention to his plight, and he is saved by two security guards (who respond to the ghastly sight they encounter with the exclamation 'Jesus Christ'). Phil is first presented in long-shot, allowing us to observe his suffering from a distance, before the film cuts to a close-up of him struggling with the noose around his neck, caught between a state of wanting to die, and yet struggling to live. (Phil attempts to end it all in the place where he has previously earned his living, and which has now had its own life-source terminated.) The image succeeds in being simultaneously farcical, absurd and disturbing, both melodramatic and emotionally authentic.

The next image is of Phil being wheeled into hospital, with only his huge clownish feet sticking out from the foot of the trolley, as if he has been reduced to a body-part (workers had been referred to as 'hands' in earlier periods of British industrial history). Danny, observing the patient being brought in from his hospital bed, ironically recognises that it is Phil through the 'cartoon-like' image of the clown's feet: previously, Danny has not appeared to recognise his son's troubles when confronted with them, face-to-face. 'Have you lost your marbles?' asks Danny, as they are later seated in close proximity on a hospital bench. 'I've lost everything else', replies Phil, before listing the items he has lost: 'house, kids, job, self-respect. . .'

Phil's misfortunes constitute the narrative thread for this middle section of the film. After the failed suicide attempt, his character is revealed sitting disconsolately by a canal. Jim tells him to 'stop being a bloody drama queen' (as if, perhaps, the film itself is acknowledging that the plot has become excessively melodramatic and pessimistic by this stage of the proceedings). Phil is welcomed back into the fold by Jim and the gang, despite his admission that he, in fact, voted for the pit to close.

In the working-men's club, the male group is broken up by the return of the banished Gloria, who offers to devote her wages to enable the band to take part in the final at the Albert Hall. Gloria's role in the narrative at this point evokes Propp's concept of a 'magical donor',[56] a helper and facilitator, who provides the necessary financial means for the band to compete. Jim talks of 'guilt', and Gloria of 'dirty money', and

Jim's grudging remark – 'I hope you've budgeted for booze' – is the only indication that he is willing to accept her offer on behalf of the men.

The band, consequently, embarks on its final journey to perform at the Albert Hall. As band members wait to be given their cue to take to the stage, a female announcer on the internal intercom service has difficulty in pronouncing the words 'Grimley colliery' (to which Ernie sarcastically observes, 'I bet she's glad they closed the bugger'). Harry (Jim Carter), who has assumed the role of replacement conductor for the sick Danny, conducts without a baton in the style of a 1950s 'rock and roll' performer. Framed with the audience behind him in the impressive Albert Hall arena, he conducts in a charismatic, impassioned style. Midway through the band's performance, an ailing Danny emerges onto the concert-hall platform, like a 'ghost from the past', acknowledging, with an appreciative glance, the high standard of their playing.

Danny's lifetime aspiration is seemingly accomplished when his group of musicians win the competition, but the cruel irony of events is that he has come round to the sceptical way of thinking which was prevalent amongst the band members at the beginning of the narrative, about the real worth of musical performances in the midst of mass unemployment and dashed hopes.

The final unexpected plot-twist is that his acceptance speech becomes an act of disavowal, as his 'final' emotional journey ends in a public display of anger and dismay. His refutation of the trophy becomes part of a refusal to consider music outside of its social and economic contexts, with his 'anti-acceptance' speech emphasising the rights of human beings to possess the right to work and a future. He castigates a government that has 'destroyed our industry . . . our communities, our homes, our lives, all in the name of progress'.

His condemnatory speech is made more powerful by the fact that a film audience may have been led (through the deployment of comic banter and buoyant, inspirational music throughout certain sections of the narrative) to possibly expect some form of optimistic or hopeful conclusion, which the film, in the end, resolutely refuses to provide. Danny's views and sentiments at this point echo the observations of Raymond Williams in a *New Socialist* article written during the miners strike of 1984–85 in which he rebukes 'the logic of a new nomad capitalism, which exploits actual places and people and then . . . moves on'.[57]

The closing shots of the film complete the movement away from work which has been evolving throughout the narrative. As the beleaguered community winds its way home in a victory celebration on an open-top bus, the performance of what Danny refers to as 'Land of Hope and bloody Glory', as the Houses of Parliament pass by in the background, suggests that notions of democracy and social justice in British society may be growing apart in British culture as the century draws to a close.

The characters, however, appear finally reconciled to each other, if not to their fate, so not everything is lost. There is an impression, though, that after the hustle and bustle of the ceaseless activity conveyed in the narrative up to this closing moment of reflection, what lies ahead for the men is the disturbing prospect of a somewhat stilled and silenced society, composed of too much leisure time and not enough work (a prospect which the film anticipated in the opening scene featuring the man who has become resigned to his plight, and sits reading his newspaper, while his two neighbours talk over him as if he doesn't exist or matter).

The Full Monty: 'Sheffield – a city on the move'

The male characters in *The Full Monty* are similarly presented as attempting to escape from the boredom and spiritual emptiness caused by unemployment, but in their case industrial disaster has already occurred by the beginning of the story. *The Full Monty* opens with a rueful look-back at images of the past, as captured in a promotional documentary feature *Sheffield – City on the Move* (Coulthard Productions, 1971) which is screened over the credits. This film is at pains to present Sheffield as a progressive, vibrant city, with a thriving steel industry (so the narrator informs us) providing an economic basis for the social improvements in housing and shopping areas which are taking place. The documentary informs us that 'steel employs some 90,000 men', but that 'it's not all hard work for the people in Steel City', and the short film draws upon images of people dancing in discos, and scenes of local football teams in action to illustrate the leisure aspects of Sheffield.

City on the Move appears to be referring to the present and suggests an enthusiasm about the future prospects of the city. It is therefore disconcerting for audiences when the screen subsequently fades to black, followed by a caption which reads '25 years later'. A film that has been presented as topical and current turns out to actually be a period piece, detailing hopes for a future which were never to be quite realised. *The Full Monty* will proceed to offer an 'unofficial', non-documentary view of life and economic prospects in 1990s Sheffield, which can subsequently be compared with the sense of relentless enthusiasm prevalent in *City on the Move*. Alexander Walker in his *Evening Standard* review of *The Full Monty* wryly interpreted the significance of the documentary as 'a reminder of the booming Britain that was intended to be in which everyone would have a job and no one need go naked'.[58]

The economic and social history of Sheffield between the early 1970s and the mid-1990s is not outlined in *The Full Monty*, and the film lacks the strong sense of cultural tradition which underpins *Brassed Off*. In *The Full Monty*, the central character, Gaz (Robert Carlyle), and his friends tend to live in the present, rather than remembering what has been lost, and are rather cynical, if not entirely pessimistic about the future. *The Full Monty*, in certain respects, can be seen as continuing the story of *Brassed Off* about what happens to a group of Yorkshire men after they have been made redundant, although it is unlikely that the ex-miners of the latter film would ever consider stripping for a living.

The narrative proper of *The Full Monty* begins with two men, Dave (Mark Addy) and Gaz, and Gaz's son, Nathan (William Snape), moving through an abandoned factory, carrying a large steel girder, which Gaz apparently hopes to sell as scrap metal. The abrupt transition from a documentary film, claiming that facilities and prospects in Sheffield are improving all the time, to this contrasting scene, set amid unmistakable signs of urban decay, creates an immediate sense of dramatic irony and comic incongruity.

Gaz's plans are quickly revealed as impractical, when father, son and friend are locked in the disused factory by a passing security guard, and end up trying to escape by standing upon a car which is slowly sinking into a canal. Having once been employed in this very factory 'for ten years', the men are now reduced to scavenging and appropriating from its remains. A brass band associated with the defunct steel factory (the British Steel Stocksbridge band) is glimpsed passing by, creating another link with *Brassed Off*.

Father and son become separated in the farcical antics of trying to get the girder out of the factory, and Nathan expresses disapproval at the immature attitudes and behaviour displayed by his father. A relationship that forms a sub-text within the narrative in *Brassed Off* (Phil's relationship with his son, Shane) will become a central focus of *The Full Monty*. When the gang of three are shortly reunited, Dave complains about his jeans having been soaked in the watery escape from the factory. Gaz replies that he 'should have taken' his 'kit off', unconsciously alluding to the more ambitious scheme which will shortly occupy his mind and dominate the rest of the film. Gaz invites his son to accompany him to the 'job club' – 'it'll be a good laugh', he suggests bizarrely – but Nathan, tiring of his father's relentless escapist and elusive dreams, goes home instead.

The following sequence in the film takes place at the job club, where the leader (in a teacher-like manner) is warning the men that he wants to see their CVs finished by the time he returns to the room. As soon as he leaves, however, the men take out playing cards, and start bickering amongst themselves. The impression is that these men are trapped in an intolerable situation, and are starting to regress to the level of recalcitrant schoolboys. Gerald (Tom Wilkinson), who is wearing a suit and typing on a computer, complains (like Nathan) about Gaz's attitude and behaviour, but he is told, 'You forget, Gerald, you're not our foreman any more . . . you're just like the rest of us'.

This exchange leads to a fight between Gerald and Gaz, accentuating the impression of a school classroom situation getting out of control. It is notable that there are no unemployed women present in the room, and, as in the scene depicting the 'rescue centre' serving as a makeshift job centre in *Brassed Off*, an underlying sense of despair and depression amongst the men can be detected, beneath the boisterous humour and abrasive banter.

The film proceeds to sketch the personal relationships and contexts within which the men live. Gerald has not dared to inform his wife that he has lost his job, and so pretends to go out to work each day. Dave feels that with his lack of a job and accompanying weight problem, he cannot possibly be attractive to his wife. Gaz is estranged from his ex-wife, who has settled with a new partner in a more affluent part of town. Lomper (Steve Huison) is rescued by Dave from killing himself by inhaling poisonous fumes in his car. When Lomper returns home, and finds his elderly and crippled mother struggling to get up the stairs, she says to him, 'I thought you'd gone', without specifying where she thought he was headed. She, herself, will be dead before the close of the narrative.

Both *Brassed Off* and *The Full Monty* structure their narratives around the concept of 'putting on a show', and Gaz and his fellow performers spend as much time practising their dance moves as they do taking their clothes off. Gerald's skill at ballroom dancing suggests that he may prove to be an effective choreographer, but Gaz and Dave only secure his co-operation after they thwart his interview for a new job, by making his beloved garden gnomes appear to be attacking each other, in a kind of 'Punch and Judy' show taking place behind the backs of the men interviewing him. Gerald finds himself fatally distracted, especially at the moment when one gnome head-butts and smashes another!

As he subsequently informs Gaz and Dave, at the joyless job club, he has lost the opportunity of much needed work through their actions. The gnome scene treads a fine line between comedy and cruelty. As cinema spectators, we can be drawn towards laughing at Gerald's attempts to keep a straight face, while his normally static gnomes are darting about in rapid motion. However, when an angry and emotional Gerald demands of Gaz, 'Why did you do it?', it is telling that he has no real answer, just as Andy offers no reply to Gloria's question in *Brassed Off*, 'If my job's so bloody irrelevant, how come you hate me so much?' Both films suggest that long-term unemployment and an accompanying sense of social despair may lead to men taking leave of their senses, and not always considering the possible consequences of their actions and attitudes.

Gerald's outraged despair is quelled in the following emotionally understated outdoor scene, where Gaz, Dave and Gerald settle their differences. Gerald is presented with a model wheelbarrow for his rockery, and a repaired gnome, whose bruised head reflects something of Gerald's own pain and dismay. In its setting and bittersweet sentiment, the scene echoes the sequence in *Brassed Off* where a despondent Phil is sitting forlornly by a disused canal, and is taken back into the male group, despite admitting that he voted for redundancy.

The Full Monty, having reconciled the main characters to each other, sets about auditioning for other men willing to help realise Gaz's dream of staging a successful male strip show. Bruce Jones, who played the father desperately trying to raise money for his daughter's communion dress in Ken Loach's *Raining Stones*, appears briefly as a man apparently prepared to try anything in these difficult times. In a medium close-up shot, composed within a still frame, the camera observes his uneasiness with the demands of stripping. He finally halts the audition, and signals a desire to collect his children outside, adding that this scenario is 'no place for kids'. Gaz's son, Nathan, is present throughout many of the rehearsals, and the film never seems disturbed by the thought of his presence. This may, however, be to do with the essential 'innocence' of the spectacle, and the film's desire to re-orient audiences into taking a more relaxed and positive attitude towards the human body and nakedness.

The auditions take place in the abandoned (but still guarded) steel factory, as if the men are inexorably drawn back to a place where they used to belong and have a social role. Gerald hides his face behind a newspaper on realising that one of the applicants, Guy (Hugo Speer), is the man who plastered his bathroom. Such examples of the breakdown of conventional British social class divisions between the characters testifies to the more subversive undercurrents of the film, and to its 'carnivalesque' philosophy, which can imagine a world where men can be naked with each other, without sexual desire necessarily emerging, or people thinking that the situation is peculiar or improper.

Nevertheless, the men are speechless at the size of Guy's penis (he is a 'well-hung' guy), and Lomper later will take the opportunity of escaping from a police raid to kiss and fondle Guy, suggesting that sexual as well as social despair may have led to his suicidal condition in the opening stages of the narrative. In the privacy of his bedroom, Dave will later ask his wife whether she has ever been out with a black man, a reference to his own feelings of sexual inadequacy.

In his *Observer* review of *The Full Monty*, Philip French declared that 'two sequences between Dave . . . and his wife (the admirable Lesley Sharpe) are more tender, moving and convincing than any conventional Hollywood cinema'.[59] An extract from a Hollywood picture of the 1980s, *Flashdance* (Adrian Lyne, 1983), within the narrative, will also serve to distinguish *The Full Monty*'s treatment of relationships from popular Hollywood productions, although it is notable that *Flashdance* was a Twentieth Century Fox production, and *The Full Monty* was distributed by Twentieth Century Fox Searchlight, after Film Four had rejected the film.[60]

The extract from *Flashdance* (1983) occurs when Gaz and Dave steal the video of the film from the local supermarket, in order to learn from its dance moves. This successful Hollywood film has an added resonance and meaning for the former steel workers, in that the central female character, Alex Owens (Jennifer Beals), is a welder by day and a dancer by night. Whilst watching the film, Dave focuses on the poor quality of her welding techniques, rather than the exceptional nature of her dancing, noting, for instance, that her 'mix is all to cock'. The other men are amused by Dave's obsession with detail and his concern for realist accuracy over an uncritical enjoyment of Hollywood spectacle. The film *Flashdance*, itself, shows little interest in Alex's job as a worker in a steel factory, despite the apparent novelty of her involvement in such an occupation, and is much more fascinated by her night-time position as an exotic and somewhat avant-garde dancer in a local bar.

A slighting review in *Sight and Sound* described *Flashdance* as a movie that 'is in fact nothing more than a series of dance montage sequences, shot in loving close-up but unable to open out any kind of articulate emotional perspective', the reviewer concluding that 'The effect is numbing'.[61] This account underestimates the vitality of the central performance, and the exhilarating quality of the dance sequences, I would contend, and I think it could be claimed that the makers of *The Full Monty* were influenced by *Flashdance*'s storytelling techniques of fast editing, relatively short scenes, sympathy for the 'underdog', and celebration of a character who possesses an unquenchable urge to realise a creative ambition.

Alex in *Flashdance* really desires to become a ballet dancer, but she lacks confidence to apply for the local ballet school, feeling that she is from the wrong social class. In view of *The Full Monty*'s view of male stripping as one possible route for the disenfranchised Sheffield men, it is ironic to note that in Adrian Lyne's film Alex dives into a local strip-bar, and actually pulls off the stage a female friend who has descended into stripping for a living, artistic dancing having proved to be unprofitable. Alex suggests that stripping is a form of degradation. 'Call that dancing?' she enquires of her friend, making 'a living, rolling around' with no clothes on. When she finds money stuffed into her friend's garter, the dollar notes fall into the wet street of the gutter, as if it is 'dirty money' (Gloria's phrase for her earnings in *Brassed Off*), and thus, permanently tainted. The relationship between the Hollywood and the British film is, thus, more complex than may appear initially to be the case.

Alex appears to succeed in achieving her ambition, although the narrative ends in a freeze-framed shot (as will *The Full Monty*), leaving her future unsketched. She gives a superlative, gymnastic performance in her audition piece, enhanced in the film by the use of a dance double in key sequences, and the imaginative use of camera angles in the finished film. The final shot is of her running towards her steelyard boss (Michael Nouri), who is also now her boyfriend.

With the insertion of this intertextual reference to a modern Hollywood film dramatising the 'impossible dreams of ordinary people', the goals and aspirations of these men to succeed as male strippers, may seem quite realistic and feasible in comparison. Alex's aspirations in *Flashdance* are not easily achieved, and *The Full Monty* is certainly keen to illustrate the difficulties the Sheffield men face in their desire to realise their own less culturally respectable 'dream'. What *The Full Monty* does possess (in contrast to parts of *Flashdance*) is a sense of wry humour about the tale being narrated, and a sense that other people's cultural ambitions may always appear ridiculous or bizarre from certain perspectives.

Gerald's increased willingness to enter into the 'dream world' of his comrades, despite his reservations – 'I used to have a proper job', he observes – is nowhere better demonstrated than when he allows the men to practise stripping off in his front room. Any homoerotic undertones conjured up by their activities are dissipated by the unexpected arrival of 'loan sharks', who threaten to take away his material possessions in lieu of payment for the sum of £120 which is owed by Gerald. A half-naked Dave tells the men to 'piss off', and the sight of what appears to be a homosexual orgy taking place in a suburban house, encourages the debt collectors to flee from the house!

A similar scene in *Brassed Off*, where Phil's house is emptied because of the debts he owes, ends with him being knocked to the ground by one of the debt collectors *and* concludes with his possessions being taken away. Crucially, at this juncture, he lacks the support of his fellow miners, but whereas in *The Full Monty*, the men move emotionally closer together as the narrative proceeds, in *Brassed Off*, the men tend to become fragmented and increasingly at odds with each other. The contrasting conclusions of these two comparable scenes are an illustration of certain subtle differences between the two films. (Gerald's possessions are eventually taken away from him, so the reprieve is somewhat temporary.)

In a subsequent practice session, Nathan inadvertently reveals that his father has been in prison, a detail that appears to relate Gaz to Stevie, the character played by Robert Carlyle in *Riff-Raff*. The son emerges as the only person willing to finance Gaz's dreams, even taking out his £100 savings in order to bankroll the venture. Their relationship increasingly acquires the tone of a contemporary British version of the father and son relationship depicted in *Bicycle Thieves* (Vittorio De Sica, 1948), and, as Alexander Walker noted in his review of *The Full Monty*, it was, perhaps, not insignificant that the producer of the latter was 'one Uberto Pasolini'.[62]

Newly revitalised, the men are able to imbue even the deadening and humiliating experience of signing on at the labour exchange with a sense of rhythm and life, as they spontaneously start moving in unison to the sound of a Donna Summer track playing overhead. Gerald, though, remains sceptical about their chances of success. 'You're too old, you're too fat, you're pigeon-chested', he tells the others, and when the men are arrested for indecent exposure during another rehearsal in the disused steel factory, it seems as if the venture is unrealisable and doomed.

The notoriety of the group's arrest, however, leads to a frenzy of interest in their 'one night only' performance, which leads to two hundred tickets being sold. Ironically, at the last moment, Gaz is the only member of the group to have second thoughts, and initially, he refuses to appear on stage. In front of an excited crowd, the other men take to the stage dressed in the uniform of security guards, a final symbolic overturning of repressive structures of authority.

Nathan succeeds in convincing Gaz that his place is out there with the other men, and so, to the sound of Tom Jones exclaiming, 'You give me reason to live', Gaz takes his place with the other performers. Shots of the audience reveal that Dave's wife and Gaz's ex-wife are amongst the audience, and both appear to be enjoying the spectacle. Dave's discarded shirt is caught by his wife, and Gaz throws his belt to ex-wife, Mandy (Emily Woof), suggesting that channels of communication between the sexes have been re-opened and potentially revivified by the close. Dave introduces their act by stating that they may be neither pretty, good, nor young, but they 'are here', and for their sheer nerve and presence, the spectators and, seemingly, the film applauds them.

Having taken the men to the culmination of their objective, and the climax of their act, the film concludes with an image of the men filmed from the rear, indicating that they have nothing left to shed or hide, and have shaken off some of the 'dead weight of the past', and been prepared to present themselves to an enthusiastic female audience as 'naked as the day' they were born.

In *Brassed Off*, the band is last seen fading away into the darkness of a London evening, amidst an atmosphere of social and economic gloom. At the close of *The Full Monty*, the group's triumphant performance is captured (and ended) in a freeze-frame shot, as if the price to be paid for their moment of success is to be frozen forever into an eternally still moment within history.

Conclusion

In his essay, 'Entertainment and Utopia' (1977), Richard Dyer argues that 'Entertainment offers the image of "something better" to escape into . . . that our daily lives don't provide',[63] and the concepts of brass band playing and stripping in the respective films would seem to offer the prospect of a temporary escape from the more mundane and depressing features of the men's lives. Dyer notes that a kind of yearning for what he terms 'historical utopianism'[64] is implicit in the genre of the musical, but in the comedy-dramas *Brassed Off* and *The Full Monty* there is no prospect of the men's musical and dance performances taking place in some kind of utopian (or even particularly hopeful) setting.

For Danny in *Brassed Off*, music offers both a link with the past, and the possibility of transcending unpropitious conditions in the present, but the film makes clear that a divisive and seemingly irrevocable break between past and present economic and cultural traditions is being enacted as the narrative unfolds. Hence, there is a pervasive mood within *Brassed Off* which creates a kind of 'Last of England' or 'Last of Ealing' impression as the narrative progresses.

Thomas Elsaesser in his influential essay 'Tales of Sound and Fury: Observations on the Family Melodrama' (1972), offered a definition of melodrama as 'a dramatic narrative in which musical accompaniment marks the emotional effects', and suggested that 'Music in melodrama . . . is both functional (i.e., of structural significance) and thematic . . . because used to formulate certain moods – sorrow, violence, dread, suspense, happiness'.[65] In *Brassed Off*, music is used to underline and articulate particular emotional states, with the rousing 'William Tell Overture' at the close suggesting lowly members of the community rising to stake their rightful place in society. The poignant rendition of Elgar's

'Pomp and Circumstance March' on the journey home reflects the colliery band's sense of battered pride, and their determination as a group to keep on playing to the bitter end.

In *The Full Monty*, the men respond to music through their body language, and the popular songs deployed by the men in their dance routines evince a feeling of nostalgia for the 1970s, a period when the steel industry in Sheffield was still functioning to some degree. Songs such as 'You Sexy Thing' by Hot Chocolate and 'Hot Stuff' (performed by Donna Summer) are used somewhat ironically in the film, as the men initially appear far from sexy and appealing. The masculine bodies in *The Full Monty* may be deemed redundant by industrial capitalism, but, by the close, the male strippers have succeeded in what Herbert Marcuse in *Eros and Civilisation: A Philosophical Inquiry into Freud* (1955) described as the aim of 'making the human body an instrument of pleasure rather than labour'.[66]

In his study, Marcuse also claims that 'Men can die without anxiety if they know that what they love is protected from misery and oblivion'.[67] The most disturbing implications of *Brassed Off* are, I would suggest, contained in this observation. When Phil is swinging from the coal pithead in a failed attempt to commit suicide, or Danny is thinking about the coal-corrupted nature of his insides, neither character can rest assured in the knowledge that their immediate family or the social and cultural traditions which they most value will continue after they are gone. This factor, paradoxically, does encourage Phil and Danny to fight for their beliefs, taking the film beyond conventional generic classifications of comedy, melodrama and tragedy in the process.

If *Brassed Off* is a more tragic narrative than *The Full Monty*, that may be because it has a greater sense of the important working class and cultural traditions which are in danger of being lost forever, and of musical and social talents which are perpetually overlooked by the media. The men in *The Full Monty*, in contrast, are able to explore and exploit contemporary obsessions with sexual spectacle and 'sensationalist' exposures in contemporary British culture.

Both narratives are indebted to certain traditions of Ealing comedy and films produced within the British 'new wave' cycle of films. *The Titfield Thunderbolt* and *Brassed Off* each depict communities who strive to combat the impending closure of an institution deemed essential to the local area's sense of social identity and economic needs. The villagers in the southern community featured in *The Titfield Thunderbolt* succeed in their aims, while the northerners in *Brassed Off* have their hopes crushed.

Passport to Pimlico and *The Full Monty* construct their respective stories out of juxtaposing elements of the 'ordinary' and the 'fantastic' within the same narrative. Each film dramatises the consequences of pursuing a particular form of logic to an extreme conclusion, and poses a specific question. How can the inhabitants of Pimlico be foreign if they live in London? How can a group of not especially attractive men make a success of taking their clothes off in public? The comic and dramatic elements of both films are contained in the narrative strategies involved in finding answers to these questions.

In his study *The Fantastic: A Structural Approach to a Literary Genre* (1970), Tzvetan Todorov suggests that concepts of the 'fantastic' must always be defined in relation to notions of 'the real', and claims that the 'fantastic' occupies and denotes a period of uncertainty when sceptical individuals are confronted by extraordinary events.[68] This definition would apply to the situations of both *Brassed Off* and *The Full Monty*.

Brassed Off is also attracted to the kind of saucy humour associated with the films of George Formby and the 'Carry On' series. For all its striving for a more democratic and accountable form of society, *Brassed Off* is still committed to a way of perceiving the world which draws heavily upon the framework of the 'mother-in-law' joke, and is fascinated by the prospect of a comic world where women are to be desired or feared, but certainly not entrusted with positions of power or responsibility. George Orwell in 'The Art of Donald McGill' (1941) described such a world as one where 'marriage is . . . a comic disaster' and the 'rent is always behind and the clothes up the spout'.[69] In *Brassed Off*, Jim and Ernie try to escape from their wives in order to chat up Gloria, but the wives get wind of what is happening, and follow them on the excursion in typical seaside postcard fashion.

Orwell defined a 'dirty joke' as 'a sort of mental rebellion, a momentary wish that things were otherwise'.[70] The men in *The Full Monty* begin by treating the business of stripping as something of a 'dirty' or absurd 'joke', but they come to realise that timing, dancing skills and precision of movement are all vital to the success of a performance, and they become vaguely aware that such a philosophical entity as sexual politics may exist. In pursuing an occupation associated with women (of exposing their bodies for the pleasure and edification of spectators), the men are forced into some kind of empathetic relationship with female experience. The male characters in *Brassed Off* (by way of a contrast), remain rather too tied to appraisals of the female role in society that are outdated and unhelpful. In this sense, they may represent a type of male 'dinosaur' facing extinction, while *The Full Monty* strippers can be witnessed mutating (however reluctantly and bizarrely), into 'new men'.

In his study of *British Cinema in the 1980s*, John Hill suggested that *Brassed Off* and *The Full Monty* could not 'have worked so effectively as *comedy*' if they 'had actually been made during the early 1980s'[71] when struggles to keep heavy manufacturing industries open were an ongoing concern. Both films, in that sense, are about what has already transpired.

Brassed Off was produced on a budget of £2,530,000, and took £2,873,429 at the UK box office, making the film dependent on overseas sales to make a significant profit.[72] In the light of such financial considerations and calculations, *Brassed Off* can be partly interpreted as an allegory about the difficulties facing an indigenous cinema, struggling to survive in a situation where it is difficult to raise funding for native films in a market dominated by American imports, and in which there is a lack of distribution and exhibition outlets for British films.

This contemporary cycle of comedy-dramas exploring the intricacies of regional communal life may already have peaked in British film culture, which may be an appropriate response to the elegiac mood of *Brassed Off*, in particular. The most obvious successor to Mark Herman's film has been *Billy Elliot* (Stephen Daldry, 2000), a narrative also concerned with cultivating a specialised cultural interest within the confines of a troubled mining community in a recent and embittered period of British social history. *Billy Elliot* contains less explicitly humorous material than either *Brassed Off* and *The Full Monty*, partly because it is set in the midst of the miners' strike of 1984–85, a time of harsh conflicts and unforgiving attitudes, and also because the transcendent activity at the centre of the film (ballet dancing) takes the individual away from his community, and does not have its creative roots in the local area.

The local mining community in *Billy Elliot* is depicted as torn between those who are for and against the strike (the miners in *Brassed Off* are also shown to be divided between those who are in favour of accepting redundancy, and those who wish to keep the pit open), and the town is portrayed as existing in a war-like atmosphere, resulting in a heavy police presence.

The eponymous Billy (Jamie Bell) finds in dance a release from the surrounding emotions of bitterness and resentment. His talents are harnessed into an example of 'high culture' which his father (Gary Lewis) sees as effeminate, elitist and irrelevant, especially, when considered in relation to more traditional working-class masculine pursuits, such as boxing and mining. In *Billy Elliot*, ballet is presented as something (at first) which is alien to the local mining community, although, ironically, its 'alien' quality (what one might term its 'otherness') is in fact one of its major appeals for Billy.

The antipathy and contempt displayed by Billy's father and brother towards the notion of practising and valuing the art of ballet becomes a tragi-comic motif in the film – tragic in the sense that the men's own culture and way of life based around working down a coal mine is shown as existing in an advanced state of irrevocable decline, and comical in the ways in which the film generates humour out of what might be perceived as an incongruous and unusual situation (a miner's son who desires to become a professional ballet dancer).

In *The Birth of Tragedy* (1871), Friedrich Nietzsche argued that comedy was a kind of illegitimate offshoot of Greek tragedy:

> But when a new artistic genre did spring into life, honouring tragedy as its predecessor and its master, it was frighteningly apparent that although it bore its mother's features they were the features she had borne during her long death struggle ... It was in comedy that the degenerate figure of tragedy lived on, a monument to its miserable and violent death.[73]

In *Billy Elliot*, as in *Brassed Off* and *The Full Monty*, a kind of tragedy of the working classes is being played out, with the more comic or farcical elements of the narratives serving to lessen some (but not all) of the pain experienced by the striking or unemployed miners featured in the films. In the two films set in mining towns, the coal miners are depicted as being engaged in a 'long death struggle' to keep the local pits alive, and, as spectators of the films, we witness the 'miserable and violent' death throes of a culture which has previously been defined by shared values and combined efforts at the workplace. Billy Elliot, in taking up the occupation and 'dream' that he does, has to extricate himself from the community, and assume a position within a very different type of society and workplace.

A major feature linking the 1990s communal comedy-dramas discussed was that they aspired to draw attention to a large number of characters in particular settings, who felt that circumstances had brought them to a kind of emotional standstill and social impasse. These were not narratives which suggested that a number of sequels and related films could easily be generated from the original works, and that added to their elegiac quality. I would conclude, however, that the past and present films discussed in this chapter illustrate the strengths of this particular sub-genre within British cinema, and, at the very least, seek to contradict and dispute Mrs Thatcher's famous claim that there is 'no such thing as society'.[74]

Notes

1　The sub-heading 'Things Can Only Get Better' comes from a 1993 song by D:Ream, which was used as the theme tune to the Labour party's election campaign in 1997. The website www.worldsocialism.org/spgb/nov98/ getbettr.htm1 (accessed 2 February 2005) describes the tune retrospectively as 'the relentless backing track to an illusion'. A political memoir by John O'Farrell, *Things Can Only Get Better: 18 Miserable Years in the Life of a Labour Supporter, 1979–97* (Black Swan, London, 1998), draws upon the phrase to refer to the sustained period between the dates of the title in which the Labour party was out of office.

2   Chris Peachment, review of *Up 'n' Under*, *Daily Telegraph* (25 January 1998).

3   Tom Charity interviews Mark Herman, *Time Out* (30 November 1996).

4   Mark Herman interviewed by Devin O'Leary, *Weekly Alibi* (6 November 1997). Available online at www.filmvault.com/filmvault/alibi/b/ brassedoff_f.html (accessed 2 February 2005).

5   Simon Beaufoy interviewed in *Story and Character: Interviews with British Screenwriters*, edited by Alistair Owen (Bloomsbury, London, 2003), pp. 286–7.

6   Christopher Williams, 'The Social Art Cinema: A Moment in the History of British Film and Television Culture' in *Cinema: the Beginnings and the Future*, edited by Christopher Williams (University Of Westminster Press, London, 1996), p. 192.

7   *Ibid.*

8   Philip French, review of *The Englishman Who Went Up a Hill But Came Down a Mountain*, *Observer* (6 August 1995).

9   Tom Hutchinson, review of *Waking Ned*, *Hampstead and Highgate Express* (19 March 1999).

10 Raymond Williams, *The Country and the City* (Chatto and Windus, London, 1973), p. 165.

11 *Ibid.*

12 *Ibid.*, p. 176.

13 James. F. English, *Comic Transactions: Literature, Humour, and the Politics of Community in Twentieth Century Britain* (Cornell University Press, Ithaca NY and London, 1994), p. 9.

14 *Ibid.*, p. 9.

15 Simon Critchley, *On Humour* (Routledge, London, 2002), p. 68.

16 Martin Green, *A Mirror for Anglo-Saxons* (Longmans, London, 1961: first published in 1957), p. 48–9.

17 *Ibid.*, p. 50.

18 Charles Barr, 'Opening up the Drama Archives', *Listener*, 96:2484 (November 1976), p. 651.

19   David Sutton, *A Chorus of Raspberries: British Film Comedy 1929–39* (Exeter University Press, Exeter, 2000), p. 5.

20 Marcia Landy, *British Genres: Cinema and Society 1930–1960* (Princeton University Press, Princeton, 1991), p. 337.

21 Graham Greene, review of *Shipyard Sally* (18 August 1939) in *The Pleasure-Dome: The Collected Film Criticism 1935–40*, edited by John Russell

Taylor (Secker & Warburg, London, 1972), p. 239. Cyril Connolly, reviewing *Shipyard Sally* in the *New Statesman and Nation*, 18:441 (5 August 1939), described it as 'miserably unreal', and unsure of whether 'it is a musical comedy or a Powerful Drama'. Connolly went on to claim that such examples of 'English humour' were really synonyms for what he termed a 'fear of life, fear of death, fear of anti-fascism, fear of sentiment, intelligence, sex, a cosy English fear of anything and everything' (p. 214). The unidentified film reviewer of the *New Statesman and Nation*, 18:459 (9 December 1939) was no more complimentary about the latest release by Gracie Fields' male counterpart, George Formby. The reviewer described Formby as possessing 'a North Country accent, a gigantic expanse of teeth, and a sort of self-effacing "little man" appeal'. The commentator concluded that Formby 'sings pleasantly . . . and makes broad jokes with disarming sangfroid, but that does not seem to be enough and the mystery of his wide popularity remains unsolved' (p. 821).

22 Graham Greene, review of *Shipyard Sally* (18 August 1939).

23 *Ibid.*

24 David Bordwell and Kristin Thompson, *Film History: An Introduction* (McGraw Hill, New York/London, 1994), p. 455.

25 Charles Barr, 'Projecting Britain and the British Character: Ealing Studios', *Screen*, 15:2 (summer 1974), p. 138.

26 English, *Comic Transactions*, p. 20.

27 Duncan Petrie, *Creativity and Constraint in the British Film Industry* (Macmillan, London, 1991), p. 155.

28 Jeffrey Richards, *Films and British National Identity: From Dickens to Dad's Army* (Manchester University Press, Manchester, 1997), p. 137.

29 Bordwell and Thompson, *Film History: An Introduction*, p. 455.

30 John Ellis, 'Made in Ealing', *Screen*, 16:1 (spring 1975), p. 123.

31 Anthony Carthew, 'Shop-steward Sellers shows us up', review of *I'm All Right Jack*, *Daily Herald* (14 August 1959).

32 John Hill, *Sex, Class and Realism: British Cinema 1956–1963* (British Film Institute, London, 1986), p. 154.

33 Philip Simpson, 'Directions to Ealing', *Screen Education*, 24 (autumn 1977), p. 14.

34 According to the *BFI Film and Television Handbook* (1999) edited by Eddie Dyja, *Up 'n' Under* was produced on a budget of £2 million. The film went on to make £3,206,994 at the UK box office, making it the third most popular British film in 1998. Source: *BFI Film and Television Handbook* (2000). Details of situation comedy dates of transmission are taken from Mark Lewisohn, *Radio Times Guide to TV Comedy* (BBC Books, London, 1998).

35 John Godber, 'Notes', Introduction to *Up 'n' Under* (Amber Lane Press, Oxford, 1985).

36 Brian Glover died on 24 July 1997: www.imdb.com/name/nm0323093 (accessed 8 March 2005). Gary Olsen died 19 September, 2000:

www.imdb.com/name/nm0647653 (accessed 2 February 2005). Ian
Bannen, the leading actor in *Waking Ned*, died in a car accident in November, 1999 (www.imdb.com/name/nm0000846, accessed 8 March 2005),
making the fatal road accident that resolves the narrative more disturbing
than amusing on subsequent viewings.

37   Roger Scruton, *England: An Elegy* (Chatto and Windus, London, 2000),
     p. 246.
38   Alexander Walker, 'Scam among the shamrocks' *Evening Standard*, review
     of *Waking Ned* (18 March 1999).
39   Tristan Davies, 'Who's Hugh in Wales?' *Daily Telegraph* (10 September
     1994), pp. 12–13.
40   Eddie Dyja (ed.), *BFI Film and Television Handbook* (1996), p. 28.
41   Alexander Walker, review of *Brassed Off*, *Evening Standard* (31 October
     1996).
42   Ian Johns, 'It's that Ealing Feeling', *The Times* (1 August 2002), p. 15.
43   Perry Anderson, *English Questions* (Verso, London, 1992), pp. 303–4.
44   David N. Ashton, 'Unemployment' in *Beyond Thatcherism*, edited by
     Phillip Brown and Richard Sparks (Open University Press, Milton
     Keynes/Philadelphia, 1989), p. 25.
45   John Hill, *British Cinema in the 1980s* (Clarendon Press, Oxford, 1999),
     p. 200.
46   'Sympathetic Images', Ken Loach interviewed by Gavin Smith, *Film Com-
     ment*, 30:2 (March/April 1994), p. 60.
47   *Ibid.*, p. 60.
48   *Ibid.*, p. 62.
49   *Ibid.*, p. 63.
50   UK Cinema Box office receipts for *Riff-Raff* taken from the *BFI Film and
     Television Handbook* (1993), edited by David Leafe, p. 38.
51   Geoffrey Macnab, review of *Brassed Off*, *Sight and Sound*, 6:11 (Novem-
     ber 1996), p. 44.
52   Karl Marx, *The Eighteenth Brumaire of Louis Bonaparte* (Progress Pub-
     lishers, Moscow, 1967: first published in 1869), p. 10.
53   Information on Joaquin Rodrigo (1901–99) taken from www.worldof
     classicalmusic.com (accessed 8 March 2005).
54   Eric Hobsbawm in *Age of Extremes: The Short Twentieth Century
     1914–1991* (Michael Joseph, London, 1994) claims that approximately
     2,000 British volunteers fought in Spain for the Republican cause. Hobs-
     bawm suggests that the Spanish Civil War 'even in retrospect, appears as
     pure and compelling as it did in 1936' (p. 160).
55   Alexander Walker, review of *Brassed Off*, *Evening Standard* (31 October
     1996).
56   Vladimir Propp in the *Morphology of the Folktale*, translated by Laurence
     Scott (second edition, revised and edited by Louis A. Wagner, University of
     Texas Press, Austin and London, 1968), refers to the narrative functions
     of donors and helpers (magical agents) in his appendix 1: 'Materials for a

tabulation of the tale' (pp. 123–4). Propp notes that the hero of a tale might have two objectives: 'goal as an action (to seek out, to liberate, to rescue); goal as an object (a princess)', p. 123. Young hero, Andy (Ewan McGregor), in *Brassed Off* fails to 'rescue' the mine in the film (what Propp refers to as the 'liquidation of misfortune or lack' within a narrative, p. 153), but he does gain, latterly, the 'princess', who, in turn, saves him and the men from their immediate spiritual despair. Gloria is wrongly accused of being a 'false hero' (p. 125) by the men, although she is rehabilitated (just) by the close.

57 Raymond Williams, 'Mining the Meaning: Key Words in the Miners' Strike' (1985) reprinted in *Resources of Hope: Culture, Democracy, Socialism*, edited by Robin Gable (Verso, London/New York, 1989), p. 124. Williams concludes that 'what lies ahead of us, within that alien order, is a long series of decisions in which one industry after another will declare more and more people redundant' (p. 124). *Brassed Off*, through Danny's address to the Albert Hall audience (and, implicitly to spectators of the film) comes to a remarkably similar conclusion to that of Williams. In his biography of *Raymond Williams* (Routledge, London, 1995), Fred Inglis traces the demise of the British mining industry to the failure of the 1984–85 strike: 'The miners were crushed . . . when they went back to work behind their union banners and their local brass bands, they went back to the certain loss of . . . jobs, neighbourhood, union, culture, everything' (p. 289). After his suicide attempt in *Brassed Off*, Phil talks of having lost his 'house, kids, job, self-respect. . . ' The *Guardian* reported that in 2003 there were only '15 pits remaining in the UK, employing 8,000 miners': see the Patrick Wintour article entitled '£60 million package will save four pits', 12 February 2003, p. 2.

58 Alexander Walker, review of *The Full Monty*, *Evening Standard* (22 August 1997).

59 Philip French, review of *The Full Monty*, *Observer* (31 August 1997). French concludes that 'much of its political and sexual meaning resides in the absence of glamour or triumphalism'.

60 Alison Boshoff, 'Channel 4 bares its soul over rejection of *The Full Monty*', *Daily Telegraph* (16 April 1998), p. 13. The article reports that Channel 4 had invested money in the script development of *The Full Monty*, but decided (according to Paul Webster, chief executive of Film Four) that the film was too similar 'in subject matter and style' to *Brassed Off*, which the 'television company chose to invest [in] instead after a "beauty contest" between the two projects'. Webster comments that 'We felt that the two films served the same community and had the same concerns about unemployment and dignity', but admits that in the light of *The Full Monty*'s international commercial success, 'You can only hope that you don't make that mistake again' (p. 13).

61 'Double Takes', *Sight and Sound*, 52:3 (summer 1983), p. 183.

62 Walker, review of *The Full Monty*.

63 Richard Dyer, 'Entertainment and Utopia', *Movie*, 24 (spring 1977), p. 3.

64 *Ibid.*, p. 13.
65 Thomas Elsaesser, 'Tales of Sound and Fury: Observations on the Family Melodrama' (1972), reprinted in *Movies and Methods Volume II*, edited by Bill Nichols (University of California Press, Berkeley and London, 1985), p. 172. In the essay, Elsaesser notes that 'In England, Dickens . . . relied heavily on melodramatic plots to sharpen social conflicts' and point out the 'existence of extreme social and moral contrasts' (p. 170). The naming of the town Grimley in *Brassed Off* draws upon a British comic tradition of naming places in ways which may symbolise key aspects of their being (the mining town in Dickens' *Hard Times* (1854), for instance, is named 'Coketown').
66 Herbert Marcuse, *Eros and Civilization: A Philosophical Inquiry into Freud* (Allen Lane and the Penguin Press, London, 1966: first published in 1955), p. 13.
67 *Ibid.*, p. 188.
68 Tzvetan Todorov, *The Fantastic: A Structural Approach to a Literary Genre*, translated by Richard Howard (Cornell University Press, Ithaca NY, 1975: first published in France, 1970), p. 25.
69 George Orwell, 'The Art of Donald McGill' (1941) in *Decline of the English Murder and Other Essays* (Penguin Books, in association with Martin Secker & Warburg, London, 1980), p. 152–4.
70 *Ibid.*
71 Hill, *British Cinema in the 1980s*, p. 168.
72 UK cinema production costs and box office figures for *Brassed Off* taken from the (1997) and (1998) *BFI Film and Television Handbooks*, edited by Eddie Dyja.
73 Friedrich Nietzsche, *The Birth of Tragedy*, translated by Shaun Whiteside and edited by Michael Tanner (Penguin, London, 1993: first published in Germany, 1871), p. 55.
74 Margaret Thatcher quoted in *Woman's Own* interview, October, 1987. Reference taken from Arthur Marwick, *A History of the Modern British Isles 1914–1999: Circumstances, Events and Outcomes* (Blackwell, Oxford, 2000, p. 312. Renton (Ewan McGregor), the central character in *Trainspotting* (Danny Boyle, 1995) echoes this sentiment when he declares, 'There was no such thing as society, and if there was, I was most certainly not a part of it'. The films discussed in this chapter would all contest such a statement and 'world view'.

1 'I hope you feel as good as you look': Danny (Pete Postlethwaite) appreciates the presence of Gloria (Tara Fitzgerald) and her contributions to the band (*Brassed Off*).

2 'A community at large': the Grimley colliery band and its supporters pose for a group photograph outside the Albert Hall in London (*Brassed Off*).

3 Nathan (William Snape), Dave (Mark Addy), Gaz (Robert Carlyle), Lomper (Steve Huison) and Gerald (Tom Wilkinson) look to the future. Gerald has just been presented with a repaired garden gnome as a peace offering (*The Full Monty*).

4 Eddie (Jack Smethurst): 'This is a respectable neighbourhood. We don't like ignorant loud-mouthed rabble-rousers. Understand?'
Bill (Rudolph Walker): 'Perfectly. When are you leaving?' (*Love Thy Neighbour*).

5 Eddie fears the worst as Bill and his workmates pretend to be cannibals. 'You wouldn't like me, I'm all gristle', he declares in a desperate effort to appeal to their sense of good taste (*Love Thy Neighbour*).

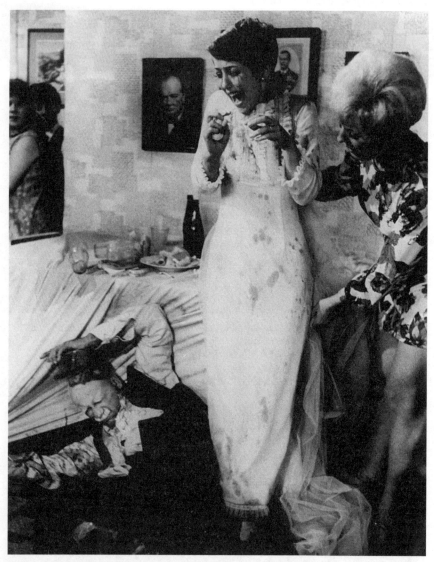

6 'He's ruined my wedding': Rita (Una Stubbs) despairs at the drunken behaviour of her father (Warren Mitchell). A portrait of Winston Churchill looks on at this image of late 1960s British social behaviour (*Till Death Us Do Part*).

7 'Send us victorious': Alf and his son-in-law, Mike (Anthony Booth), watch the 1966 World Cup final in which England defeat West Germany 4–2. In his excitement at the result, Alf will temporarily forget his prejudiced views and kiss the man to his left (*Till Death Us Do Part*).

8 George (Om Puri) and Ella (Linda Bassett) enjoy a special screening of a favourite Bollywood movie at their nephew's cinema in Bradford (*East is East*).

9 William (Hugh Grant) is so caught up in his own feelings of loss and loneliness that he does not see the newspaper headlines referring to the 'glamour photographs' of Anna (Julia Roberts) (*Notting Hill*).

10 Private lives and public places: Anna and William get to know each other better (*Notting Hill*).

11 David (Hugh Grant) becomes Prime Minister of Britain. Issues of foreign policy and domestic affairs will figure prominently in his political and personal plans (*Love Actually*).

2

Racial discourses, ethnicity, and the 'comic mode' in contemporary British cinema

Black Film Bulletin: Have you always been interested in making films with a black theme?

Simon Channing-Williams (producer of Secrets & Lies, *1996)*: No ... What do you mean by black? Black in terms of having black people or black in terms of its humour?[1]

This chapter will examine a particular group of British films produced during the 1990s which sought to explore issues of national, cultural and ethnic identity in the form of narratives combining comic *and* dramatic plot developments, incidents and perspectives. Such films as *Leon the Pig Farmer* (Vadim Jean, Gary Sinyor, 1992), *Wild West* (David Attwood, 1992), *Bhaji on the Beach* (Gurinder Chadha, 1994), *Secrets & Lies* (Mike Leigh, 1996), *My Son the Fanatic* (Udayan Prasad, 1998), and *East is East* (Damien O'Donnell, 1999) constituted a vital and innovative sub-genre within 1990s British film culture. These films meditated on what it meant to be Jewish, black, British-Asian or African-Caribbean in contemporary Britain, and were identified by many critics as operating within comic frameworks evoking memories of earlier traditions of cultural and cinematic humour in British society, whilst also seeking to engage with issues of race and ethnicity from new and stimulating points of view.

Hugo Davenport in the *Daily Telegraph*, for instance, described *Leon the Pig Farmer* as a 'demented comedy of manners', which extracted 'much comic mileage from *kosher*' customs and cultural codes of conduct, whilst drawing upon an element of 'ripe, seaside postcard naughtiness'.[2] Philip French in the *Observer* categorised *Wild West* as 'funny, sad and tough ... and full of sly observation',[3] and Leonard Quart in a *Cineaste* review of *Bhaji on the Beach* defined the film as 'a work of

social realism suffused in charm and a deft sense of comedy'.[4] Alexander
Walker of the *Evening Standard* summed up *Bhaji* as a 'complex excursion into multi-ethnic manners' which was 'funny' and 'racially truthful'.[5]

Nigel Andrews in the *Financial Times* described a later film about
British-Asian life, *My Son the Fanatic*, as 'grimly funny', and claimed
that the film showed 'golden-age liberalism meeting its nemesis . . . in
today's ideological solemnities'.[6] James Christopher of *The Times* interpreted *East is East* as a 'gleefully irreverent comedy', which nonetheless
presented a 'flinchingly real' depiction of a 'bruising culture clash',[7]
although Anthony Quinn in the *Independent* expressed a sense of unease
that the 'comedy' of the narrative was 'upended in the final quarter by
some incongruously grim domestic violence'.[8] Christopher Tookey in the
Daily Mail, however, suggested that *East is East* possessed that 'treasur-
able Ealing-comedy quality of helping to redefine Britishness',[9] while
Nigel Andrews in the *Financial Times* felt that the film was 'funny, in a
"Carry on up the Khans" style' of comedy.[10]

Jonathan Romney, writing in the *Guardian*, suggested that *Secrets &
Lies*, a drama about a black woman discovering that her biological
mother was white, succeeded in being 'Hilarious and gruelling',[11] while
Quentin Curtis in the *Daily Telegraph* concluded that Mike Leigh's film
contained the potential to be therapeutic and socially beneficial: 'Leigh
has made a humane comedy that not only laughs at the agonies of class
and racial difference, but also helps to heal them'.[12]

It is clear from these selected critical summations that the role and
purpose of comedy and the 'comic mode' within these narratives are perceived as being very varied in tone, style and content, and the respective
films are subjected to a number of differing interpretations and evalua-
tions from reviewers. This chapter will examine how these particular
1990s films attempt to explore themes of social, cultural and ethnic identity by drawing upon a range of comic forms, styles and approaches. I
shall also consider the relationship between the films' status as generically hybrid texts, and their fluid and exploratory conceptions of cultural and ethnic identity.

Earlier British traditions of depicting ethnic groups in a 'comic'
manner or irreverent style have long been subject to debates about the
social and political implications of 'joking' about first- and second-
generation Asian, Indian and African-Caribbean communities in Britain.
In an essay entitled 'The Whites of their Eyes: Racist Ideologies and the
Media' (1981), Stuart Hall claimed that such practices served to rein-
force social divisions around unhelpful and pernicious notions of
'otherness': 'Telling racist jokes . . . reproduce[s] the categories and rela-

tions of racism, even while normalizing them through laughter . . . The time *may* come when blacks and whites can tell jokes about each other in ways which do not reproduce the racial categories of the world in which they are told. The time, in Britain, is certainly *not yet arrived*.'[13]

Sarita Malik in 'Is it 'cos I is black: the Black Situation in Television Comedy', the title of a chapter in her study *Representing Black Britain: Black and Asian Images on Television* (2002), argued that 'Much of the British comedy tradition needs to be recognized as working within this culture of racism, while using the alibi of comedy to give the illusion of being outside of it'.[14]

This chapter will consider the legacy of certain British comic treatments of race relations and ethnic representations in film and television, as established in the late 1960s and 1970s. The pertinence of Hall's and Malik's observations will be considered in relation to feature film versions produced from two popular (but controversial) television situation comedies of this period – *Till Death Us Do Part* (1965–75) and *Love Thy Neighbour* (1972–76) – both of which raise questions about the ethics of generating comedy through depictions of racist attitudes, actions and discourses. The question of whether 'race relations' can ever be considered a 'laughing matter' will be examined. Are these particular 1960s and 1970s situation comedies now no longer either funny or acceptable?

A case study of the film *East is East* (1999) will provide an opportunity to explore issues arising out of potentially offensive treatments of racial and cultural themes in the 1990s. This commercially successful comedy-drama, based around a British-Asian family struggling to reconcile liberal and absolutist ideological beliefs, was able to present a vision of 1970s Britain as conceived from a late 1990s perspective. The film's particular form and style of humour (like *Till Death Us Do Part* and *Love Thy Neighbour*) was deemed by some commentators, however, to be in questionable aesthetic and political taste. Cary Rajinder Sawhney in an essay 'Another Kind of British: An Exploration of British Asian Films' (*Cineaste*, 2001) noted that *East is East* 'was perceived by some parts of the [Asian] community as reinforcing negative stereotypes of Moslems (and Asians generally), raising the old question of whether they are laughing with us or at us'.[15]

As in the communal-comedy-dramas discussed previously, several of the films to be analysed display a concerted interest in issues pertaining to the role of communities and particular social groupings in contemporary British society. Just as the miners in *Brassed Off* are depicted as a fragmented and fragile sub-section of society, with no discernible economic future in the short or long term, several of the alliances formed within the ethnic comedy-dramas of the 1990s can be interpreted as existing within a similarly tenuous and open-ended condition.

Leon the Pig Farmer, for instance, juxtaposes the counties of Surrey and Yorkshire, compares a stockbroking and a farming family, and offers gleeful caricatures of both white, northern working-class culture, and Jewish, white middle-class southern culture. *My Son the Fanatic* sets British pluralist views about a person's right to pursue pleasure in a consumer society against opposition from Muslim authoritarian traditions, frowning upon hedonistic behaviour enjoyed and pursued for its own sake.

East is East explores such conflicts within the context of a family home in Salford, while in *My Son the Fanatic* both the more mundane and exotic features of Bradford society are counterpointed with the intellectual and emotional appeal of 'imaginary homelands' (to draw upon the title of Salman Rushdie's collected essays published in 1991),[16] semi-mythical places which can provide disaffected ethnic groupings in British society with alternative forms of inspiration and guidance.

Such cultural contrasts and challenges lead to the formation of a series of comic and highly dramatic situations. The members of the Asian women's community group who travel from Birmingham to Blackpool in *Bhaji on the Beach* have to decide whether concepts of female unity and mutual support might, finally, be more important than a rigidly conceived adherence to traditional Asian creeds of conduct and belief. *Wild West* and *Secrets & Lies* both revolve around London-based Asian and black characters, who question and reject imposed or unambiguous definitions of their cultural identity and social position, opting instead to be open to a greater range of influences and possible courses of action, enabling them to determine their own personal history and sense of self. *Secrets & Lies* specifically explores what happens when the racial or ethnic 'other' (who may have been banished from memory), turns up at the front door, and seeks entry into an all-white household, already heavily steeped in conflict.

Before exploring the comic and dramatic possibilities created by such dilemmas and scenarios, however, two examples of British comedies engaging with themes of cultural integration and diversity from a less restrained and 'politically correct' era will be examined and probed.

'To love (or hate) thy neighbour?' Situational comedy and racial conflicts in 1970s British film and television culture

In The Alf Garnett Saga *(Bob Kellett, 1972), Alf (Warren Mitchell) and Else (Dandy Nichols) are babysitting Enoch, a black child from next door:*

Alf: What d'y bring that thing in here for? Bloody coon.

Else: What do you mean? He's as English as you. He was born here, wasn't you Enoch?

Alf: Born here? It must have been a bloody hot day, the day he was born!

In Love Thy Neighbour *(John Robins, 1973), Eddie (Jack Smethurst) and Arthur (Tommy Godfrey) are discussing the differences in skin colour between Jamaican-born Bill (Rudolph Walker) and British-Pakistani Winston (Azad Ali):*

Eddie: He's paler than you, but he's browner than what we are.

Arthur: That's because he's a Paki.

Eddie: He's not as black as you, because they don't have as much sun in Paki-land as they do in Africa.

Winston: Please, I am from Putney.

Arthur: They don't get a lot of sun in Putney, either, do they?

Eddie: Blimey, it's not that long ago that you lot descended from the apes.

Bill: We all descended from the apes

These two extracts of dialogue from *The Alf Garnett Saga* and *Love Thy Neighbour* provide a sense of the films' controversial and outspoken attempts to dramatise issues of race and colour by way of allowing a free flow of racist insults and innuendos to be perpetuated by the central (and, on occasion, by the subsidiary) characters of the narratives. The exchanges between these various figures are based around a level of frankness, and a lack of subtlety, which can appear shocking and unacceptable today, but which was nevertheless conceived of as 'light entertainment' (in other words, suitable viewing for nearly 'all of the family') during the early 1970s.

The assertions and assumptions of characters in the scenes cited above do tend to be counterpointed by the observations of other characters, such as Else and Bill, who take a more thoughtful, rational and enlightened view of the racial or cultural situations being discussed. The presence of these other non-racist (or in some cases less racist) characters meant that the programmes could not necessarily be considered as unambiguous propaganda for offensive or dubious ideological positions. Howard Jacobson in his study of comedy *Seriously Funny: From the Ridiculous to the Sublime* (1997) suggested that jokes consisted of 'a plot, a set of characters' and a 'complex of warring voices',[17] and *Till*

Death Us Do Part and *Love Thy Neighbour* certainly provided plentiful examples of the latter.

Bill, in the *Love Thy Neighbour* sequence quoted above, evokes Darwin's theories of evolution in response to Eddie's racial slur about black people descending from apes, but logical thinking and liberal-minded debate in these texts has to compete with the more tangible (if socially conservative) pleasures offered to audiences by characters such as Eddie Booth and Alf Garnett daring to speak the 'unspeakable', or think the 'unthinkable'.

The language and imagery deployed by these two characters, and their drawing upon such terms as 'coon', 'Paki' and 'apes', could always be potentially utilised by spectators who desired to inflame (rather than ease) racial tensions and relations in 1970s British society, with the result that the supposed 'anti-heroes' – Garnett and Booth – were always capable of being appropriated as positive figures by television viewers and cinema audiences who agreed with what they said, and the manner in which they expressed themselves.

In the quoted extract of dialogue from the *Love Thy Neighbour* film, racist remarks are not restricted to the central character (who is noted for his fanatical racism), but are also uttered by a more sympathetic member of the cast, Arthur, who works in the same factory as Eddie, and, who is generally presented as a normal, ordinary character, enjoying reasonably good relationships with his fellow black and Pakistani workers. Arthur's observation about Winston – 'That's because he's a Paki' – illustrates that the racist ravings of Alf Garnett or Eddie Booth could be almost subliminally reinforced by supporting characters occasionally resorting to the same kind of language and attitudes in a less explicit manner.

The naming of black characters, Enoch and Winston, in the two respective films suggests an obvious reference to senior Conservative politicians, Sir Winston Churchill (1874–1965) and Enoch Powell (1912–98). The 'joke' underpinning the use of the names might be that in a truly multi-cultural society, even names associated with white Conservative Party politicians could be extended to include black children born in Britain, thus serving to break down ingrained cultural and ethnic distinctions regarding signifiers of Britishness. Alf Garnett, inevitably, sees the act of christening a black child Enoch in the early 1970s as neither ironic nor iconic, but as a calculated outrage ('Bloody sauce!') on the part of the black parents.

Stuart Hall in his essay 'The Whites of their Eyes' (1981) accepted that 'the appearance of blacks, alongside whites, in situation comedies' might have helped to 'naturalise and normalise their presence in British society', but concluded that the 'comic register in which [the comedies] are set' had the effect of insulating viewers from a recognition of 'their incipient racism'.[18] In his book *British Low Culture: From Safari Suits to Sexploitation* (1998), Leon Hunt noted that 1990s 'Terrestrial television' had 'steered clear of *Love Thy Neighbour* and been cautiously selective in its repeats of *Till Death Us Do Part*'.[19]

The 55 television episodes of *Love Thy Neighbour* have also not been repeated on the satellite channels such as *Granada Plus* and *UK Gold* that specialise in repeating archive comedy and drama television programmes, implying that its brand of insult-strewn humour is now considered unsuitable for transmission. Episodes of *Love Thy Neighbour* were unexpectedly made available to purchase on DVD from the summer of 2003 onwards, however, suggesting a certain change in attitude amongst those holding the rights to the programme.[20]

Although much of the humour displayed in the television episodes and feature films might, when viewed from a retrospective 1990s perspective, be seen as more childish than threatening, or deemed over-reliant on a kind of incessant and inane process of 'name-calling', it is important to recall that in the context of when *Till Death Us Do Part* and *Love Thy Neighbour* were originally produced and transmitted, debates about race, ethnicity and national identity in Britain were taking place within a highly charged social and political context.

Arthur Marwick in *A History of the Modern British Isles 1914–1999* (2000), records that immigration from the West Indies, Pakistan and India to Britain increased from 28,000 to 136,400 between 1953 and 1961.[21] Brian Spittles in *Britain Since 1960: An Introduction* (1995) reports that in 1967 Kenya began expelling citizens of Asian origin, and that by February 1968 a thousand Kenyan Asians were entering Britain each week.[22] This situation of enforced exile was followed by the decision of General Idi Amin, dictator of Uganda, to expel the entire Asian population from Uganda in 1971 and 1972.[23]

In a speech delivered in the West Midlands in April 1968, Conservative politician Enoch Powell responded to these developments by predicting that by the year 2000 'Whole areas, towns and parts of towns across England' would be 'occupied by sections of the immigrant and immigrant descended population'.[24] This prospect, in Powell's view, needed to be avoided by government attempts to stop the 'further inflow' of immigrants, 'and by promoting the maximum outflow' of those who had already settled in Britain:

> We must be mad, literally mad, as a nation to be permitting the annual inflow of some 50,000 dependants, who are for the most part the material of the future growth of the immigrant-descended population. It is like

watching a nation busily engaged in heaping up its own funeral pyre . . .
Only resolute and urgent action will avert it even now. Whether there will
be the public will to demand and obtain that action, I do not know. All I
know is that to see, and not to speak, would be the great betrayal.[25]

Brian Spittles notes that Powell was 'immediately dismissed from the
shadow cabinet' by leader Edward Heath, but records that Powell
'retained supporters within the Conservative Party', and amongst
London dockers, who 'within days' called a 'spontaneous strike and
marched to the House of Commons to voice their approval of Powell'; a
response which 'caused a great deal of embarrassment and bewilderment
to many radicals and liberals'.[26]

The character of Alf Garnett was notably an East End dockyard
worker, and the cultural conflicts of Love Thy Neighbour took place
within the housing estate of an outer-London suburb, Richmond-upon-
Thames. In The Alf Garnett Saga (1972), Alf tells his wife that Enoch
Powell opposes the Conservative Party's desire to join the Common
Market, claiming that 'Old Enoch's against it . . . He don't want no more
bloody foreigners over here'. In Love Thy Neighbour, Eddie delivers a
speech to his wife in response to Bill's father coming to visit from
Trinidad, which is sympathetic to Powell's views as expressed in a 1972
speech, delivered in Ramsgate, where he spoke of 'hundreds of
thousands of our fellow citizens' who feel 'as if they are trapped or tied
to a stake in the face of an advancing tide'.[27] In the film, Eddie declares
of his black next-door neighbour, 'I knew it, he's moving the whole
bloody tribe in . . . I don't want any more nig-nogs living next door . . .
Before we know where we are, we'll be overrun with them. Maple
Terrace will become a suburb of Trinidad.'

The insults exchanged between the opposing characters in the films'
screenplays are consequently intensely politicised and potentially inflam-
matory when considered in the context of their original reception and
production. Hanif Kureishi in his essay 'The Rainbow Sign' (1986),
which accompanied the published screenplay of My Beautiful Laundrette (Stephen Frears, 1985), argued that 'Powell allowed himself to
become a figurehead for racists', and that, similarly, the prevalence of
'Television comics' using 'Pakistanis as the butt of their humour' during
the 1970s constituted a 'celebration of contempt in millions of living
rooms'.[28] Kureishi, thus, linked the speeches of Enoch Powell and the
'comic' tirades of figures such as Eddie Booth and Alf Garnett, and
found them both contributing to an atmosphere of increased racial
intolerance and potential conflict.

A fantasy sequence in Till Death Us Do Part (Norman Cohen, 1969),
presents Garnett dreaming that he has an audience with the Queen and

the Prime Minister of 1969, Harold Wilson. Alf complains about there being 'too many foreigners' in 1960s British society, declaring that 'Old Enoch Powell, he's got the right idea. Chuck 'em all out, especially the black ones'. Garnett goes on to suggest to Her Majesty that the position of Prime Minister should have been offered to Powell, who had, as noted above, been removed from the Conservative shadow cabinet in 1968 by Edward Heath, following his speech about immigration and repatriation. Garnett's comments in this dream sequence were extremely topical and contentious, as he seeks to rewrite history from the point of view of a fantasising racist. The scene concludes with Garnett asking the pipe-smoking figure of Harold Wilson how he would feel if his next-door neighbour at Downing Street, the Chancellor of the Exchequer, Roy Jenkins, 'sold his house to a family of coons'.

The film version of *Love Thy Neighbour* also makes one brief reference to actual political figures. A competition question about good neighbours – 'Do you share the same political beliefs?' – is 'answered' by the film with a glimpse of Bill removing Eddie's poster of Harold Wilson in his front window, which claims 'Labour will get things done', and replacing it with a poster of Edward Heath, who is identified as a 'Man of Principle'. Between the period 1964 and 1976, British political elections were dominated by the figures of Wilson and Heath. Wilson was elected Prime Minister in 1964, 1965 and 1974, and Ted Heath was victorious in the 1970 election.[29] The 'comic' conflicts between Alf and his family, and Eddie and Bill were consequently shaped and influenced by these wider political and ideological swings and tendencies in British society, as personified by the opposing Labour and Conservative party leaders, Wilson and Heath. When Margaret Thatcher replaced Heath as Conservative leader in 1975, and Harold Wilson retired from his position as Prime Minister in 1976, a period in politics and British film and television comedy came to a close.[30]

Stuart Allen, the producer of *Love Thy Neighbour*, suggested in a 1972 *TV Times* article that the show was 'about integration. We want to cool things, and we think we're going to succeed'.[31] Salman Rushdie in an essay 'The New Empire within Britain' (1982) expressed scepticism, however, about this notion of 'integration', which he felt 'meant in practice ... that blacks should be persuaded to live peaceably with whites, in spite of all the injustices done to them every day'.[32] This formulation might be perceived as pertinent to the implied moral of *Love Thy Neighbour*, that racial harmony might eventually be forged out of visible disharmony and distrust, by characters who nonetheless express their deepest and most ordinary fears without restraint or censorship.

The film adaptations of *Till Death Us Do Part* and *Love Thy Neigh bour* were part of a trend within British film production (partly initiated by *Till Death Us Do Part* in 1969, and lasting until approximately 1980), which sought to capitalise upon the popularity of certain television situation comedies by adapting them into feature-length narratives to be shown in cinemas.

In *The Dialogic Imagination* (1975), Mikhail Bakhtin argued that 'Everything that makes us laugh is close at hand, all comical creativity works in a zone of maximal proximity'.[33] Such a conceptualisation was perfectly in tune with the aesthetic principles of television situation comedy, and the regular use of close-ups and medium-shots to frame events and interactions between characters, but visual styles appropriate for television were less obviously suitable for cinematic presentations. Equally, the extended running-time of the film adaptations did mean that the narratives had to develop a new plotline roughly every 30 minutes.

The *Monthly Film Bulletin* reviewer of *Till Death Us Do Part* claimed that 'the didactic purpose of the original' television series was completely absent from the 1969 film version, and noted that 'watching the film at a public showing one noticed that the audience consistently laughed with Alf rather than at him'.[34] The critic here makes an interesting distinction between the more private responses to the series when transmitted in the confines of people's homes, and the more observable responses of spectators to its projection in a public space. The film itself provided a kind of background history to the Garnett family, following the fortunes of the Garnetts and the East End of London from the outbreak of war in 1939 to the winning of the World Cup against Germany in 1966. *The Alf Garnett Saga* (1972) lacks this historical perspective and symmetry, and takes place in an early 1970s setting in which the family have been moved to a high-rise flat, the power is constantly being switched off due to disputes by workers in the public sector, and Alf and his son-in-law are both worried that Rita (Adrienne Posta) may have been made pregnant by a black man.

Love Thy Neighbour (1973) contains a number of story elements. Bill and Eddie's wives (Kate Williams and Nina Baden-Semper) enter a competition aimed at rewarding good relationships between black and white neighbours. Eddie and Bill are simultaneously involved in a dispute about union membership, which escalates into a racial conflict in the factory where they both work. Until 2003, episodes of the television series had not been made available on video nor on DVD, so the 1973 film version produced by Hammer films had, until then, been the only example of the series available for contemporary home viewing. The film consequently assumed something of the status of a 'video nasty', partly because of what Leon Hunt in *British Low Culture: From Safari Suits to Sexploitation* termed its 'sense of the forbidden, the unsaid, the repressed'.[35]

The film's narrative opens with shots of Buckingham Palace, the white cliffs of Dover, country fields, and a leisurely game of cricket, each image evoking idealised and idyllic symbols of 'Englishness'. These images are accompanied by a male voice on the soundtrack quoting from Shakespeare – 'This happy breed of men' – and extolling the virtues of Britain as 'a land where all men are equal, irrespective of race, creed or colour'. The film then abruptly cuts to the sight of Eddie Booth accusing his neighbour, Bill Reynolds, of being a 'bloody black trouble-maker', and the film proper begins. A gap is immediately opened up between flattering and 'officially sanctioned' images of British society and culture, and this starker image of a harsher, unprepossessing 'reality'. The narrative will proceed to depict early 1970s Britain as culturally depressed, economically stagnant, and plagued by industrial disputes, none of which contributes to promoting or encouraging states of harmonious co-existence between differing ethnic groups.

Bill objects to paying his union dues to Eddie, who is the factory trade union official, partly because of his racist views. This results in a strike in which the workers and strikers become differentiated by their skin colour. The black workers want to form the ABU (the All Black Union) and continue working, while the white workers vote for strike action, and refuse to recognise any other union. Winston, a British-Pakistani character, caught in the middle of the dispute, exclaims that he does not know to which side he belongs, or to whom he should express an alliance. 'You're not white', Bill informs him, in response to his enquiry. 'He's not bloody black, either', counters Eddie. The film is not concerned with exploring his particular social and cultural dilemma, and his character remains outside the terrain which the narrative has selected for its attempt to portray 'black versus white' conflicts in comic terms, but it is notable that the Pakistani character is here presented as a doubly alienated figure, unclaimed and disavowed by both white and black communities in the British workplace.

Earlier in the narrative, Eddie has remonstrated with the figure of an Indian bus conductor, played (in one of the stereotyping conventions of the 1960s and 1970s) by a white actor (Norman Chappell), in black make-up.[36] The comic elements of this sequence are partly developed out of the conflation of identities, with the Indian voice emerging 'ventriloquist-like', from within the white character-actor coated in black dye. Eddie, subsequently, refers to the Indian character as 'Ali Babi' and 'Gungha Din', before being thrown off the bus for insulting behaviour.

In the film, insults such as 'King Kong', 'nig-nog go home', 'jungle boy', 'savages', 'sambo senior', 'Did I just see my mother go out with a golliwog?' are all uttered by the central white character. The black character responds with such expressions as 'white-honky', 'pale-skinned loudmouth', and 'ignorant poof'. Such self-perpetuating racial insults constitute the primary means by which the narrative generates its comedy. This paranoid obsession with the language of colour distinctions makes the use of even 'innocent' phrases such as 'looking on the black side' (or the less innocent term 'blacklegs', a reference to strikebreakers) problematical for characters in the course of the narrative.

When the two wives, Barbie and Joan, have their one argument in the film, it is over the nature of Joan's defence of the language used by her husband (that he only calls 'a spade a spade'), which leads to Barbie accusing even Joan of calling her 'a spade'. Even though the film promotes itself as a comedy, which therefore shouldn't be taken *too* seriously, the narrative reveals how racial insults can escalate and lead to a state of civil unrest and social unease.

In the film's most provocative and disturbing sequence, Bill provides Eddie with his worst nightmare by pretending (along with his black workmates) to be a cannibal, who is prepared to cook Eddie in a boiling cauldron and eat him. 'We've declared war on the white man', and reverted to the 'law of the jungle' declare Eddie's kidnappers, as they bundle him into the work's canteen. ('You wouldn't like me, I'm all gristle', declares Eddie in a desperate effort to appeal to their sense of discrimination and good taste.)

This astonishing scene is played for what one might term 'serious laughs', is accompanied by the non-diegetic sound of atmospheric drumming on the soundtrack, and features the black men stripped to the waist. Bill dons a pair of vampire-like fangs to add to the sense of terror and unease, and is framed leering menacingly over Eddie as he lies in the canteen 'cauldron'. The men circle the melting pot, and only the addition of some potatoes and vegetables and the use of utensils from the factory canteen by the 'cannibals' indicate that the scene, if shown separately from the rest of the narrative, was not necessarily to be taken at face value. Even so, there is still a sense of uncertainty as to what will be the final outcome of the black men's 'joke' on Eddie, which is only resolved when Eddie faints from shock, and Bill and the other 'cannibals' leave this primeval 'scene of the crime' for fear of being discovered by the firm's cleaning women.

Eddie, at this point, is presented with a situation which threatens to go beyond language and laughter, at the same time as he is graphically faced with having to accept responsibility for the effects of his own discourses and references (the kidnapping is a response to his description of the black workers as 'a bunch of savages'). The black workers, in an almost literal and metaphorical sense, force him to 'eat his words', even if it means that they have to regress to one of the earliest stereotypes of black representations, the image of the native savage.

The comedy in *Love Thy Neighbour*'s parody of such images emerges from the essentially unheroic character of Eddie Booth being forced to see his distorted view of black cultural history affirmed in a way which suggests that the 'revelation' might cost him his life. Black audiences could possibly gain some pleasure in seeing the irrepressibly indignant and hostile character of Eddie Booth fear, for once, that he has met his match. The sequence could also be read, however, as promoting negative and regressive images of black masculinity and history, and implying that the anxieties and fears expressed by such figures as Enoch Powell (and Eddie) about black communities gaining a threatening 'upper-hand' by stealth and numbers may have some basis in a kind of heightened fantasy, which is always capable of becoming a reality if left unchecked. 'It was only a joke, he didn't actually eat you', declares Eddie's wife, when he returns home. 'He might have done if I hadn't have fainted', replies Eddie, suggesting that for him the incident wasn't merely a joke.

This confrontation in the works canteen might be interpreted as an example of the film's willingness to push its characters towards extreme states of being in which conflicts (even if they are treated essentially comically, rather than dramatically), are brought out into the open. It would be difficult to argue, however, that *Love Thy Neighbour* and *Till Death Us Do Part* were fundamentally aimed at improving society, and indeed both texts depicted characters who appeared trapped in an endless cycle of repetition from which there was no escape, unless Booth and Garnett, as the main perpetrators of all the disputes, suddenly decided to alter their views and behaviour.

The comic structures of the television episodes of *Love Thy Neighbour* and *Till Death Us Do Part* were dependent on racial and social conflicts being revived on a weekly basis, and so neither series could change or develop its narrative patterns or character traits very easily without undermining the fundamental premises on which the programmes were based. Hence, perhaps, the peculiarly tortured nature of each series' 'world view', with Alf always 'going down the pub' as his family refused to accept his arguments, and Eddie always insisting on having the last (and usually racist) word.

The various points of narrative closure in the film version of *Love Thy Neighbour* do, however, seek out ways of going beyond such deadlocked situations. Eddie's mother, Annie Booth (Patricia Hayes), strikes up a romantic relationship with Bill's Jamaican father (Charles Hyatt), suggesting that the Booth and Reynolds families can be brought closer together. When Bill and Eddie finally shake hands and pledge to put aside their differences in order to claim their prize in the 'Good Neighbour' competition, a caption appears on screen, stating, 'No, this is not the end'.

The narrative actually concludes with Eddie learning that he is now related to Bill, through his wife's brother having (without Eddie's knowledge) married Barbie's sister. 'Welcome to the family, brother Eddie', announces a gleeful Bill, as the three couples – one white, one black and one mixed-race couple – briefly share the same social space. The statement – 'That really is the end' – is flashed onto the screen, over a freeze-framed shot of Eddie's face, now presented as half-black, half-white, over which the film's credits unfold.

Eddie's character would probably conclude that this inter-racial marriage (to which he is tentatively related) serves to diminish and taint his status and ideological position, by rendering him somewhat less purely 'white' than before. In terms of the overall verbal and visual conflict depicted in the film, Eddie's final 'fantastical' mutation into a half-white and half-black man might be read as a progressive moment which signals the possible eventual breaking down of rigid black and white binary oppositions, creating opportunities for a more genuinely multi-cultural and inter-connected society to emerge in decades to come.

The Alf Garnett Saga (1972) also concludes on the issue of mixed-race relationships, but does not suggest that a positive or progressive denouement can be reached. Alf has to face the possibility that his daughter may have engaged in an adulterous affair with a black singer (Kenny Lynch), leading to a chance that she may give birth to a black child. The film ends with Alf having scorched himself, after causing a fire in his bedroom by smoking in bed. Else remarks that 'The way you look now, you'll suit a black grandson'. 'Piss off, you fat cow', replies Alf, remaining socially unreconstructed or tamed until the very end.

In *Till Death Us Do Part* (1969), one scene depicts Garnett at his daughter's wedding reception, putting his arm around a black woman and stroking her arm. 'Watch it, it comes off,' she replies, referring to her skin colour, after he has made a demeaning reference to the jungle. 'The coon's got a sense of humour', declares Garnett, before drunkenly staggering around the room. The scene ends with Alf being pushed backwards by a young woman, and consequently spilling his drink over the wedding dress worn by his daughter Rita (Una Stubbs), before crashing to the floor. This 'fall from grace' might be read as Alf's physical punishment for his indomitable racism, although he equally possesses a cartoon-like, comic resilience, which means that he will always upright himself and, in due course, resume his former outlook and way of responding to the outside world.

In *The Alf Garnett Saga*, the only occasion in which Alf is friendly to a black character is when he experiences the effects of a 'trip', after having taken his son-in-law's LSD by mistake ('Where's he going? He didn't say nothing to me about a trip', enquires Else innocently). He subsequently fantasises that he is yachting with Edward Heath and limbo-dancing to the sound of a Caribbean band. The drug also makes him embrace a black couple in the local pub, declaring them to be the 'salt of the earth', and highly desirable members of society, who 'add a bit of colour to life'.

Only the side-effects of hallucinogenic drugs can 'cure' Alf's incorrigible racism, it appears, and if Eddie has reached a stage of possessing 'mixed' feelings about black people by the close of *Till Death Us Do Part*, it is still unlikely that he can be considered a reformed or radically altered individual. Thus, these programmes and films were able to dramatise, in a farcical and exaggerated manner, anxieties and concerns about relationships between different ethnic groups in 1970s British society, but were generally not able to go beyond a regular re-stating of the white leading figure's contempt for black people, and his unease about the social effects of the immigration process.

I have sought to demonstrate that the strategies of these 'comic' narratives may (in certain respects) have been more complex than has generally been accepted, and that the film versions of the respective situation comedies do contribute to the overall (if inevitably somewhat contentious) achievements of the series as a whole. The television episodes and cinema films could, perhaps, be commended for their vitality and willingness to be volatile and outrageous, even if the central white characters within the texts are far from admirable.

Equally, a limitation of both the television episodes and the accompanying films is that the scenarios tend to privilege the experiences and settings frequented by the white characters. The lack of a drama-based narrative, capable of taking the plots in a more serious and varied direction, and of cultivating a more socially extensive viewpoint on ethnic interactions, does mean that the humour tends to be repetitive and, at worst, rather futile and nasty. Characters from (and spectators of) *Till Death Us Do Part* and *Love Thy Neighbour* were thus doomed to experience a strong sense of *déjà vu* with each new episode, until there was no way that situations could be developed beyond a certain point, and both series finally came to an end.

New approaches to engaging with (and representing) issues of ethnicity and cultural identity were clearly needed, and the following section

will briefly discuss the movement which took place in the 1980s from sit-
uation-comedy-type treatments of such themes towards a more serious
drama-oriented approach. *My Beautiful Laundrette* (Stephen Frears,
1985) will be discussed as an example of a film which combines drama
and ambivalent comic observations about British-Asian life in mid-
1980s Britain, in ways making it something of a template for the later
1990s British films which set out to explore ideas about ethnic groupings
and conflicting emotions in British society.

My Beautiful Laundrette (1986), a 1980s ethnic 'soap opera', and Rita, Sue, Bob and Aslam Too

In 1982, Channel 4 began transmissions, and one of its founding aims
was to encourage more independent filmmaking by under-represented
groups and communities.[37] The channel encouraged the growth of film
and video workshops examining contemporary black culture in Britain,
and Sarita Malik in an essay on 'Black British Cinema of the 1980s and
1990s' (1996) reported that two-thirds of black and Asian films in distribution in Britain during the 1980s were documentaries.[38]

There was a danger, however, that the documentary or avant-garde
films emanating from such workshops could be considered overly esoteric, a factor potentially reducing their political impact and opportunities to reach a broad range of viewers and spectators. *My Beautiful
Laundrette* (1985) was a Channel 4 film which sought to construct
ethnic characterisations outside of 'politically correct' notions and lim-
iting, self-contained generic distinctions, and in the process create a story
whose key characters might be of interest to audiences who nonetheless
didn't quite know how to respond to them on an emotional level.

Screenplay writer Hanif Kureishi attempted to depict a range of subject positions and cultural themes, within a narrative form centred upon
the themes of illicit love, mixed-race relationships, and the presence of
racist behaviour in British society. In an introduction to the published
screenplay of *My Beautiful Laundrette* (1986), Hanif Kureishi claimed
that the film was envisaged as 'an amusement, despite its references to
racism, unemployment and Thatcherism. Irony is the modern mode, a
way of commenting on bleakness and cruelty without falling into
dourness and didacticism.'[39]

The wry humour and idiosyncratic outlook prevalent within the narrative was thus partly the result of a semi-tragic situation in which racial
conflict and social inequality were still perceived to be rife in British
society. The film was different in tone to the abrasive manner, static characterisations, and comic approaches typical of *Till Death Us Do Part*

and *Love Thy Neighbour*, but the film shared with these programmes a desire not to produce 'positive' or quietist representations of British society, or to adopt a pious or censorious attitude towards the conduct and language of its central characters.

My Beautiful Laundrette drew upon a range of naturalistic, romantic and comic modes of narrative expression. Part of the film's radical aesthetic and idiosyncratic appeal was to suggest that the continued fragmentation of consensual values in British society had opened up the possibility for new economic and sexual alliances to be formed which cut across established and conventional demarcations, based on skin colour and ingrained cultural differences.

The film was released during the midway point of Margaret Thatcher's eleven years as Prime Minister (1979–90), and just as *Till Death Us Do Part* and *Love Thy Neighbour* were influenced by the discourses of Labourism and Conservatism which dominated the political landscape of the 1970s, *My Beautiful Laundrette* meditated on what Mrs Thatcher and her brand of Conservatism symbolised for British society by the period of the mid-1980s. Margaret Thatcher's policies and philosophical credos are acknowledged as pervasive and powerful forces in the narrative, but the film does not suggest that her influence is only destructive or baleful. Instead, the logic of unbridled free enterprise is shown as applying equally to criminal operations involving drugs and pornographic videos, and the renovating of an amenity such as the local laundrette.

The eponymous laundrette is, of course, far from beautiful, particularly after it is vandalised by white racists. Significantly, in terms of its symbolic significance as a meeting place for various ethnic members of the local community, it is extremely damaged by the close, but not quite destroyed. Characters within the film strive to resist being defined in an overly rigid or predetermined fashion, and, as a result, a kind of 'unofficial' and 'alternative' vision of multi-cultural Britain is tentatively outlined.

Frears and Kureishi's film does not flinch, however, from depicting inter-racial relations in inner London as fuelled by antagonisms similar to those displayed by Bill and Eddie in *Love Thy Neighbour* – only in these 1980s instances of racial conflict farcical comic antagonism is replaced by scenes of street violence suffused with a tangible sense of danger and menace. *My Beautiful Laundrette* has comic moments, and contains a series of ironic observations about 1980s Britain, but it does not suggest that examples of racial prejudice and hatred can be converted into comic material.

The more hopeful and optimistic elements of the film are largely based around the relationship between Johnny (Daniel Day Lewis), a white former National Front sympathiser (who admits 'I ain't made much of myself'), and Omar (Gordon Warnecke), a young Asian male, anxious to impress his extended family. Johnny and Omar's interactions are constantly threatened by external forces, and by shifting balances of power within their own relationship. Omar needs Johnny to repel the menacing group gathering outside the laundrette, but as Johnny maintains connections with the disaffected group (and was formerly supportive of their racist ideologies), neither Omar nor spectators of the film can ever be sure of his real loyalties or future intentions.

Part of the eroticism of their relationship may indeed emanate from this sense of social uncertainty, with its hint of a masochistic reworking of the traditional colonial servant–master relationship.[40] Johnny, subsequently, remains a fluid character, involved with two distinct cultures and not quite embracing or renouncing either (although at the close of the film he does oppose the menacing behaviour of his former associates).

The narrative concludes with the laundrette (like the house in Sam Peckinpah's *Straw Dogs*, 1972), nearly destroyed by English thugs, conveying a sense of Britain as an increasingly lawless place. The final shot is of Omar and Johnny tending to each other's wounds, the sensuality of their relationship still intact, even if the localised social and economic structure which generated their coupling is now shattered. Racism in the film is not presented as an amusing and inevitable part of everyday British life, but as a destructive force, particularly identified with those groups of men who are disenfranchised from experiencing the material rewards of what the businessman Nasser (Saeed Jaffrey) refers to as 'the new enterprise culture'.

Rita, Sue and Bob Too (Alan Clarke, 1987) was a film which also offered its own unique perspective on British society in the 1980s, but in ways which looked back to the more outspoken and contentious examples of British comedy discussed earlier. With its harsh view of relationships and stark northern setting, only partially alleviated by the pleasure-seeking activities of its central white characters, *Rita, Sue and Bob Too* develops a somewhat curious sub-text in the final third of its narrative, when it presents a mixed-race relationship between Sue (Michelle Holmes) and an Asian male, Aslam (Kulvinder Ghir).

Sue initially declares that she has never been out with a 'Paki before', but suspects that he will turn out to be just the same as all her other boyfriends, and the film seems to bear out the truth of her observation, as Aslam is finally displaced from the narrative after hitting Sue, and is last glimpsed running away from a police car after neighbours have reported the presence of a suspicious figure in the area.

Alan Clarke's film, which John Hill in *British Cinema in the 1980s* (1999) suggests 'virtually abandon[s] perspective altogether',[41] features a scene in which Aslam tries to intercede with Sue's father in the course of a family dispute. The father (Willie Ross), in a drunken and demented state, warns Aslam to 'Keep out of this, you black bastard'. 'There's no need for that', replies Aslam attempting to reason with him, adding self-deprecatingly, 'I can't help being a Paki'. 'Yes, you fucking can', says Sue's father, pursuing his own Alf Garnett/Eddie Booth-like example of deranged reasoning to its logical conclusion. Sue and Aslam appear to inhabit a kind of social wasteland, which does not encourage communication or understanding between differing cultures and communities.

My Beautiful Laundrette had succeeded in creating British-Asian characters that were lively and unpredictable, but there were no unambiguous indications about how such cultural representations could be extended and updated within a fragmented and piecemeal indigenous film industry, which itself lacked a stable production base and a clear sense of its own identity. It was possible to wonder if *Laundrette* was so original and idiosyncratic that its personalised view of a multi-cultural environment could not be easily imitated or transcended.

Consequently, filmmakers in Britain at the beginning of the 1990s who wished to explore themes of ethnicity and cultural relations in their own work had to draw upon those indigenous traditions from the recent past which could be salvaged, and those that were still in a tentative state of development. A feature linking the 1990s films to be discussed in the following section is that they tended to be formulated around interesting and problematical dramatic situations, which allowed a number of characters to express varying and contrasting points of view on issues arising from the central concerns of the storylines. Such scenarios represented an attempt by directors and writers (unlike in *Till Death Us Do Part* and *Love Thy Neighbour*) to go beyond the reiterating of fixed positions by characters, and to illustrate the complexities of the situations depicted.

Developing notions of ethnic comedy-drama in 1990s British cinema

The key British films exploring issues of ethnicity and cultural identity produced during the 1990s were the result of a general movement away from both documentary and more broadly conceived comic narratives. Earlier British cinematic and television traditions were not completely renounced, however, and *East is East* (1999), as I shall discuss in the case study, appeared to gain a certain level of creative inspiration and artistic freedom from its 1970s setting, and from drawing upon some of the more culturally contentious comic paradigms and attitudes associated with that era.

Leon the Pig Farmer (1992) was also influenced by traditions of British television situation comedy, as demonstrated by its use of stereo-typical characterisations and larger-than-life plot developments. *Wild West* (1992), in contrast, was an idiosyncratic attempt to reproduce the kind of ethos prevalent in 1960s Cliff Richard musical comedies about 'putting on a show', but within the confines of a much less idealised and romanticised setting (the Asian band in the film live on a 'run-down' estate in Southall, London).[42]

Bhaji on the Beach (1994) resurrected the tradition of community-centred, multi-narrative dramas produced by Ealing Studios in such films as *It Always Rains on Sunday* (Robert Hamer, 1947), *Train of Events* (Basil Dearden/Charles Crichton/Sidney Cole, 1949), and 'Home Front' British Second World War movies, films which featured a series of diverse characters brought together by a shared common experience, and who find their lives changed in the process. By making first- and second-generation Asian women characters the central figures in such a mosaic pattern of intertwined stories, the filmmakers, Gurinder Chadha and Meera Syal, were promoting more extensive indigenous cinematic representations of race and gender with regard to issues of 'Britishness' and cultural identities within Asian communities. The film's privileging of Asian women characters in its narrative was also something of a riposte to such films as *My Beautiful Laundrette*, which had predomi-nantly focused on male desires, anxieties and aspirations.

My Son the Fanatic (1997) heralded the return of Hanif Kureishi to writing films about British-Asian life in a drama based around 'a comic clash of generations and cultures',[43] exploring the lack of common ground between Muslim fundamentalist and liberal Western values, as embodied in a conflict between a father and son, and raising the ques-tion of which of them in the end is the more deluded or misguided in their beliefs.

Secrets & Lies (1996) was another family drama from the period (a serious and sincere narrative, punctuated with moments of irony, and instances of caricature), and striking in that it focused on a black rather than an Asian central character. The film represented Mike Leigh's con-certed attempt to produce an intimate psychological drama about a white working-class mother and her black daughter eventually coming to terms with each other, and their respective situations.

A number of recurring themes can be identified in this small but sig-nificant group of films: the multi-faceted nature of 'home' for first-, second-and third-generation immigrant families; the complex relationships between 'roots', 'origins' and conceptualisations of the 'future'; the difficulties of reconciling inherited cultural identities with personal desires for freedom of expression; the positioning of the 'other' or the 'outsider' in British culture, both internally and externally; the relationship of Asian and Afro-Caribbean communities to white, working-class lifestyles; the persistence of racist attitudes and humour in British culture; the mixing of genres and identities in post-modernist, multicultural societies.

Homi K. Bhabha in *The Location of Culture* (1994) referred to the 'unhomeliness' that is the 'condition of extra-territorial and cross cultural initiations',[44] and several of these films, dramatising the experiences of second- and third-generation immigrants to Britain, are imbued with a pervasive feeling of sadness and uncertainty as to whether British society represents for characters a kind of home and haven, or rather an unfriendly and ultimately temporary place of residence.

Julia Kristeva in her study *Strangers to Ourselves* (1991) posed the question 'Can one be a foreigner and happy?', implying that visitors to another culture and place may always feel somewhat out of place in the new society in which they reside.[45] Kristeva suggests that psychological factors may sometimes lie behind the foreigner's desire for exile, leading to a lasting sense of dislocation in time and space: 'should one recognize that one becomes a foreigner in another country because one is already a foreigner from within?'[46] She goes on to claim that individuals who have broken from their original surroundings, cultural reference points and beliefs may face 'a life in which acts constitute events because they imply choice, surprises, breaks, adaptations, or cunning, but neither routine nor rest'.[47]

By focusing on the elements of 'choice' and the occurrence of 'breaks' in the everyday lives of their characters, and contrasting memories and representations of the homeland with the vivid reality of the present, the 1990s British films under discussion were able to draw upon melodramatic, social realist, and comic narrative elements in their stories and accounts of ethnic experiences of life in contemporary Britain. The films also conveyed an impression that endings to the various stories were not predetermined or predictable, and very much represented work in progress.

Thus, the Asian women's group in *Bhaji on the Beach* travel from Birmingham to Blackpool for a 'female-fun-day', but Bombay and India remain significant cultural and religious touchstones for the older women on the bus, whilst Birmingham is described as 'the land that time forgot' by the youngest members of the group. The film ends with the women embarking on a journey home with some dramatic situations having been resolved, but others remaining disturbingly open. *Bhaji on the Beach* appears to have been made to reflect a view that notions of British society had moved on from eras when people could simply be classified as black, Asian, white, Indian, and so on. This was not to suggest that such categories were not still important, both politically and socially, but, as Gurinder Chadha stated, 'People like me have a plurality of influences and my work is about a celebration of this mixing and mingling'.[48]

Bhaji on the Beach, similarly, contains a number of generic elements within its narrative composition. Principally, the film is a drama, telling the story of a group of women engaged on a day-trip, and the narrative unfolds in a series of parallel stories interlinked and introduced in the style of a television 'soap opera'. These relatively low-key stories are, however, interrupted by satirical and playful dream sequences in which serious concerns are 'played out' in the form of extended jokes and reflections on tensions and ideological conflicts within the represented community.

Women characters within the film constantly engage in a type of animated comic banter, which also evokes the comic textures of the more male-dominated worlds of *Till Death Us Do Part* and *Love Thy Neighbour*. *Bhaji on the Beach* is also keen to celebrate the simple pleasures of Blackpool promenade and sea front (see Gracie Fields in *Sing As We Go*, 1934), and to illustrate how the characters experience the location as a space of relative freedom.[49]

The narrative focuses upon the anxieties and concerns of three women characters in particular: Hashida (Sarita Khajuria), who has been made pregnant by her black boyfriend, and is considering having an abortion in order to be able to fulfil her parents' hopes that she train as a doctor; Ginder (Kim Vithana), who has decided to leave her violent Asian husband Rajid (Jimmi Harkishin); and Asha (Lalita Ahmed), a middle-aged newsagent and housewife, who feels unappreciated by her family, and, as a result of her general anxieties and fears, experiences strange visionary hallucinations in which an image of the Hindu god Rama watches over her menacingly.

Asha's visions enable the film to break away in an almost subliminal comic fashion from its linear, realist-oriented structure, and to point towards alternative constructions of 'reality' based on lurid fantasies about Ginder and Hashida. Asha is unnerved by what she perceives as disloyalty and treachery within the group of women, and imagines that Ginder is poisoning her husband's family, and that Hashida has been so corrupted by Western ways that she has mutated into a heartless, disrespectful, blonde woman, brazenly trampling over the traditional pieties and rituals of Hindu culture. Alexander Walker of the *Evening Standard* described 'the brief fantasy sequences of Indian gods rebuking Asian girls who've gone native' as Chadha's 'sole concession to wholly Asian filmgoers' and a 'satirical plus' for the narrative.[50] (*Till Death Us Do Part* and *The Alf Garnett Saga* also notably contained fantasy sequences which represented Alf's wildest desires and deepest anxieties.)

The unnerving scenarios taking place in Asha's subconscious hint at how the more exotic scenarios associated with Bollywood cinema might treat such subject material, and the returns to a mundane reality heralded by the end of the fantasy sequences might conceivably result in a feeling of disappointment for some spectators, as they are made to realise that the film is not constructed within the mode of 'magical realism', and thus cannot ultimately transcend its immediate and somewhat prosaic settings. This is finally a very British film, where the settings are not inherently aesthetically pleasing, and are composed of motorway service-stations, cafes and seaside promenades, making the film more of an 'emotional journey' than a 'road movie' in the tradition of American cinema.

Asha's hallucinations are usually concluded in the manner of a joke, with an unexpected or ironic punchline, as she is brought back down to earth unexpectedly. When she first announces that sometimes she sees 'things', the film cuts to a close-up shot of a group of men exposing their backsides in a passing mini-bus. A later dream sequence features Asha being pursued by a white Englishman, Ambrose Waddington (Peter Cellier), blacked-up as an Indian suitor. The scene ends with the rain penetrating his disguise and making the dye on his face run, suggesting that a long British comic tradition of white performers mimicking Indian characters (as in *Love Thy Neighbour*) can, perhaps, now be laid to rest, or re-visited nostalgically before being finally banished as a 'bad joke'.

Peter Brooks in *The Melodramatic Imagination: Balzac, Henry James, Melodrama, and the Mode of Excess* (1976) claimed that 'melodrama regularly simulates the experience of nightmare', and that in melodramatic narratives the 'end of the nightmare is an awakening brought about by confrontation and expulsion of the . . . person in whom all evil is seen to be concentrated'.[51] In relation to this observation, it is surely significant that it is the sceptical and doubting Asha who crucially attacks Ginder's husband at the close for his violent, oppressive conduct towards his wife and child.

The setting under the pier where this confrontational encounter takes place becomes (in the process) a kind of theatrical arena in the style of a Greek tragedy, where violent emotions are unleashed and conflicts brought out into the open. Asha, having 'awakened' to the dramatic reality of the situation, after her 'comic' visions, is consequently prepared to intervene decisively in the affairs of others, however painful and threatening the experience.

When the women head off for 'home' at the film's conclusion, the regular anxious glances made by the driver and group leader Simi (Shaheen Khan) in the rear-view mirror of the mini-bus suggest that their difficulties will be travelling with them, but at least the problems experienced by individual members of the group have been brought out into the open.

The unveiling of a cake in the shape of two large bosoms declaring 'Blackpool or bust' on the ride home, allows the women to forget their worries for a moment, and enables the film to end with the sound of laughter (rather than tears), as the group travels through the famous illuminated lights of Blackpool sea front. Symbolically, the 'body' of women in the bus have journeyed from Birmingham to Blackpool without going 'bust', and the experience, for all of its traumas, has proved therapeutic and revivifying.

The women's vulnerability to openly hostile actions and racist attitudes in public places is somewhat offset by the progress they have made in engendering a greater sense of group unity during the outing. Like the band of ex-miners drifting through London at the close of *Brassed Off*, the group may face an uncertain and painful future, but by the conclusion of the film there is an impression that the individual and parallel stories outlined at the beginning have, at least, become part of a more unified and inter-connected story.

In an interview in the *Black Film Bulletin* (1999), Gurinder Chadha described *Bhaji* as a sort of 'poor cousin'[52] to *Wild West* (1993), an earlier film about a British-Asian community. *Wild West* was a Film Four comedy-drama featuring musical performances by a group of Pakistani brothers whose dream is to become Country and Western singers. The film includes a romantic sub-plot involving lead singer Zaf Ayub (Naveen Andrews) falling in love with a beautiful Asian woman, Rifat (Sarita Choudhury), and rescuing her from an abusive husband (who, on this occasion, is white and not Asian).

Music and creative ambition are valued more highly by the brothers than notions of inherited traditions or enforced allegiances. Their disaffected mother (Lalita Ahmed, who played the troubled Asha in *Bhaji*), however, views the aspirations of her sons as an undesirable consequence of living in a dissolute society: 'There are no Pakistani cowboys', she solemnly declares. For Zaf, country music represents the prospect of liberation, and the lyrics of their songs – 'I'm going over to the other side' and 'Anyone can be somebody too' – represent a rejection of a future based overwhelmingly on inflexible codes of conduct. When one of Zaf's aunties discovers him buying pork sausages, he lies that they are for his dog. He is outwitted by the auntie, though, who counters that 'Even the dog must obey God's law'.

The comic and dramatic tensions forged out of setting fundamentalist ideals and individualist beliefs in close proximity and opposition are further explored in *My Son the Fanatic* and in *East is East*, whose very title seems to acknowledge its relationship to *Wild West*. The 'wild west' of the title refers to the name of a record company, but also serves as a coded comment on the lawlessness of contemporary British society as represented by 1990s Southall in the narrative. Hence, the comic parody of a lawless frontier town in *Wild West* increasingly becomes an implied criticism of post-industrial Britain with its barren landscape and limited opportunities for young people of seemingly *any* ethnic origin. It is notable, for instance, that the brothers turn to Nashville for creative inspiration, rather than to any particular aspects of contemporary British culture.

In *Wild West*, mother and sons are drawn to places (Pakistan/ Nashville) whose power and lure lie as much in their imaginative and symbolic connotations as in their actual physical existence. The mother of the would-be Country and Western band in *Wild West* dreams of returning to Pakistan, even though her sons tell her that 'it's real primitive back there . . . It's all repeats on the TV. A lot of people think Sgt Bilko is the new military dictator on account of him being on so often'. Zaf and his brothers are determined to resist any kind of nationalist project aimed at encouraging them to become good Asian or British citizens. The film allows 'alternative' and speculative constructions of identity to flourish, which enable the film to close with a pair of contrasting conclusions, one sad – the band's failure to sign a record deal – the other comic– suggesting that an unquenchable optimistic spirit, with the aid of an unexpected legacy, can result in the realisation of a cherished 'dream'.

The record company are only willing to sign and promote Rifat as a solo performer (without the band) because they say that she possesses the kind of 'dusky looks' which can be promoted in America, implying that female sexuality can be marketed for popular consumption in a way that an Asian Country and Western band cannot. (One of the brothers had originally feared that they could be lynched if they performed in Tennessee.) Zack despairs that the record producers 'got no sense of imagination, just like the rest of this whole damn, deadbeat country', declaring 'We're just brown faces to them'.

Wild West's ultimate commitment (unlike *Bhaji*'s) to non-realist strategies of narration does provide the film with space to develop an ending which grants the band's wish to leave Britain for the USA. Using money given to them by their mother from the sale of the family home, they jet off to Nashville in the final images of the narrative, while she takes the plane to Pakistan. Thus, the film arguably contains a 'realistic', pessimistic ending about the failure of the boys' ambitions, and another ending, predicated on notions of wish-fulfilment, where sombre failure can unexpectedly and belatedly mutate into comic hopefulness.

In his monograph on *Laughter* (1900), Henri Bergson claimed that 'A situation is invariably comic when it belongs simultaneously to two altogether independent series of events and is capable of being interpreted in two entirely different meanings at the same time'.[53] This paradigm is highly appropriate to many of the situations faced by characters in this group of 1990s ethnic comedy-dramas, and the ways in which spectators (themselves) may have mixed feelings about which courses of action characters should choose to pursue.

Characters in several of the films are torn between differing beliefs and responses, leading to feelings of mixed emotions. Om Puri's Asian taxi driver character, for instance, at the end of *My Son the Fanatic*, having lost his son to Islamic fundamentalists and his wife to Pakistan, declares ironically to his white English mistress (Rachel Griffiths), a prostitute in Bradford, 'I have managed to destroy everything . . . I have never felt worse, or better'.

The central situation of *My Son the Fanatic* (1997) was wittily summed up by Philip French in the *Observer* as 'They thought he was into drugs, but it was worse. He'd got religion',[54] referring to the film's central scenario in which Parvez is disturbed by what he sees as the extreme and damaging commitment of his son Farid (Akbar Kurtha) to unyielding fundamentalist beliefs (Parvez refers to these concepts as 'funny ideas'). The film examines the 'fanatical' elements of absolutist codes of conduct, and their relationship to ordinary lived experience, a topical subject in the late 1980s and 1990s (and one seemingly without any comic features, or obvious settlement or resolution).

In an 'afterword' to the 1995 edition of *Orientalism: Western Conceptions of the Orient*, Edward Said claimed that 'We all need some foundation on which to stand; the question is how extreme and unchangeable is our formulation of what this foundation is'.[55] Salman Rushdie had written in 1991 that he found himself 'up against the granite, heartless certainties of Actually Existing Islam, by which I mean the political and priestly power structure that presently dominates and stifles Muslim societies'.[56]

In *My Son the Fanatic*, Parvez works for a German businessman, Mr Schitz (Stellan Skarsgard), whom he mistakenly hails at the airport with a placard welcoming 'Mr SHITs'. The irony of this rather obvious joke is that the businessman turns out to actually be something of 'a shit', physically abusing Parvez's prostitute girlfriend, and finally making his own contribution to the oppressive atmosphere pervading the story. Parvez hopes to maintain his permissive lifestyle without dismantling his family, but this does not prove to be possible. The final scenes feature a bitter struggle between female prostitutes and male fundamentalists, with father and son supporting opposite sides of the conflict. Son Farid walks away from his family in the film's final images, becoming an indelible part of his 'band of brothers' and fellow fundamentalists.

Parvez's mistress suggests that they take a vacation from Bradford and travel to India, but Parvez feels that this would offer only a temporary and illusory solution to their problems, and the film's last shot is of him alone, drinking whisky, listening to jazz, and reclining on the stairs of his empty home. 'There are many ways to be a good man', he tells his son in their last exchange. Om Puri, ironically, would play a character who adopts 'hard-line' fundamentalist beliefs in *East is East*, connoting something of the schizophrenia inherent in the extremities of the 'foreigner-in-exile' situation outlined by Julia Kristeva in her study.

My Son the Fanatic is generally sympathetic to those Asian characters who seek to fit into British culture and attempt to avoid or resist the stranglehold of absolutist beliefs and isolationist stances. However, one particular scene, which reconstructs the comic ethos and 'world view' of *Till Death Us Do Part* and *Love Thy Neighbour* for a contemporary era, indicates why some ethnic groups might find emotional solace and intellectual support in philosophies which openly criticise and oppose what they see as Western-style decadence and the tendency of white English culture to mock those publicly who are designated as different or 'foreign'.

Parvez, a character sympathetic to Western culture, is put under the spotlight (literally) at a Bradford nightspot, while watching a white English comedian (Andy Devine) at work in a club named Manninghams (Manningham is an area in Bradford where, according to an *Observer* supplement on 'Race in Britain, 2001', 'young Asians' rioted for two nights in 1995:[57] ironically, the name also conjures up images of the comedian Bernard Manning, notorious for the deployment of racist material in his comic routines).

The comedian on stage decides to insult Parvez as part of his act, declaring, 'I can smell shit somewhere' on spotting Parvez in the audience, before continuing: 'It's Salman Rushdie himself. What you're smelling here folks is the Satanic arsehole . . . If you fuckers all left town on the same day, we'd all have two hours extra bleeding daylight.' This racist ridicule spreads to the audience, and a nearby spectator repeatedly throws a piece of paper at Parvez, to which his prostitute friend, Bettina, responds by hurling a drink at the perpetrator, before they are all forced to make a hasty exit from the club. The German industrialist who has invited Parvez to the club comments sarcastically that 'this is the celebrated English culture I have heard so much about', and resolves to 'inform the police of this disgust'. 'They were sitting at the next table' observes Bettina, matter-of-factly.

This sequence begins with a panning shot of a white audience enjoying the comedian, whose humorous material, initially, is not concerned with race. This serves to set the context for what will follow, emphasising that the setting and situation are of a perfectly ordinary and unexceptional nature. The ugliness and unpleasantness of his racist remarks, thus, emerge from within the confines of local 'light entertainment'. The stand-up comic's patter and manner of delivery conjures up memories of Eddie Booth's racist remarks and observations, but here there is no equivalent of a Bill Reynolds to counter the offensive and hurtful insults, and it is left to the white woman accompanying Parvez to register her disgust with what is transpiring, and to counter and disrupt the laughter of the club audience at the comedian's observations and language. Unlike Love Thy Neighbour, however, the flow of the narrative in My Son the Fanatic is interrupted after a character is revealed expressing racist views (however comically expressed or intended), and this does represent a significant change from the process of ongoing racial insults at the centre of programmes and films such as Love Thy Neighbour and Till Death Us Do Part.

Howard Jacobson, in Seriously Funny: From the Ridiculous to the Sublime suggests that 'In comedy the hyperbole of hate makes an instant ass of intolerance, while not denying you the extravagant pleasures of indulging it'.[58] Jacobson acknowledges that comedy is always double-edged, and not necessarily morally responsible, as it is always possible for a comic performer to claim 'I am only joking, don't take me seriously'. This scene in My Son the Fanatic illustrates, though, how jokes and barbed observations presented under the guise of comedy can have tangible consequences, particularly for the unlucky victims and targets of a comic's stand-up routine.

In his monograph, On Humour, Simon Critchley suggests that 'Ethnic humour is very much the Hobbesian laughter of superiority or sudden glory at our eminence and the other's stupidity',[59] and admits that 'Perhaps one laughs at jokes one would rather not laugh at . . . As such the very relativity of humour might be said to contain an indirect appeal that this place stands in need of change'.[60] The nightclub scene in My Son the

Fanatic does not imply that such humour in a public place can comfortably facilitate social improvements and increased integration. Instead, the comedian's patter leads to physical abuse, and leaves Parvez seemingly without an immediate community to which he can express allegiance, or feel that he truly belongs.

This group of 1990s British films, as a whole, testifies as to the ways in which conceptions of ethnicity and cultural identity were becoming more complex and diverse within the contours of 1990s Britain, and implies that representations of a modern indigenous multi-cultural society, consequently, needed to become more challenging and searching.

The search for an authentic personal and cultural identity on the part of key protagonists is one of the distinguishing features of several of the films, especially in *Secrets & Lies* (1996) where black optician Hortense (Marianne Jean-Baptiste) seeks out her biological mother, who gave her up for adoption. In so doing, Hortense unknowingly (or subconsciously) uncovers the white, working-class family to which she was originally denied access. Cynthia (Brenda Blethyn), it transpires, did not look at her baby girl after she was born, and subsequently never realised that the child was black. This process of looking-away initiates a series of painful and ironic misunderstandings: 'I took a couple of wrong turns', explains Hortense as the reason why she is late (21 years late, to be precise) for her half-sister's birthday party.

Judith Williamson noted in a (2001) interview ('Changing Images: Judith Williamson in Conversation with Huw Beynon and Sheila Rowbotham') that Mike Leigh's penchant for creating parodic forms of characterisation, with characters (particularly female characters) being defined by their heightened and highly mannered forms of speech, did not apply to the character of Hortense in *Secrets & Lies*, who was presented as being particularly quietly and carefully spoken:

> *Secrets & Lies* is a very funny film, but Mike Leigh didn't dare make the black woman in it comic. All the other characters are hysterically over the top, completely surreal characters, they seem almost mad, and then, right in the middle of the film, you have this black girl who is incredibly thoughtful and normal. Everybody else is caricatured.[61]

The comic and dramatic tension of the narrative is, in fact, generated out of the contrast between the stillness and quietness of Hortense and the raucous, more impulsive and unrestrained behaviour of the Rose family. Leigh may have felt that it was politically and commercially expedient not to represent the female black character in terms which could be defined as exaggerated or caricatured. Hortense's restrained and dignified persona also provides a contrast to the unmediated frankness of Cynthia and her daughter Roxanne (Claire Rushbrook) and their determination to express whatever is on their mind (a tendency which links with them with such characters as Eddie Booth and Alf Garnett, albeit minus their extreme views).

These contrasts of personality also suggest that each character can gain something from her opposite 'other half', and the film ends with an image of cultural integration and ethnic harmony, as Cynthia and her two daughters, Roxanne and Hortense, are shown appearing to be reconciled and happy in each other's company. Neither is quite as lonely or incomplete as previously, now that they are aware of the existence of their cultural 'other' and 'double'. The film concludes with Cynthia in the presence of her extended family, reclining on a sun-lounger in the backyard, declaring, 'This is the life': an ironic statement given the pain and anguish dominating the film from its very beginning, and one suggesting that racial harmony and ethnic integration can be achieved out of a process of inner and outward searching, amidst scenes of melodrama, borderline tragedy, and comic conflict.

Leon the Pig Farmer also involves characters searching for their origins, but this film adopts a humorous and bemused approach to its subject material. *Leon* concerns a Jewish man from a southern middle-class family who learns that he is the product of artificial insemination, and that his biological father is a Yorkshire pig farmer. *Leon* proceeds to imply that grotesque acts of miscegenation may serve to modify existing cultures and bridge cultural and geographical divisions after he accidentally creates a mutant pig-sheep during an act of artificial insemination undertaken on his biological father's farm. Contemplating the implications of this transmutation, he speculates that 'It might be kosher', meaning that the pig-sheep mutant might (in time) prove acceptable to Jewish culture.

This hypothesis remains only tentative in the film, and the result of Leon's experiments is left to roam unseen (and presumably die) in country woods at the end of the film. *Leon* (like *Secrets & Lies*), however, does close on a note of cultural reconciliation, with the Yorkshire and Jewish families pictured together in a restaurant, exchanging confidences and appearing comfortable in each other's company.

Despite such textual images of integration, there was still the not easily verifiable question of what kinds of audiences went to see this group of films at the cinema. Gurinder Chadha in a 1998 interview claimed that *Bhaji on the Beach* was a success 'not because black people went to see it, but because white people went to see it',[62] suggesting that while the film may ultimately be committed to bringing various ethnic groupings closer together, divisions within British culture may resist such overtures.

This group of films, on the whole, I would contend, reflected a desire by filmmakers in Britain to move beyond the reductive and inflexible binary oppositions of 1970s situation comedies and yet avoid the sense of esoteric isolationism engendered by some of the films produced out of the 1980s workshop movements. This impulse may, in part, have been due to the fact that the financing and commercial reception of a significant number of 1990s films became more internationally oriented during the decade.

Ian Christie in an essay 'As Others See Us: British Film-Making and Europe in the 90s' (2000) reported, for example, that *Secrets & Lies* was 'largely funded' outside Britain by 'France's CIBY 2000' network,[63] and Andrew Anthony in an article entitled 'British Cinema' (*Observer*, 1999) noted that Mike Leigh's film 'made more money in Paris alone than it did in the whole of Britain'.[64] Sales of British films abroad were also increasingly important in the 1990s. Gurinder Chadha proudly claimed that *Bhaji* was sold 'to every territory in the world', and 'did well' in America, which helped it to make an eventual profit on its £1 million budget[65] – the film in fact took only £309,715 during its original UK cinema release.[66]

Some of the other films engaging with issues of race and ethnicity were also not particularly successful at the UK cinema box office when originally released. Mark Steyn, while reviewing *Bhaji* in the *Spectator*, claimed that its predecessor, *Wild West*, was 'a box office dud'.[67] Sarita Malik in the *Journal of Popular British Cinema* reported that BBC films pulled out of financing *East is East* after *My Son the Fanatic* received what executives felt was a 'lukewarm response' from cinema audiences, which left the corporation 'reeling'.[68] Thus, it was by no means a foregone conclusion in such circumstances that *East is East* (which I shall discuss next) would ever be produced, or that it would turn out to be very popular with British cinema audiences.

Case study: *East is East* (1999)

This examination of *East is East* will seek to explore how this particular film extends many of the themes, dilemmas and conflicts outlined so far in the chapter, and consider the ways in which the film explores connections between comic modes of expression and racist discourses, and audaciously combines elements of 'low comedy' with moments of intensely serious drama.

East is East, a Film Four production, opened on 200 screens across Britain, 'instead of the art-house average of 10 or 15 prints in circulation around the country',[69] according to the *Independent on Sunday*, and

gained cinema admission receipts of over £7 million in relation to its production budget of £2.4 million.[70] This made the film by far the most commercially successful of the ethnic comedy-dramas produced during the
1990s. BBC films, ironically, as noted above, decided to withdraw their
financial and developmental participation in the film because, according
to producer Leslee Udwin, 'there were no star names in it', and 'it was,
they thought of limited appeal'.[71] (Channel 4 made a similar decision with
regard to *The Full Monty*, which was later openly regretted.)

East is East was adapted from his successful stage play by Ayub Khan-
Din, whose own familial and cultural experiences are interwoven into
the text. In its redrafting of autobiographical material into dramatic fiction, the film evoked (at certain moments of its narrative) Terence
Davies' account of Liverpool family life in the 1940s and 1950s, as
reconstructed in *Distant Voices, Still Lives* (1988). Both *Distant Voices*
and *East is East* conclude with images of the father being ejected from
the narrative, but only in Davies' more tortured and avant-garde,
mosaic-style narrative, is the father implicitly punished for his sins by
death.

The filmic style adopted by director Damien O'Donnell seeks to play
down *East is East*'s origins in a theatrical stage play by imbuing the
narrative with a sense of constant motion and movement, created by
fast editing within scenes, skilful use of a varied range of musical accompaniment to the visual images, and a tendency to present particular
viewpoints from unusual angles (suggesting a world in the process of
being turned upside-down). This fluid and brisk style is in stark contrast
to some of the techniques evident in Mike Leigh's study of ethnic family
tensions in *Secrets & Lies*, which deploys long takes and relatively static
camera positions in the quest to discover and reveal its own particular
emotional truths.

Om Puri appeared as two diametrically opposed characters in *My Son
the Fanatic* and *East is East*, exemplifying two sides of the debate about
the extent to which first-, second- and third-generation immigrant communities should seek to assimilate themselves into British culture by
playing down their religious and political beliefs. In the former film, he
plays a Pakistani taxi-driver who embarks on an affair with a prostitute,
and worries about the 'funny ideas' his son is formulating. He is shocked
by the boy's sympathies for Islamic fundamentalist beliefs, and longs for
a time when his son will 'tire of his moral exertions'.

In *East is East*, Puri plays a Pakistani chip-shop owner, who, with the
passion of a true zealot, tries to force his British-Asian children into
accepting the tenets of the Muslim faith: 'You not English, English
people never accepting you. In Islam, everyone equal see, no black man,

or white man', he informs his recalcitrant son Tariq (Jimi Mistry). This idea of the 'double' haunts both characterisations, and at the end of each film Puri's character has been rejected by his children, and his marriage is in an extremely damaged state, suggesting that whichever side of the cultural dichotomy is privileged or highlighted, the end result may be the same.

In *Engaging Characters: Fiction, Emotion, and the Cinema* (1995), Murray Smith defined the co-text of a film as the 'set of values, beliefs and so forth which form the backdrop to the events of the narrative'.[72] In *East is East*, discourses of Muslim isolationism, patriarchal authoritarianism, white English racism, and teenage rebellion are all circulating within the narrative, which, via its early 1970s setting, is able to present these discourses and patterns of behaviour as being at new stages of development. Consequently, the spectator is encouraged to construct readings of the film by discriminating between the claims of the competing polyphony of voices, values and discourses propelling the narrative forward.

One brief exchange in *Secrets & Lies* points to a subject area which will form the basis of an entire narrative in *East is East*. In the former film, a young Asian man is having his picture taken for his 'Auntie', and laconically explains to photographer Maurice (Timothy Spall) the reason for the picture: 'It's time I got married'. 'Pick a bride time, is it?' replies Maurice, pragmatically. In *Secrets & Lies*, such moments point to the multitude of stories which could be developed and explored. Mike Leigh's film, however, proceeds to explore clashes and misunderstandings between white and black characters, and does not dramatise the tensions and difficulties hinted at in this reference to arranged marriages in Asian and Indian culture.

East is East begins by detailing how Nazir (Ian Aspinall), the eldest son of the Khan family, refuses his own arranged marriage. To mark this act of ungrateful transgression, a family portrait of him is later shown fading away on the wall, denoting his separation from the family, and he is consequently pronounced dead by his own father (even though George knows that Nazir is actually living in Eccles). By fleeing the family home, and abandoning the Muslim cultural tradition, he sets in motion a spirit of defiance which the other children will reluctantly and haphazardly continue.

Tariq develops a non-Muslim, British identity as 'Tony', and Nazir himself becomes known as 'Mr Nigel', an implicitly gay partner in an Eccles boutique. Abdul (Raji James) and Maneer (Emil Marwa) are depicted as more dutiful sons, whilst Meenah (Archie Panjabi), the only daughter, is lively and free spirited. The youngest, Sajid (Jordan

Routledge), attempts to shield himself from the world by viewing it solely from the perspective of his parka-hood. He is too young to be subjected to an arranged marriage, as he himself points out, but he suffers the pain of an enforced circumcision, when his father decides to 'bloody fix him' (referring to him as if he were a cat or a dog, in urgent need of neutering).

George Khan, as portrayed by Om Puri, is a complex figure. Speaking a kind of broken English throughout ('I ask you who doing this', is a fairly typical utterance), he is also capable of seeking violent retribution, when thwarted in his desire to instil Muslim values in his children. We sense that underneath his self-assured demeanour, George is a deeply divided character. On a family outing to Bradford, he reveals that he came to Britain in 1937 to appear in a film about Anglo-Indian relations and colonial wars, uttering lines such as 'I kill bloody English' (see also Ambrose, the amateur actor in *Bhaji on the Beach*, who recalls dressing up to play Indian figures in Anglo-American films about Britain's relationship with India).

East is East examines how, in his role as a patriarchal Pakistani father, George may be trying to sustain a part beyond its limits of cohesion and reasonableness, and – like those similarly frustrated figures from 1970s situation comedies, Alf Garnett and Eddie Booth – will seek to discredit those who stand in the way of creating the kind of community he wishes to establish and validate.

In the opening stages of the narrative, George is depicted trying to make out the details of a radio report on East Pakistan's fight for independence during its conflict with India and West Pakistan in 1971. Neither George nor the film's audience can discern the exact state of the war because of the noise and bustle of the fish-and-chip shop in which the scene is set. The indirect manner in which this conflict is presented may suggest that the film itself is indeed not concerned with these wider international historical issues, that they do just perhaps constitute background listening.

East is East is clearly more concerned with the personal dimensions of the story it is conveying, but the film does go on to imply that these wider political currents may influence George's behaviour and attitudes. Towards the end of the film, watching a television news broadcast of the failure of East Pakistan to achieve independence makes him aware of the vulnerability and divided nature of the Pakistani state, and leads to a renewal of his own attempts to impose a form of 'home rule'.

George's efforts to crush any opposition to his plans and authority lead to the most distressing scenes within the narrative. As George tries to find out which members of his family have destroyed the special watches set aside for the planned wedding ceremonies, his feelings of outrage and bitterness are (ironically) unleashed on his two most loyal supporters within the family – Maneer and Ella (Linda Bassett). Maneer is beaten for remaining silent on the question of who is responsible for the damage, and Ella is attacked for daring to answer George back. As George turns into a vicious wife-beater, the camera records the helplessness of Maneer, and the restrained tears of Sajid, as they respectively listen to and witness the violent actions of their father.

Ella is menaced at her place of work, the family fish-and-chip shop, and the drawn blinds of the entrance to the shop denote not only that the shop is closed for business but that events almost too terrible to observe are occurring behind the shutters. Thus the film at this stage distances itself from George when he resorts to domestic violence and becomes manically intolerant, suggesting that underneath what may have appeared to be initially funny or farcical within the narrative lies something much darker and disturbing. If the film as a whole wishes to operate within the generic sphere of comedy-drama, this sequence is a forceful reminder that there are still moments within the narrative which consist of pure drama, from which no moments of humour or light relief can be extracted.

The scenes of violence, I would contend, are particularly shocking to an audience because they form such a contrast to the previous moods of earthy humour pervading the narrative, and force spectators of the film to re-assess their views and impressions of George, and recognise that he is a character who must be taken seriously (and, in the end, defeated, if democracy and decency are to prevail within the Khan household).

The scenes of George's destructive and hurtful behaviour illustrate how life within the family can suddenly darken in mood and atmosphere, and the family unit become a battleground in which members fight for survival, and for what they believe is right. The film will proceed to demonstrate how George is finally defeated and overthrown by the uprising of his intransigent family (although Ella continues to support him whenever she can), who stage a series of revolts over his authoritarian tendencies and ruthless methods of persuasion.

East is East's fascination with dual and potentially antagonistic discourses is, in fact, introduced in the opening sequences of the film, which feature the Khan children taking part in a Christian Whitsun parade. Meena is framed holding an icon of Christ on the cross, as two of her brothers mutter such irreligious sentiments as 'Check out the nurses', suggesting that religious worship can be fun and life-affirming. This sense of harmony and shared beliefs is suddenly broken by the intervention of Ella, who frantically warns her children that their father is back early from the mosque. The sons and daughter scuttle down a side-street in a hurried, hectic fashion to avoid incurring the wrath of George, whilst carrying the icons of Jesus and the Virgin Mary. The effect is to create a sense of urgency and farce, with the sight of Christ on the cross speeding through a Manchester back-alley appearing comic and (possibly) faintly scandalous to the spectator. Even at this early stage of the narrative, the film seeks to present familiar images in a new perspective, and is prepared to disorient spectators.

The sequence which follows also depicts a religious occasion being disrupted, when Nazir abandons his own wedding. Whereas the Khan teenagers can be shown rejoining the Whitsun procession at a later stage, after a circuitous detour, the film emphasizes that once the Muslim ceremony has been interrupted and rejected, once the 'spell' of the occasion has been broken or questioned, there can be no return to a state of original innocence.

The narrative structure of the film is based around three arranged marriages, each of which ultimately fails to take place. The effects of the debacle of the first planned wedding are presented as painful and dramatic, whilst the concluding two arranged marriages are depicted as comic and farcical in tone, although all three occasions have serious dramatic consequences for the family's future and emotional well-being.

The extended scene which draws the narrative to a close focuses on the problems engendered by the very concept of arranged marriages. In this ill-fated encounter, the appearance of the brides-to-be is revealed prior to the event, marking a break with the ritualistic tradition as depicted in the first marriage. Contrary to the attractive woman who is revealed at the final moment as Nazir's selected bride (the published screenplay describes her as 'stunningly beautiful'[73]), and who is the real victim of his simultaneous flight from Muslim and heterosexual cultures, the two women chosen as brides for Abdul and Tariq are caricatured to appear extremely unattractive and undesirable. Both wear black-framed glasses, have large faces and buck-teeth. Even George has initially winced at their appearance when presented with a framed portrait of them, before pronouncing the girls 'beautiful'. This remark is clearly in the film's terms ironic and insincere, but George's response illustrates that aesthetic concerns will not stop him trying to realise his ambitions. (Ella, once relations with the prospective in-laws have irretrievably broken down, will describe the two daughters as 'monstrosities'.)

The film, from this stage in the proceedings, pushes its own dramatic and comedic logic of holding no character or philosophy sacred to the extreme, and out of the resulting anarchy will emerge a somewhat desperate struggle to identify and re-establish shared meanings and values by the close of the story. The last two arranged marriages are aborted in the final examples of a series of escalating social embarrassments and tensions. A model of a woman's pubic area and thighs made by art student Saleem (Chris Bisson) ends up in the lap of Abdul and Tariq's prospective mother-in-law, who is predictably horrified. An image symbolising women who won't stay in the subordinate places mapped out for them finally defeats George's hopes of forging a cultural, economic and spiritual link between the areas of Salford and Bradford, two northern towns and cities associated with providing key settings for the British 'new wave' cinema of the late 1950s and 1960s.

East is East's own period setting of the early 1970s is evoked by images of space-hoppers, with their propensity to burst and then lie deflated in the street being used to connote the fragility and ephemeral quality of some of the decade's more colourful innovations (and social hopes?). The film, as a whole, does not succumb to post-modern nostalgia about the recent past, preferring instead to recreate it in the spirit of what Bakhtin in *The Dialogic Imagination: Four Essays* (1975) referred to as 'contemporaneity', a form of 'contemporary reality' which implies 'a simultaneity of times' in which conceptions of past, present and future are linked together.[74]

For cinema audiences of *East is East* in 1999, the film's allusions to problems within British society, circa 1971 (racial unrest in economically depressed towns, organisations permitted to promote racist viewpoints, philosophical and practical debates about whether disparate communities should be more integrated with each other), appear still relevant to analyses of the state of multi-cultural Britain in the late 1990s. In *East is East*, the past is not so much another country, but one with rather disturbingly similar concerns to the present.

The links connecting British culture from the 1970s to the 1990s, and the film's refusal to romanticise or fetishise the recent past, are exemplified in a pivotal scene juxtaposing sights and sounds from the 1970s children's series *The Clangers* with the Khan family's disconsolate emotions, after George has aggressively and unflinchingly berated them for their resistance to his plans. Mother, sons and daughter are pictured mutely watching the series, the extracts from the programme adding a surreal, defamiliarising tone to the scene, and functioning as a kind of meta-commentary on the family's disturbed psychological state.

The 'alien' family of the Clangers was composed of a Major Clanger, who was recognised as the most important member, and a Mother Clanger who worried when the Tiny Clangers misbehaved and tried to open up the boundaries of their world.[75] The inclusion of this imaginary world into the world of the Khan's serves an ironic purpose. The line

'That made them laugh' is intoned by the narrator of the Clangers just as the Khans are pictured at their most solemn and perplexed. The innocence and childish fun of the Clangers is thus counterposed with the increasing distress felt by the family.

The intertextual elements point the narrative away from its mood of overwhelming melancholy, and heighten an audience's awareness that they (like the Khan family) are watching a constructed fiction. The TV narrator's references to the 'lonely planets, with no life on them at all' echo, in allegorical form, the family's own feelings of alienation, and allude to the difficulties of putting down roots in an inhospitable landscape. 'No trees, only rock', observes the programme's narrator, as the film cuts to a shot of George (the 'Major Clanger' of his family) in a separate room of the house. George, too, at this stage, seems like a character from another time and place, an alienated and forlorn figure, who might have been happier living in a distant past when children were less recalcitrant and influenced by twentieth-century Western values and beliefs.

The uneasy silence in the family living room (apart from the strange noises produced by the Clangers) is broken by Tariq, who rails against what he reads as his mother's acquiescence in their collective oppression. 'You can both fuck off if you think I'm getting married to a fucking Paki!' he declares. This results in the youngest son cowering to his mother, and Meena appearing shocked and bewildered. Tariq, with his embittered language, could be interpreted as bringing racism directly into the family home, and hence insulting and threatening his own brothers and sister. Equally, he resists what he sees as impositions on his liberty, by voicing his opposition through harsh and hateful language.

Tariq's outburst is shocking, because from an outsider's perspective it can appear as an example of self-contempt. The cruel irony of the language deployed in his disavowal is that this is precisely the kind of language which white racists might use in relation to British-Asian families such as the Khans.[76] In *The Dialogic Imagination*, Bakhtin referred to the concept of alien language as 'a language not one's own, at any level', and acknowledged the power contained within the 'unofficial side of speech, with its rich store of curses', capable of pushing 'to the limit the mutual non-understanding represented by people who speak in different languages'.[77]

This scene works within the paradigms outlined by Bakhtin as to how communication between fragmented groups may disintegrate into mutual loathing and incomprehension. George and his children are ultimately not speaking the same kind of language, and either they do not understand each other, or they understand each other only too well.

I shall consider how the film ultimately seeks a way to break beyond this cultural, ethical and linguistic deadlock (which we saw affected *Love Thy Neighbour* and *Till Death Us Do Part*) in the final section of my case study.

'Come and hear Enoch speak!' is the invitation offered to passers-by in the street by Mr Moorhouse (John Bardon), George's racist neighbour, in two sequences from *East is East* which allude to the symbolic power of Enoch Powell (a controversial figure much cited in Alf Garnett's 'comic' rants, as noted earlier) during the 1970s.[78] With regard to these scenes from the film, Claire Monk, writing in *Cineaste* (2001) interpreted them as evidence of what she termed the film's depoliticisation of 'Britain's recent past', and evidence of a screenplay which 'barely' acknowledges the 'racism being inflamed at that time'.[79]

It may well be that commercial considerations, and a desire to succeed in achieving a level of populist appeal, influenced the amount of space allotted to this aspect of British social history. I will seek to illustrate, however, that in the two scenes where Powell's influence *is* evoked and suggested, the disturbing and disruptive nature of his pronouncements are acknowledged, and conceivably debunked, through the economical use of humour and levels of irony.

In the first scene, a poster of Enoch Powell's face is highlighted promoting a speech to be given by him in Salford town hall. This visit predictably encourages some local people to become openly hostile to black and Asian ethnic communities. George's neighbour Mr Moorhouse and his grandson, Earnest (the spelling of his name in the screenplay suggests the well-meaning 'earnestness' of his character), are depicted distributing leaflets to advertise this talk by the Conservative Member of Parliament. In the opening image, George Khan is framed next to the posters as he makes his way to the fish-and-chip shop. The sequence is predicated on glances directed at each other by the characters on opposite sides of the road, and on the comical ways in which virulent racial hatred is subtly undermined by the actions of Earnest (Gary Dalmer). Mr Moorhouse shouts 'Let's send the buggers home' when noticing George in the street, the incident recalling the personal disputes at the heart of a wider malaise in *Love Thy Neighbour*. The encounter, in which George does not speak, reveals that for all his attempts to subject others to the authority of his own discourses within the confines of the family home, he (in turn) risks being objectified and undermined by the disapproving gaze and language of others, when stepping out into public spaces.

In the scene, Earnest is depicted enthusiastically handing out leaflets aimed at fanning the flames of racial tension and discrimination, whilst

ironically interrupting these activities to shout a greeting to George
Khan ('Salaam-alacum') which earns him a rebuke from his grandfather,
and a puzzled stare from the subject of his interpellation. It could be concluded from this disjunction between Earnest's words and deeds that he
is involved in actions without fully understanding what he is doing, or
being expected to represent. His spontaneous address to George also
suggests how he might ultimately resist attempts at indoctrination.

The implications of this sequence are responded to in another short
scene featuring the poster of Enoch Powell prominently displayed in the
front window of Moorhouse's terraced house opposite the Khan's home.
This particular scene serves as a kind of riposte to the veiled menace and
unresolved tension implicit in the earlier sequence. Here the street location is a play area for young children and teenagers, who are presented
as more culturally integrated and at ease with each other than the adults
in the earlier scene. (Meena, for instance, is shown accompanied by two
white girls on her way home from school.)

Events in this scene are initiated by Earnest (referred to by Meena in
another of the double discourses of the narrative as 'Pongo'), who invites
Meena to play football with him. She seizes the opportunity to physically and symbolically attack both the racist neighbour and the 'mythic'
figure of Powell who fuels and legitimises his racism. Meena kicks
Earnest's football through the poster of Powell in the front window, hitting the 'man behind the man', so to speak, before (in a typical 'slapstick'
technique) leaving the innocent party (Earnest) to bear the brunt of the
racist's wrath.

This moment exemplifies the potential of humour to take aim at a
number of culturally over-determined targets in a single instance, suggesting that would-be tyrants are always capable of being brought down
to earth by what Freud termed the comic process of 'unmasking'.[80] On
this occasion, the use of comedy functions as a form of wish-fulfilment,
implying that beleaguered communities are always capable of fighting
back when least expected. Equally, the conclusion to the scene suggests
that the forces of oppression may be shattered, but not necessarily
destroyed. As the camera pans in to frame the face of Earnest's racist
grandfather through the broken glass of the window, we note that his
awesome and farcical appearance (his face bears the imprint of flying
food) is still, however, capable of emptying the street simply by the intensity of his gaze. Mr Moorhouse, his face registering both hatred and
shock, rages at Earnest to 'Come back here, you little bastard', suggesting that racists are not easily defeated, but are not immune from sudden
and successful counter-attacks either.

'Never the twain'?

In the closing section of the film, Sajid gives a V-sign to the Pakistani visitors from Bradford, and announces their arrival with the phrase, 'The Pakis are here!' His mother does not chastise or correct the boy for his language or terminology; only a shot of George Khan looking askance at what he faintly hears, hints at the complex layers of prejudice and discrimination circulating within the discourses of the film. Sajid's exclamation could be read as another example of verbal negativity, or even (as racist commentators might claim) of self-delusion. It could be argued that the film is seeking to destroy the sacred power and mystique of racist language, by allowing it to be voiced by victims and aggressors alike, implying that no communities are immune from discrimination and hatred, and that any social grouping may on occasion resort to the use of hurtful and offensive comments and viewpoints.

Only in the final moments of the narrative is there an indication that certain characters might succeed in escaping from the sense of solitude and of being misunderstood they have experienced throughout the film. In a concluding sequence, George is allowed a brief respite from his feelings of alienation, failure and regret by the exchanging of a greeting in Arabic with another lonely figure, Earnest. When George is expelled from the family home ('It's over', Abdul tells him), Earnest catches him at his lowest moment and greets him with the expression 'Salaam-alacum' ('God be merciful upon you'). George replies, 'Waalacum-salaam' ('And you too').

These mutual blessings are ironic given that the situations created by George have resulted in his family spiritually rejecting him, while young and impressionable Earnest has received only blows and abrasiveness for his own attempts at social integration. Nevertheless, this scene of pathos between two exiled characters does suggest a kind of tentative breakthrough, in comparison to the ideological blockages and divisive language prevailing elsewhere. Here, the cultural exchange between sender and receiver is invested with a sense of mutual dignity and respect, based on underlying notions of the need for disempowered individuals to seek some form of shared language and common ground. A fleeting moment of recognition between these two ultimately marginalised figures is, thus, circuitously and movingly achieved.

George Khan's separate marriages in Pakistan and Britain have rendered the official status of his own children somewhat ambivalent (the mother refers to George's children living under his 'bastard roof'), and Earnest, too, is called a 'little bastard' by his grandfather. The scene is indicative of how audience expectations have been subtly subverted and disrupted by the end of the film. Earnest, the grandson of a racist figure of the community, is a character whom one might expect to express racist statements, given his upbringing. The ironical twist of the film is that Earnest is, in fact, prepared to utter a welcoming phrase in an Arabic tongue in an effort to reach out to other cultures, while two of the Khan sons are themselves prepared to speak contemptuously and 'comically' of 'Pakis'.

Language in the film is thus always double-edged, but *East is East* does attempt to distinguish between the language of democracy and discourses of totalitarianism and oppression. In so doing, the film is not pious or high-minded, and does believe in some of the virtues of plain-speaking inherent in the phrase 'calling a spade a spade'. George is not interested in the concept of shared cultural discourses, and so is left somewhat marooned by the close. The brief exchange with Earnest, at the close, nonetheless, suggests that there may still be hope in the future, if George can accept defeat and a reduced sense of linguistic potency.

The final fate of the Khan family is left open in the closing shots, and there is no attempt to detail, in the manner of Victorian literature, those characters that go on to live fulfilled or disappointing lives. Abdul's parting comment to George before he leaves the house – 'It's over' – indicates a desire to inject a note of finality into the proceedings, but George has not previously revealed an inclination to accept the setting of limits to his authority.

The failure of George's plans and aspirations at the end of the narrative also mirrors the failure of East Pakistan to achieve independence in 1971. Stanley Wolpert in *A New History of India* (1989) states that 'Pakistan emerged from this third undeclared war with less than half its population, its army and economy on the brink of collapse, its myth of Muslim unity destroyed, its spirit sorely deflated'.[81] The final image of George, glimpsed in the dawn-light of the family fish-and-chip shop, accepting 'half-a-cup' of tea from Ella, is of a man whose own 'myth of Muslim unity' has been dented, and whose spirit is also 'sorely deflated'.

The film ends with shots of the Khan teenagers leaving the house, and merging into the frantic activity of the street, which is once again peopled by children, now that the onerous figures of Mr Moorhouse and George are no longer highly visible. The implication of this open-ended conclusion might be that family life of whatever culture continues despite all upheavals and that in terms of the chronology of the film, 1971 will soon turn into 1972 (the year in which *Love Thy Neighbour* began transmission, and *Till Death Us Do Part* returned to British television screens after a four-year absence).

Conclusion

In his *Evening Standard* review of *East is East*, Alexander Walker noted that 'East and West once co-habited in the same redbrick English street in the TV series *Love Thy Neighbour*. We've progressed since then: *East is East*'s first-generation Asian-Brits now put "Hate Thy Father" at the top of their agenda'.[82] When summarised in such terms, it may not seem as if the film necessarily represents that much of an aesthetic or ideological advance upon the kinds of situation comedies discussed previously, which tended to reject subtleties of character and nuances of plot in favour of a more general air of noisy conflict in which characters rarely had any narrative time to reflect on the reasons underlying their behaviour and attitudes.

However, notably, *East is East* does represent a return to northern culture, as opposed to the outer-London suburban housing estate featured in *Love Thy Neighbour*, and the East End setting where Alf Garnett sought to make his views public. *East is East*, with its theatrical origins, can be placed in a tradition of filmed plays set in the north of England (for example, *Hindle Wakes* (Victor Saville, 1931), *Hobson's Choice* (David Lean, 1953) and *Spring and Port Wine* (Peter Hammond, 1970). *East is East*'s similarities in theme to the subject-material of these three films – rebellious young men and women who reject their parents' codes of conduct and deepest wishes, in a quest to fashion their own lives – place the film within a British dramatic and cinematic tradition of narratives about frustrated northern characters who face the prospect of stunted existences if they do not register their protests against conformity.

The Salford setting of *East is East* also suggests a certain relationship to the 'Weatherfield' Manchester setting of the Granada television serial *Coronation Street* (1960 onwards), which was criticised in an essay by Stephen Bourne in *Black Images in British Television: The Colour Black* (1989) for the absence of ethnic characters from its storylines, despite its setting: 'Of all the soap operas to have achieved success and popularity in Britain, *Coronation Street* has probably failed more than any other to have represented black and Asian people'.[83] In the late 1990s, the serial has tried to rectify this omission by having an Asian family run the corner shop, and featuring such actors as Saeed Jaffrey (who appeared in *My Beautiful Laundrette*), Chris Bisson (who plays Saleem in *East is East*) and Jimmi Harkishin (who starred in *Bhaji*, and had a brief part in *East is East*) in featured roles.

East is East's links with aspects of northern 'comic realism' (as exemplified by such traditions as the British 'new wave' films of the 1960s, and *Coronation Street*), imbues the narrative with a sense of integrity and purpose, so that for all its pithy and insult-strewn language and emphasis on bodily functions, the film never becomes merely a series of loosely connected scenes, without any wider overall meanings or points of reference, as was sometimes the case with the feature-film versions of popular situation comedies adapted from television.

East is East does convey a sense that its makers consciously sought a mass audience for the film, and one of the ways in which that was achieved (as the deleted scenes included in the DVD and video retail editions of the film indicate[84]) was by downplaying the sense of social tragedy and cultural deadlock hovering away at the edges of the narrative. The film does not shy away, however, from showing some of the possible consequences of intolerance, or by suggesting that the kinds of oppositions dramatised within the family can be easily resolved.

This dramatic and philosophical paradigm can also be applied to the endings of *Bhaji on the Beach*, *My Son the Fanatic* and *Secrets & Lies*, all of which illustrate a creative tension between what one might term the optimistic and socially hopeful tendencies of the comic mode, and the more downbeat and pessimistic impulses of a certain type of social-realist drama. These films do seek to go beyond the typical 1970s situational-comedy framework outlined earlier, which tended to imply that cultural interactions between differing ethnic groups were doomed to exist in repetitive and somewhat futile cyclical patterns.

The plots of the 1990s films discussed in this chapter highlight the pain and uncertainty suffered by the central characters – who may feel torn between a loyalty to the religious, spiritual or familial side of their character and a desire to transcend superficial or simplistic ethnic definitions of their personal identity – leaving many of the films with an impression of unresolved tensions as they conclude their stories.

One of the boldest aspects of *East is East* was its determination to present its Asian characters as rounded individuals who were capable of being racist, stubborn and isolationist, while still maintaining a kind of comic exuberance (which could also be claimed for the figures of Alf Garnett and Eddie Booth, despite their otherwise obvious failings as role models).

East is East tries to salvage what it can from the 1970s traditions of British comedies about ethnicity and problems with the coloured neighbours next door, and, where possible, re-appropriate some of the sub-genre's terms of abuse, perhaps with a view to lessening some of their power to wound and hurt. Speaking the language of one's enemy is always a difficult and potentially dangerous practice, as it can lead to a general escalation in virulent abuse and the formation of situations where there are no limits to what can be uttered or argued.

My Son the Fanatic, Bhaji on the Beach and *East is East* all contain examples of racism by white British characters, but they also suggest that Asian characters can be bigoted, repressive and self-righteous on occasions. The films do not revel in racist language enjoyed for its comic pleasure or cruelty, but suggest that prejudiced views, in general, militate against the creation of a genuinely multi-cultural society, and a healthy British film and television culture.

In aiming to reach a mixed and wide audience, the films hold out the possibility of demonstrating that racist behaviour and separatist attitudes are undesirable and divisive in a modern society, without ever being pious or utopian in the process. The racist insults conveyed and perpetuated in *Love Thy Neighbour* and *Till Death Us Do Part*, in the television episodes at least, were accompanied by the sound of audience laughter, suggesting that in certain circumstances racist terminology could be funny. In *Bhaji on the Beach* and *My Son the Fanatic*, examples of racism by white characters are presented as horrific and demeaning, but the women in *Bhaji on the Beach* are still depicted as capable of laughing as a community at the end of their trip to the seaside, despite the moments of high drama experienced during the day.

American film reviewer Pauline Kael, writing about the British 'new wave' cinema of the 1960s, and referring to such films as the racial murder-mystery *Sapphire* (Basil Dearden, 1959), and the industrial-conflict comedy *I'm All Right Jack* (John Boulting, 1959), suggested that there was a whole tradition in British films of what she termed characters living 'without grace', who exist in 'little ugly rooms, and . . . get on each other's nerves', and whose 'speech is charged with petty hostilities'.[85]

Till Death Us Do Part, Love Thy Neighbour, My Son the Fanatic and *East is East* can all be seen as embracing and extending that tradition, which can be seen as a positive movement in so far as second or third generations of immigrant communities may now be experiencing a greater sense of belonging in British culture, but negative, to the extent that some of the original hopes held by immigrants to Britain may have been betrayed or seem lost and elusive.

The lack of an extended and expansive dramatic space to formulate and cultivate individual dreams and aspirations may lead to a succession of disputes which become sour and petty, and one would have to acknowledge that several of the 1990s films discussed do contain characters who dream of escaping from Britain to America or Pakistan in search of a more fulfilling and authentic existence.

If films such as *Bhaji on the Beach* and *East is East* are prepared to depict British-Asian or African-Caribbean characters in an unflattering light, or make fun of their foibles and viewpoints, they do so in order to extend and deepen the range of ethnic characterisations available in British cinema; and, unlike *Till Death Us Do Part* and *Love Thy Neighbour*, these films emanate from a culturally mixed (rather than prominently 'white') production base, adding a wider range of cultural influences to the resulting narratives.

Comedy as a form is often envisaged as something of a disaffiliated and independent genre, and so is always capable of mutating into new dramatic forms when least expected. The comic mode, when effectively mixed with dramatic and compelling explorations of ethnicity in 'everyday' British society, is thus particularly well suited to depictions of 'hybrid' groups and communities, who may be involved in the process of formulating new identities and priorities, but do not necessarily wish to forget or deny the emotional, spiritual and cultural journey which they have undertaken, en route towards a new future, spiritual home or 'promised land'.

Notes

1 Interview with Simon Channing-Williams, conducted on 6 October 1998 by *Black Film Bulletin* in *A Fuller Picture: The Commercial Impact of Six British Films with Black Themes in the 1990s* by Onyekachi Wambu and Kevin Arnold (British Film Institute and *Black Film Bulletin*, London, 1999), p. 59.
2 Hugo Davenport, review of *Leon the Pig Farmer*, *Daily Telegraph* (25 February 1993).
3 Philip French, review of *Wild West*, *Observer* (16 May 1993).
4 Leonard Quart, review of *Bhaji on the Beach*, *Cineaste*, 20:4 (1994), p. 48.
5 Alexander Walker, review of *Bhaji on the Beach*, *Evening Standard* (20 January 1994).
6 Nigel Andrews, review of *My Son the Fanatic*, *Financial Times* (4 November 1999).
7 James Christopher, review of *East is East*, *The Times* (4 November 1999).
8 Anthony Quinn, review of *East is East*, the *Independent* (5 November 1999).
9 Christopher Tookey, review of *East is East*, *Daily Mail* (5 November 1999).
10 Nigel Andrews, review of *East is East*, *Financial Times* (30 April 1998).
11 Jonathan Romney, review of *Secrets & Lies*, *Guardian* (23 May 1996).
12 Quentin Curtis, review of *Secrets & Lies*, *Daily Telegraph* (24 May 1996).
13 Stuart Hall, 'The Whites of their Eyes: Racist Ideologies and the Media' (1981), reprinted in *The Media Reader*, edited by Manuel Alvarado and

John. O Thompson (British Film Institute, London, 1990), p. 18.

14 Sarita Malik, *Representing Black Britain: Black and Asian Images on Television* (Sage Publications, London, 2002), p. 106.

15 Cary Rajinder Sawnhey, 'Another Kind of British: An Exploration of British Asian Films', *Cineaste*, 24:4 (autumn 2001), p. 61.

16 Salman Rushdie, *Imaginary Homelands: Essays and Criticism 1981–1991* (Granta Books in association with Penguin, London and Harmondsworth, 1991).

17 Howard Jacobson, *Seriously Funny: From the Ridiculous to the Sublime* (Viking, London, 1997), p. 36.

18 Hall, 'The Whites of their Eyes', p. 17.

19 Leon Hunt, *British Low Culture: From Safari Suits to Sexploitation* (Routledge, London, 1998), p. 55.

20 Episodes of *Love Thy Neighbour* from series one and two were made available to buy on DVD in Britain by early 2005 (licensed by FremantleMedia Enterprises).

21 Arthur Marwick, *A History of the Modern British Isles 1914–1999: Circumstances, Events and Outcomes* (Blackwell, Oxford, 2000), p. 260.

22 Brian Spittles, *Britain since 1960: An Introduction* (Macmillan, London, 1995), p. 97.

23 *Observer Race in Britain Special Edition* (25 November 2001), p. 4.

24 Text of Enoch Powell's speech delivered in the West Midlands, April, 1968, reprinted in the *New Statesman* (17 April 1998), pp. 14–19.

25 *Ibid.*

26 Spittles, *Britain since 1960*, p. 98.

27 *Ibid.*, p. 99.

28 Hanif Kureishi, 'Introduction', *My Beautiful Laundrette and The Rainbow Sign* (Faber & Faber, London, 1986), p. 12.

29 Information on prime ministers and election dates taken from Spittles, *Britain since 1960*, pp. xxiii–xvi.

30 *Ibid.*, p. xvi.

31 Stuart Allen quoted in '*Love Thy Neighbour*', article from *TV Times*, 1972, reprinted in *Black and White in Colour: Black People in British Television since 1936*, edited by Jim Pines (British Film Institute, London, 1992), pp. 28–31.

32 Rushdie, *Imaginary Homelands*, p. 137.

33 M.M. Bakhtin, *The Dialogic Imagination: Four Essays*, edited by Michael Holquist (University of Texas Press, Austin, 1981), p. 23.

34 *Monthly Film Bulletin* review of *Till Death Us Do Part*, writer not identified, 36:421 (February 1969), p. 36.

35 Leon Hunt, *British Low Culture*, p. 55.

36 For example, Kenneth Williams was an Indian Raj, the Khasi of Kalibar, in *Carry On up the Khyber* (Gerald Thomas, 1968), and Peter Sellers played an Indian character in *The Millionairess* (Anthony Asquith, 1960) and *The Party* (Blake Edwards, 1968).

37 Amon Saba Saakana in 'Channel 4 and the black community' in *What's this Channel Fo(u)r?: An Alternative Report*, edited by Simon Blanchard and David Morley (Comedia Publishing Group, London, 1982), claimed, however, that 'Channel Four's administration is bereft of any type of political philosophy which can place it in sympathy with the aspirations of black people' (p. 123).

38 Sarita Malik, 'Beyond "The Cinema of Duty"? The Pleasures of Hybridity: Black British Film of the 1980s and 1990s', in *Dissolving Views: Key Writings on British Cinema*, edited by Andrew Higson (Cassell, London, 1996), p. 207.

39 Kureishi, 'Introduction', *My Beautiful Laundrette and The Rainbow Sign*, p. 43.

40 David Thomson describes the process of cultural exchange in *My Beautiful Laundrette* as 'The Indo-Paks . . . hiring the unemployed white kids as workers, and having them as lovers. It's a way to soothe the fascist breast': 'Listen to Britain', *Film Comment*, 22:2 (March/April, 1986), p. 60.

41 John Hill, *British Cinema in the 1980s* (Clarendon Press, Oxford, 1999), p. 184. Hill concludes that the film refuses 'to engage seriously with the Asian characters . . . or to tackle the questions to which the relationships between the Asian and white characters . . . give rise' (p. 184).

42 Ashwani Sharma (Principal Lecturer in Media and Cultural Studies at East London University) presented a stimulating paper entitled 'Comedy, Race and Britishness' at the 1994 Leicester Film and TV Studies Summer School, which made a number of pertinent and stimulating observations about the film *Wild West* (1992).

43 *My Son the Fanatic*, described as a 'comic clash' of cultures and generations on the cover of the video retail edition (VHS, VC3719, Feature Film Company).

44 Homi K. Bhabha, *The Location of Culture* (Routledge, London, 1994), p. 9.

45 Julia Kristeva, *Strangers to Ourselves*, translated by Leon. S. Roudiez (Columbia University Press, New York, 1991), p. 4.

46 *Ibid.*, p. 14.

47 *Ibid.*, p. 7. 'Constantly feeling the hatred of others . . . hatred provides the foreigner with consistency . . . Hatred makes him real, authentic so to speak, solid, or simply existing', suggests Kristeva (p. 13) in a description which might offer a partial explanation of the behaviour and attitudes of the father in *East is East*.

48 Gurinder Chadha quoted in Alkarim Jivani, 'Argy Bhaji', *Time Out* (19–26 January 1994), p. 19.

49 Blackpool is a symbolic presence at the end of the Channel 4 documentary *Bernard's Bombay Dream* (broadcast on 26 June 2003, produced and directed by Norman Hull), profiling the comedian Bernard Manning, who is often accused of racist humour (although he claims in the programme that 'A joke is a joke', and that one should 'never take a joke seriously').

The documentary ends with Manning returning from Bombay to Black-pool, and praising the virtues of Blackpool as emblematic of the British nation as a whole, and, particularly in comparison to Bombay: 'Lovely sea front. Nice cool breeze. Not like India. Flies all over the fu**ing place . . . What a wonderful country we live in', he declares, as he walks along the seafront.

50 Alexander Walker, 'Chips with chilli sauce', review of *Bhaji on the Beach*, *Evening Standard* (20 January 1994).

51 Peter Brooks, *The Melodramatic Imagination: Balzac, Henry James, Melo-drama, and the Mode of Excess* (Columbia University Press, New York, 1984: first published in 1976), p. 204.

52 Interview with Gurinder Chadha (12 November 1998) in Wambu and Arnold, *A Fuller Picture*, p. 38.

53 Henri Bergson, *Laughter* (1900) in George Meredith, *Comedy: An Essay on Comedy*, edited by Wylie Sypher (Johns Hopkins University Press, Baltimore and London, 1980), p. 123.

54 Philip French, review of *My Son the Fanatic*, *Observer* (3 May 1998).

55 Edward Said, 'Afterword', *Orientalism: Western Conceptions of the Orient* (second edition, Penguin, Harmondsworth, 1995: first published 1978), p. 333.

56 Rushdie, 'One Thousand Days in a Balloon' (1991), in *Imaginary Home-lands*, p. 436.

57 *Observer Race Special* 2001 (25 November 2001), p. 10. Christie Davies in *Ethnic Humour Around the World: A Comparative Analysis* (Indiana University Press, Bloomington and Indianapolis, 1996: first published in 1990), suggests that 'The pattern of ethnic jokes does change systematically in response to profound social and economic changes, but it does so slowly and often after a marked time-lag' (p. 139).

58 Jacobson, *Seriously Funny*, p. 36.

59 Simon Critchley, *On Humour* (Routledge, London, 2002), p. 70.

60 *Ibid.*, p. 75.

61 'Changing Images: Judith Williamson in Conversation with Huw Beynon and Sheila Rowbotham', in *Looking at Class: Film, Television and the Working Class in Britain*, edited by Huw Beynon and Sheila Rowbotham (Rivers Oram Press, London/New York/Sydney, 2001), p. 105.

62 Gurinder Chadha quoted in Wambu and Arnold, *A Fuller Picture*, p. 38.

63 Ian Christie, 'As Others See Us: British Film-making and Europe in the 90s', in *British Cinema of the 90s*, edited by Robert Murphy (British Film Institute, London, 2000), p. 77. The £150,000 budget for *Leon the Pig Farmer* was raised by the filmmakers after the script was rejected by the BFI, British Screen and Channel 4, according to Hugo Davenport in a review of the film in the *Daily Telegraph* (25 February 1993).

64 Andrew Anthony, 'British Cinema', *Observer*, 3 January 1999. In contrast to the film's popularity in France, Nick Thomas in the *BFI Film and Television Handbook*, edited by Eddie Dyja (1998), describes the British

box-office performance of *Secrets & Lies* as 'respectable if not earth shattering' (p. 36).

65 Wambu and Arnold, *A Fuller Picture*, p. 38.

66 Box office figures for *Bhaji* taken from the (1996) *British Film and Television Handbook*.

67 Mark Steyn, review of *Bhaji on the Beach*, *Spectator* (5 February 1994). According to the *BFI Film and Television Handbooks* of 1993 (edited by David Leafe) and 1995 (edited by Nick Thomas), *Wild West* generated receipts to the value of £30,349 at the UK box office, in relation to a production budget of £1.32 million.

68 Sarita Malik, 'Money, Macpherson and mind-set: the competing cultural and commercial demands on Black and Asian British films of the 90s', *Journal of Popular British Cinema*, 5 (2002), p. 94.

69 Matthew Sweet, 'With *East is East* poised to become this year's *Full Monty*, British Asian cinema has made the mainstream its own', *Independent on Sunday*, *Life Etc* (10 October 1999), p. 1.

70 Box office and production figures for *East is East* taken from the 2000 and 2001 *BFI Film and Television Handbooks* edited by Eddie Dyja.

71 Leslee Udwin interviewed in *Black Filmmaker*, 3:9 (21 June 2000), p. 6.

72 Murray Smith, *Engaging Characters: Fiction, Emotion, and the Cinema* (Clarendon Press, Oxford, 1995), p. 194.

73 *East is East* screenplay (Film Four Books, London, 1999), p. 14.

74 Bakhtin, 'Glossary', *The Dialogic Imagination*, p. 426.

75 See *The Clangers* website, www.clangers.co.uk.

76 The *Daily Mail* (17 June 2003) reported that two High Court judges ruled that 'The word Paki is racially offensive and not merely an abbreviated form of Pakistani'. Lord Justice Auld, in a case referring to a football supporter who was charged with 'chanting of a racialist nature', ruled that 'It is odd and a shame that this is so in this country, but the unpleasant context in which it is so often used has left it with a derogatory or insulting, racialist connotation' (p. 28).

77 Bakhtin, *The Dialogic Imagination*: 'alien' language (p. 430); 'the unofficial side of speech' (p. 238); 'mutual non-understanding' (p. 356).

78 Enoch Powell in a collection of essays entitled *Still to Decide* (edited by John Wood, Elliot Right Way Books, Surrey, 1972), claimed in a chapter on immigration that 'Of the great multitude, numbering already two million, of West Indians and Asians in England, it is no more true to say that England is their country than it would be to say that the West Indies, or Pakistan, or India are our country'. His conclusion was 'In these great numbers they are, and remain, alien here as we would be in Kingston or in Delhi . . . The process is that of an invasion . . . in the sense that a people find themselves displaced . . . by those who do have another country and whose home will continue to be elsewhere for successive generations' (p. 190).

79 Claire Monk, 'Projecting a new Britain', *Cineaste*, 26:4 (2001), p. 35.

80 Sigmund Freud described 'unmasking' as equivalent 'to an admonition: such and such a person, who is admired as a demigod, is, after all only human like you and me'. See *Jokes and Their Relationship to the Unconscious* (1905), edited by James Strachey and Angela Richards (Penguin, Harmondsworth, 1981), p. 263.

81 Stanley Wolpert, *A New History of India* (Oxford University Press, Oxford, 1989: first edition published in 1977), p. 390.

82 Alexander Walker, review of *East is East*, *Evening Standard* (4 November 1999).

83 Stephen Bourne, 'Soap Operas', *The Colour Black: Black Images in British Television*, edited by Therese Daniels and Jane Gerson (British Film Institute, London, 1989), p. 122.

84 The four deleted scenes on the retail DVD and video editions of *East is East* are generally quite sombre and meditative in tone. The first extra sequence has the Khan teenagers contemplating how they might like to be categorised (Saleem suggests 'Anglo-Indian') in response to Peggy using the expression 'Paki'. The final sequence depicts how the mild-mannered Abdul is goaded into violence by racist comments made by his workmate Mark (Gary Lewis) towards a group of black sailors in the *Britannia* public house. The scene ends with Abdul returning home in tears as his father is praying, and illustrates some of the reasons why George may be sceptical about becoming too integrated into British culture. It is clear that taken together, the excluded scenes do not present 1970s Britain as a welcoming 'land of opportunity' for the Khan children.

85 Pauline Kael, 'Commitment and the Straitjacket' (1961), in *I Lost it at the Movies* (Jonathan Cape, London, 1966), p. 77.

3

Romantic comedy and new beginnings in 1990s British cinema

Gareth (Simon Callow): Tom, how's the speech coming along?

Tom (James Fleet): It's pretty good, I think. Something for everyone . . . tears . . . laughter . . . [1]

This chapter will explore the genre of romantic comedy in relation to British cinema, with particular regard to the emergence of this particular generic form as a high-profile feature of British film production during the 1990s. Following the international commercial success and critical interest generated by *Four Weddings and a Funeral* (1994), a number of films exploring the complicated relationships and courtship patterns of young couples in contemporary British society were released. Such films included *Sliding Doors* (Peter Howitt, 1997), *Fever Pitch* (David Evans, 1997), *Martha: Meet Frank, Daniel and Laurence* (Nick Hamm, 1998), *This Year's Love* (David Kane, 1999), *Gregory's Two Girls* (Bill Forsyth, 1999) and *Notting Hill* (Roger Michell, 1999).

Prior to the success of *Four Weddings and a Funeral*, romantic comedy tended, in the main, to be a generic form associated with Hollywood rather than British cinema. This chapter will go on to consider some of the key critical issues at stake when the romantic and comedic aspects of romantic comedies are filtered through a specifically 'British' aesthetic and cultural perspective, and will examine the two most influential films within this particular cycle of British films: *Four Weddings and a Funeral* (1994) and *Notting Hill* (1999).

Both films were predicated upon a wry consideration of the possibilities for Anglo-American relationships in modern Britain, and could be seen as symptomatic of a wider desire by British film producers, directors and writers to forge closer working relationships between British and Hollywood production companies, and to demonstrate that Britain was capable of producing films with outstanding appeal to international audiences. The chapter concludes with a discussion of *Love Actually* (Richard Curtis, 2003), considering the film in terms of its status as a kind of 'ultimate' Richard Curtis/Hugh Grant British romantic comedy, and a film which explores male–female interactions within a London setting, and in the context of Britain's political and social relationships with Europe and America.

Prior to these case studies, I will discuss some of the important features and aspects of the genre known as 'romantic comedy', and explore a number of issues raised by its status as a hybrid or dramatically versatile form of narrative, before examining particular traits and traditions in British cinematic romantic comedies from the period of the 1930s to the 1990s.

Conceptualising the 'comic romance'

Northrop Frye in *Anatomy of Criticism: Four Essays* (1957) linked specific genres with particular seasons, associating tragedy with autumn, comedy with spring, and romance with summer.[2] Frye noted that one of the distinctive features of comic narratives was their tendency to conclude in scenes of happiness and triumph for the central protagonists. Such emotionally pleasing or satisfying resolutions impressed audiences as 'desirable', rather than as 'true', argued Frye, who suggested that such endings were often engineered through careful plot 'manipulation', which symbolised 'a victory of arbitrary plot over consistency of character'.[3]

The combination of romantic and comic themes within a single narrative enabled two distinct dramatic modes to be brought together ('spring' and 'summer'), in forms which allowed spectators to follow with interest the twists and turns of a particular relationship, safe in the knowledge that within this mixture of romance and comedy events would generally turn out satisfactorily in the end. Thus, the romantic elements of a narrative provided the framework for constructing a dramatic and potentially engaging storyline, while the comic features of the story could be utilised to reflect on (and illustrate) the sometimes absurd nature of romantic infatuation or sexual obsession, and the gaps between idealised views of romance and the sometimes more prosaic and less inspirational nature of characters' actual experiences of love.

Romantic comedy could, nonetheless, be seen as a genre which essentially sought to celebrate the idea of a union between two mutually attracted and well-suited lovers, even as its narratives simultaneously formulated a series of conflicting viewpoints, events and circumstances capable of keeping the couples-in-question apart until the very end.

Patrick Murray in *Literary Criticism: A Glossary of Major Terms* (1978) states that 'The great English writer' in the form of romantic comedy was William Shakespeare, who presented 'mythic' characters in 'idealized settings' at a 'distance from everyday reality',[4] and who consequently established the basis of a British or English sensibility towards theatrical constructions of romantic comedy, often featuring moments of farce, deception, disguise and last-minute reconciliations between fathers and daughters, and suitors and heroines.

In *The Unruly Woman: Gender and the Genres of Laughter* (1995), Kathleen Rowe defined romantic comedy as a socially progressive dramatic form, because of what she perceived to be its emphasis on the need 'for *a* woman, in the narrative itself',[5] and the genre's tendency to work towards establishing an order and vision of society which was improved and revivified by the end of the story. This particular form of narrative, in Rowe's view (countering possible claims that romantic comedy focused on the lives of individuals whose romantic obsessions tended to render them somewhat uninterested in society), was significant for the ways in which it sought to present a kind of totalised view of social relations in which aspects of 'work and play, the social and the sexual' were seen as intertwined with each other.[6]

Rowe identified a series of attributes which she associated with tragedy and comedy: concepts of death, the aristocratic and finality were linked with tragedy while, in contrast, sex, the bourgeoisie and circular narratives were related to comedy.[7] (In *Four Weddings and a Funeral*, we shall see how these tragi-comic distinctions are dispersed, and re-envisaged throughout the narrative.)

With regard to romantic comedy as a specifically cinematic genre, Bruce Babington and Peter William Evans in *Affairs to Remember: The Hollywood Comedy of the Sexes* (1989) defined a particular species of Hollywood romantic comedy, known as 'screwball' comedy, as 'inspired by misrule, rebellion, irrationality' and a 'topsy-turvy vision of life'.[8] Such characteristics allude to the anarchical impulses of these kinds of romantic comic films which take great delight in tearing down repressive structures of narrative and society, and imagining freer, looser forms of cultural signification and social structuring in their place.

In an article, 'Screwball Comedy: An Overview' (1986), Wes. D. Gehring, nonetheless, expressed a certain degree of doubt about the level of political and dramatic significance that could be attributed to these types of comic/romantic rebellion. He pointed out that Hollywood romantic comedies of the 1930s tended to be concerned with such 'crucial' (in other words, trivial) 'issues' as 'how to dunk a donut' correctly in *It Happened One Night* (Frank Capra, 1934), or the question of 'who gets custody of the dog in divorce proceedings' (*The Awful Truth*, Leo McCarey, 1937).[9] The genre of romantic comedy (when perceived from such sceptical viewpoints) raises questions about the extent to which the personal *is* political in such contexts, and whether the issue of individual lovers finally getting together is, in the wider scheme of things, a relatively unimportant or insignificant matter.

In the examples of seemingly nonsensical triviality offered by Gehring, one could argue a case that the treatments of the 'donut' and the role of the dog in a divorce case are used symbolically and satirically in both films to raise questions about how the respective couples should behave towards each other, and the types of values on which they should seek to base their relationships. Screwball comedies tended to emphasise the importance of play in the relationships of adult couples, and of remaining in touch with one's earlier and less sophisticated or self-conscious self. The only liaisons and marriages frowned upon in these films were those in which a relationship had become overly formal or lacking in lustre.

Within this dramatic and philosophical framework, I would suggest that such examples of romantic comedy, while open to charges of narcissism and self-indulgence on occasions, could also be considered to possess a radical ideological and aesthetic dimension based on screwball comedy's inherent tendency to react against calls for its central characters to meekly conform to social norms, and its attempts to present fresh and unpredictable images of married-life and courtship patterns between men and women.

Stanley Cavell's seminal examination of the romantic comedy genre, *Pursuits of Happiness: The Hollywood Comedy of Remarriage* (1981), produced a strong case for seven 1930s and 1940s comedies of 'remarriage' to be considered as intellectually sophisticated, dramatically nuanced depictions of challenging male–female relationships. The films analysed by Cavell were all produced between 1934 and 1941, and while he concedes that these romantic comedies have been described as 'fairy tales for the depression',[10] he is wary of critical approaches which result in reductionist readings, based on over-simplified models of relating texts to contexts, or analyses which conversely imply that the primary types of pleasures provided by these films for audiences were simply of an escapist or fundamentally illusory nature.

In line with Frye's studies of classical romance in myths, fairy tales and stage plays, Cavell stresses the significance for romantic comedies of situation, time and place: 'the narratives requires a setting . . . in which the pair have the leisure to be together . . . A natural setting is accordingly one of luxury [where] work can be postponed without fear of its loss.'[11]

The 'could-be' couple, therefore, need a place where they can see and appreciate each other's qualities more clearly and resonantly – a process of discovery which may consequently involve a certain withdrawing from everyday society, so that the couple can learn to accept and expand their views of each other, and society itself can work towards welcoming and valuing the couple on their return from a place of seclusion (a dramatic process enacted in several of Shakespeare's late plays).

Despite Cavell's sense of the life-enhancing and worthy explorations of human relationships carried out in these 'comedies of remarriage', when alluding to these particular films in his study *Contesting Tears: the Hollywood Melodrama of the Unknown Woman* (1989), he detected the presence of a 'moral cloud', and what he identified as a 'structure of unhappiness' that was not totally dispersed by the narrative conclusions of the seven romantic comedies selected for discussion.[12] This observation points to the recurrence of situations in romantic comedies which emphasise the gap between human aspiration and achievement, a gulf which may loom both disturbingly and amusingly large on occasions.

In an essay 'Romantic Comedy Today: Semi-Tough or Impossible?' (1978), Brian Henderson had earlier suggested that such phenomena as 'the doubling of the divorce rate ... the rise of the single parent, the political and social impact of feminist movements and gay right movements'[13] were not propitious developments for the producing of modern romantic comedies. The removal of censorship restrictions, and the consequent frankness of language applied to contemporary discussions of sexual and emotional matters, was, in Henderson's view, counterproductive to modern re-enactments of the more traditional paradigms and dramatic movements associated with the genre in its classical heyday.

However, Steve Neale in a 1992 *Screen* essay, 'The Big Romance or Something Wild?: Romantic Comedy Today', suggested that by the late 1980s, and following the success of films such as *Pretty Woman* (Gary Marshall, 1989), romantic comedy was once again experiencing a new lease of life in American cinema.[14] Perhaps because the genre commonly reaches out to dramatise some kind of ideal or perfect union, whilst evincing a readiness to highlight the potential pitfalls and calamitous confusions involved in instigating any kind of romance, romantic comedy has remained a popular form with film audiences.

Romantic comedy (like other generic forms and modes), has had to adjust its narrative patterns to accommodate and reflect upon changes in society, and the state of current moral and ethical debates. Women's desire for greater individual autonomy and recognition in the workplace, and the legalisation of abortion and gay sexual practices between consenting adults, are all factors which makers of British and American contemporary romantic comedies have to take into account when formulating and conceptualising their narratives. The genre may be based around certain universal and repetitive features ('boy-meets girl, boy-loses-girl etc'[15]), but the routes to happiness and romantic fulfilment undertaken by the central characters in a love story will always (to a certain extent) be faced with the problems created by certain contemporary concerns and social anxieties.

In an essay entitled 'Citylife: Urban Fairy-tales in Late 90s British Cinema' (2001), Robert Murphy sets out to examine some of the broader narrative antecedents of such films as *Four Weddings*, *Sliding Doors* and *Notting Hill*, as well as considering their underlying political significance within British culture.[16] Murphy suggests that an examination of the narrative patterns of several 1990s British romantic comedies testifies to the influence of fairy tales and folk tales on the distinguishing features of the scenarios, particularly in their emphasis on the setting of a 'magical quest' to be participated in by modern-day kinds of princesses and princes, alongside their constructing of alternative, attractive surroundings in which true lovers can discover each other (often depicting London, unexpectedly, as an 'enchanted village' in the process).[17]

The occurrence of these features in recent British films may point to the existence of a 'timeless' formal element with regard to narratives about romance, where characters may enact particular movements and actions almost as if they were pieces on a chess board, or functions in a Proppian theory of narrative.[18]

From such formalist or structuralist perspectives, the wider ideological and social significance of filmic romantic comedy partnerships might be considered questionable. Thomas E. Wartenberg's book *Unlikely Couples: Movie Romance as Social Criticism* (1999) is, in part, a concerted attempt to emphasise the political and cultural implications and dimensions of romantic pairings in British, American and European cinema. His account of potentially transgressive partnerships in a range of films, subsequently, focuses on narratives revolving around troubled relationships of 'a cross-class, interracial, or homosexual character'.[19]

Wartenberg defines an 'unlikely couple' as 'a romance between two individuals whose social status makes their involvement problematic',[20] and uses the film version of George Bernard Shaw's play *Pygmalion* (Anthony Asquith and Leslie Howard, 1938), as a British example of a couple divided by class, gender and social outlook. Wartenberg's examinations of specific films seek to suggest and demonstrate that films dramatising romantic entanglements cannot help being bound up with wider issues of race, sexuality, and pressures from certain sections of society to conform to dominant norms and axioms.

Such narratives, in Wartenberg's view, should not be viewed simply as individualistic films or generically determined tales, but ought to be examined as films capable of making contentious contributions to debates about personal freedom, and commenting upon male–female interactions in the context of specific societies encountered at critical stages of their historical development. It may be that the films selected for discussion by Wartenberg emphasise the dramatic rather than the comedic elements of their stories and characterisations. I would agree, however, that romantic comedies and romantic comedy-dramas are linked by their concern to explore the personal and political dimensions of relationships in ways which are potentially provocative, insightful and enlightening.

I will now proceed to discuss and examine a number of significant romantic, comedic and dramatic traditions and trends established in British cinema, particularly between the decades of the 1930 and 1950s, and consider some of the ways in which the films under consideration sought to combine comic and dramatic modes of narration and expression in forms capable of engaging with particular concerns of the times in which the films were originally produced.

Trends and traditions of romantic comic drama in British film culture

Algernon: I have dared to love you wildly, passionately, devotedly, hopelessly.

Cecily: Hopelessly doesn't seem to make much sense, does it?[21]

Before the important role romantic comedy assumed in British film production during the decade of the 1990s, and beyond, it could be argued that British cinema had not previously developed an instantly recognisable or sustained tradition of romantic comedy in a similar fashion or style to that of American cinema. Nonetheless, I would claim that certain key films released during the three decades of the 1930s, 1940s and 1950s did serve to construct a certain 'British' manner of engaging with romantic themes in particular distinctive and imaginative ways.

Examples of such films would include a number of Alfred Hitchcock's 1930s British films, particularly *Rich and Strange* (1931) and *The 39 Steps* (1935), 1930s and 1940s comic films starring George Formby in which the romance aspect of the narratives was a key component of the films' desire to appear optimistic during troubled times, and such seminal and diverse narratives as *The Ghost Goes West* (Rene Clair, 1936), *The Divorce of Lady X* (Tim Whelan, 1938), *Pygmalion* (Anthony Asquith and Leslie Howard, 1938), *The Demi-Paradise* (Anthony Asquith, 1943), *Brief Encounter* (David Lean, 1945), *Genevieve* (Henry Cornelius, 1953), *The Prince and the Showgirl* (Laurence Olivier, 1957), *Indiscreet* (Stanley Donen, 1958) and *The Millionairess* (Anthony Asquith, 1960).

A feature of British cinema which tends to distinguish it from its Hollywood counterpart is that British films (unlike Hollywood cinema) did not develop a strong tradition of producing 'screwball' romantic comedies in the 1930s. Aspects of 'screwball' comedy can, though, be detected in several of Alfred Hitchcock's British films released during this decade, with the comic and romantic interactions between his male and female leading characters contributing to the thematic concerns and aesthetic pleasures of the films. The 'cinematic universe' of Hitchcock's 1930s films tended to be a slightly menacing and uncertain place, however, resulting in different types of relationships to those formulated in 'screwball' comedies being established within the various scenarios of the narratives.

In *The 39 Steps* (1935) and *The Lady Vanishes* (1938), for example, the playful, but ultimately trustworthy emotional bonds formed between the characters played by Robert Donat and Madeline Carroll, Michael Redgrave and Margaret Lockwood (with their corresponding determination to protect British interests) could carry positive connotations for audiences troubled by the possibility of threats to the nation from abroad.

Hitchcock was keen to explore the sexual undercurrents existing between his male and female characters in the context of international tensions and domestic disturbances. In *The 39 Steps*, Richard Hannay (Robert Donat) and Pamela (Madeline Carroll) are handcuffed together by enemy agents pretending to be police officers. She fears that he is an escaped murderer of women, while he describes her as the 'white man's burden'; to the Scottish innkeepers providing them with refuge for a night they are a 'runaway couple'. The pair's eventual 'authentic' relationship is consequently established out of a series of disguises, antagonisms and mutual suspicions. The bleak (studio-based) setting of the Scottish moors eventually forces the prospective lovers into developing some kind of compassionate feeling towards each other. The fact that Hannay and Pamela spend a night (handcuffed) together, without being married, also renders them something of an 'illicit couple' in terms of dominant 'British' moral and cinematic discourses of the period.[22]

Earlier in his career, Hitchcock had dramatised the dynamics of a male–female partnership within the state of marriage, outside of the generic tropes of the thriller. In *Rich and Strange* (1931), he concentrated on a marriage suffering from the seeming lack of opportunities for romantic excitement in urban British culture during the period of the early 1930s. The lead characters, Fred (Henry Kendall) and Emily (Joan Barry), are unexpectedly presented with an opportunity to escape from their rather dull existence through a legacy from an aunt offering them the opportunity to embark on a world cruise. The film goes on to explore the effects of environment on their desires for passion and greater empathy with each other, and the motif of the journey, similarly, creates a space for British cinema to expand the horizons of its treatment of romantic themes.

On board ship, Emily meets a passenger, Commander Gordon (Percy Marmont), who falls in love with her, and offers her the possibility of a new life abroad with him. Emily speaks of how difficult a business is the state of being in love, because, as she says, in a relationship 'everything's multiplied by two – sickness, death, the future'. In the closing sections, Fred and Emily do indeed face illness and death together when the ship sinks, and they are stranded, but the film closes with the couple returning home, still bickering and disagreeing about their plans for the future – a conclusion which can be read as implying that this particular couple's relationship will never really progress or aspire to anything beyond a slightly mundane situation in which both partners feel that their lives should somehow be more enjoyable and exciting.

The romantic liaisons formed in George Formby's 1930s comedy films were recurrently constructed around George's indefatigably northern character falling in love with a well-spoken, middle-class girl from the south of England, who would enjoy listening to his musical renditions, and support him in his efforts to win a race and/or expose wrong-doers, spy rings and saboteurs! The films would invariably conclude with George being rewarded with a kiss from the young woman of his dreams, and consequently declaring in an affirmative fashion, 'It's turned out nice again'.

Romance in Formby's films was generically motivated, perceived as an important (if somewhat subservient) part of the narrative structure, along with the accompanying musical numbers and comic-action sequences. The romantic interludes, however contrived and perfunctory they might appear to a modern-day audience, provided an emotional basis for the otherwise episodic and inconsequential events of a Formby film-narrative. George's character's relationships with his leading ladies were not as sexually oriented as his songs, and largely involved displays of genial affection and mutual encouragement (the female role was played by a series of different performers, including Googie Withers,

Phyllis Calvert and Kay Walsh, but the characteristics of the part rarely altered). The final culminating embrace between George and his sweetheart could be read as symbolising a potential reconciliation between the 'two nations' (north and south) of British society in a period of severe economic recession, linking his films tangentially to the communal comedies discussed earlier.

David Sutton, in *A Chorus of Raspberries: British Film Comedy 1929–1939* (2000), notes that one of the most important film producers in British cinema during the 1930s, Alexander Korda, 'was drawn to essentially escapist material, whether romantic or comic',[23] and Korda's production company, London films, did release two innovative and diverse romantic comedies during the decade.

In *The Ghost Goes West* (Rene Clair, 1935), Robert Donat played two versions of the same character – Murdoch Glourie, a Scottish ghost made to walk the earth 'for ten generations' because of alleged cowardice in the face of an eighteenth-century battle against both the English and a local clan (the MacLaggans), and Donald Glourie, a modern descendant of the Glouries, forced to sell the family castle to a wealthy American (played by Eugene Pallette) because of increasing financial debts.

Donald and Murdoch are both attracted to the American businessman's daughter, a tendency which helps to inaugurate the notion of Anglo-American relationships as a possible narrative-focus for future British films. The American's first response on buying the castle, however, is to enquire 'When can we start tearing it down?' suggesting that the formation of economic and emotional alliances between British and American characters will not be a straightforward or painless process. The castle is correspondingly shipped to Florida, where it is rebuilt.

Ironically, modern-day Florida will become a place of salvation for the ghost, as an American descendant of a rival Scottish clan is present to whom Murdoch can demand a retrospective apology, freeing him to be a wandering spirit no more, and to take his leave of what he describes as a 'weary world', creating a space for his contemporary counterpart to find love in the form of the American's daughter (Jean Parker).

The film contrasts the economically depressed 1930s Scottish world, symbolised by the decaying and debt-ridden castle in the opening sequences, with the brightly lit 'new world' of America featured in the second part; the voyage by ship across the Atlantic cleverly bridging the two worlds and distinctive parts of the narrative. The film is essentially light-hearted and benevolent, but the presentation of eighteenth-century Scotland, with its wars of independence and internal rivalries, is not without a certain bitter edge, and 1930s America is depicted as a somewhat violent place, lacking in spiritual depth and established cultural traditions of its own.[24]

The Divorce of Lady X (Tim Whelan, 1937), a very different kind of romantic comedy produced by Alexander Korda, was set in the hotels and courtrooms of 'high-society' London, and centred upon the perceived capriciousness and unfathomable nature of desirable women. Leslie (Merle Oberon), an attractive single woman, forces herself into a divorce lawyer's hotel room for the night, after fog makes it impossible for the revellers at a fancy dress party to return home. (Fog, declares Leslie, is what Americans come to Britain to see; the presence of a London fog in her view allows life to become 'an enthralling adventure'.)

Logan (Laurence Olivier), the divorce lawyer on whom she imposes her presence, specialises in exposing unfaithful wives on behalf of their husbands in divorce-court hearings, and, in one speech to a jury, he accuses womankind of having attained a state of freedom and independence without having become responsible, trustworthy or productive citizens. Leslie plays upon Logan's unflattering perceptions of women in general (and herself in particular), and creates a fictitious identity which includes both a current husband and a rakish sexual past. Logan, predictably, becomes both appalled and fascinated by these images of her character – only at the very close of the narrative does he learn that she is not, in fact, the kind of person that she claimed, and he assumed her to be. The film, ironically, ends with Logan making an impassioned speech praising marriage as a blissful state (the 'most idyllic, most delightful institution in the whole fabric of our civilisation'), which should not be cheapened or weakened by acts of casual infidelity in hotel rooms.

The Divorce of Lady X, in terms of both its stylistic appearance (the film is shot evocatively in an early British cinematic use of Technicolor), and its concern with sexual politics and issues of trust in male–female relationships, would influence the production of later British romantic comedies such as *The Prince and the Showgirl* (also starring Laurence Olivier), and *Indiscreet,* in which London featured as a backdrop to the romantic complications experienced by a glamorous but mature couple played by Cary Grant and Ingrid Bergman. (*Four Weddings and a Funeral* would also display a somewhat voyeuristic fascination with a woman's sexual past, and the issue of her suitability as a long-term companion for an upper-class English male.)

The most challenging representation of the 'Battle of the sexes' in 1930s British cinema probably remains, however, the 1938 film adaptation of George Bernard Shaw's 1914 play *Pygmalion*, in which Wendy Hiller portrays Eliza, a London flower-seller, and Leslie Howard plays the dialects expert and language coach Henry Higgins, who seeks to demonstrate that anyone can speak received pronunciation English if they are taught well enough, and who seizes upon Eliza to prove his theory. Asquith's film details the somewhat harrowing experiences involved in effecting Eliza's transformation from 'common' flower-girl to an English lady, and Higgins is depicted as a sort of semi-demented scientist, who cares only for his experiments and nothing for the people around him. This makes him an effective and exacting teacher, but a limited human being.

Henry Higgins (like Laurence Olivier's divorce lawyer in *The Divorce of Lady X*) is both fascinated and repelled by the woman's life before she met him – 'She's so deliciously low', he declares of Eliza – and yet both the play and film find that there is a curious void at the centre of English upper-class society, which makes the subsequent change in her being seem somewhat superficial to the teacher, and rather damaging for the pupil, who, consequently, feels that she belongs to no particular stratum of society in particular.

In his chapter on the film, Thomas Wartenberg interprets *Pygmalion* as a bleak example of the repressive sexual and emotional climate of British culture (circa 1914–38). A notably comic instance of this English unease at matters of physical and emotional intimacy comes when Eliza gives the mildest of kisses to a hapless suitor outside the professor's house, and is immediately reprimanded by a police constable, who informs the couple, 'This isn't Paris!' Wartenberg suggests that '*Pygmalion*'s men are either bachelors or dolts, so that Eliza is left without the possibility of genuine intimacy . . . England's men are simply not fit partners for independent women like Eliza . . . The film concludes that gender roles so constituted offer no hope for genuinely reciprocal relationships'.[25]

The film (like Higgins himself) demonstrates a tension between its coldly observational and satirical strand of narrative, and the incipient romantic elements bubbling under the surface, threatening to turn the work into a more recognisable and conventional narrative about conflicts and contrasts between the sexes. This is most evident in the film's two final scenes, which slightly modify the play's original ending in which Eliza and Henry finally part after their ideological differences prove insurmountable.

The movie adaptation concludes with shots of a distressed Higgins, pacing the streets in search of the absent Eliza, who eventually returns unexpectedly to his study as he is listening to gramophone recordings of her original speaking voice. She is framed in close-up, for once displayed as towering over him, an indication of the change in the power structure of their relationship. In the closing shot of the film, however, the seated Higgins turns his back to Eliza, and the camera, and demands (in the infamous closing line), 'Where the devil are my slippers?'

Wartenberg reads this revised ending as 'an aesthetic as well as an ethical lapse', which compromises the film's 'demonstration of the destructiveness of traditional masculinist postures'.[26] Both the play and the film are aware, however, that for all its rigorous banter and frantic energy, neither the romantic nor the comedic elements of the text have been easily formulated; relationships between male and female characters are depicted as flawed and troubled, and both working-class and upper-class societies are shown to function by unspoken prejudices and axioms, making significant social change and progress in British culture difficult to initiate. In adopting such viewpoints, the film rejects any complacent acceptance or celebration of upper-class English society, and, in so doing, again distances itself somewhat from the American screwball comic tendencies of the 1930s.

The Second World War created a need for a new type of British film, one capable of placing its characters' personal relationships within the context of emerging contemporary historical and social developments. *The Demi-Paradise* (Anthony Asquith, 1943) represented an attempt to bring Russian and British cultures and characters together in one narrative, following Russia's entry into the war in 1941. Laurence Olivier (in a part far removed from his role as the insular English divorce lawyer in *The Divorce of Lady X*) appeared as Ivan Kouznetsoff, a Russian engineer, residing in Britain to oversee the development of a propeller capable of breaking up ice during perilous sea voyages. The film charts his character's initially discouraging experiences of British life as he comes across 'depressing faces', unceasing rain, and landladies who warn against 'any goings-on' within their premises.

A more personalised relationship with British culture is made possible for him only after he meets Ann (Penelope Dudley Ward), the daughter of the shipyard's managing-director, and she introduces him to her family in Barchester (Donald, in a more fantastical manner, has his social horizons broadened by meeting the daughter of an American millionaire in *The Ghost Goes West*).

The emotions subsequently generated by Ann will cause the serious and intellectual Ivan to declare that 'There is a revolution in my head!' Ann, in turn, starts to read such books as 'Women in Soviet Russia' (having earlier been handed *Crime and Punishment* as a warning about what can happen to Russian women). Ivan later makes a somewhat matter-of-fact proposal of marriage to Ann, which is, nonetheless, subject to certain stringent conditions – Ivan believes that she should wear less 'make-up', and be more sincere and less self-seeking. Ann, in turn, objects to his manner of courtship, and describes him as a 'priggish, conceited, egotistical man'.

This scene, set in a smart London nightclub, is fascinating for the mixed sympathies that it could potentially generate from male and female spectators. Ivan is understandably keen to cut through what he sees as the complacent and undynamic attitudes of the English upperclass businessmen he encounters, but Ann is also justified in being perplexed and alarmed by the self-righteous, patriarchal and implacably dogmatic nature of Ivan's view of the world.

The couple's burgeoning relationship never really recovers from this breakdown in communication and trust, and when the film moves from its pre-war phase to the depiction of a war in which Britain and Russia are now allies against Germany, personal alliances become secondary to the need to fight and destroy the enemy. Ivan describes Britain as a slumbering nation that needs to be awakened, and war in the film acts as a catalyst for Britain to be galvanised into taking decisive action against a worsening world situation.

When Ivan comes across Ann in her wartime position as a Wren in the British navy, he declares that all of the 'superficial' aspects of her character have gone away, but so, sadly, has the personal dimension and erotic spark of their relationship, and the film ends with Ivan back in the snowy wastes of his native country, relating his strange story to British sailors passing through Russia.

Before his departure, Ivan praises what he describes as the 'dreadful sense of humour' that typifies and helps to define the British people's attitudes to life, love and work. Ivan values laughter because he believes it to be bound up with notions of democracy and free speech: 'For there is no laughter where there is no freedom', he declares solemnly (in a seemingly oblique reference to the totalitarian nature of Russian life under Stalin).

The Demi-Paradise is still intensely moving for its evocation of a period in which unlikely international partnerships were formed in a determination to stop fascism from triumphing, and for its insistence that countries can learn important lessons from each other despite adhering to opposing sets of political and economic beliefs. Ironically, as Ann and Ivan drift apart, their respective countries grow closer, leading Campbell Dixon in a *Daily Telegraph* review (22 November 1943) to declare that 'Few pictures this year have been so funny and so moving in the oddest, most unexpected places'.[27]

Brief Encounter (David Lean, 1945) premiered towards the end of 1945, several months after the end of the Second World War, but was interestingly located in a kind of 'timeless' period prior to the war, and set in a fictional town similar to that of Barchester (Ann's home town in *The Demi-Paradise*). *Brief Encounter* (while clearly a traumatic romantic drama, rather than a romantic comedy) became an important reference point in British film culture for the intense and serious fashion in which it portrayed the extreme and unsettling emotions experienced by a housewife and a doctor, who have the misfortune to fall in love whilst married to other partners. As William Whitebait observed in his review of the film in the *New Statesman and Nation* (1 December 1945), tension emerges from the couple having 'to decide what – if anything – is to be done' about their plight.[28]

The tale grows out of mundane situations such as accidental meetings and missed trains, and like *Rich and Strange*, the film ultimately returns to the setting and situations outlined in the opening scene, implying a destiny that cannot in the end be averted. The comical interludes within the narrative revolving around a station master's attempts to ingratiate himself with a railway canteen manageress bear a relationship to Shakespeare's use of a comic sub-plot to parallel (from a farcical or irreverent point of view) the events and characters at the centre of the story. These burlesque and brusque moments provide the audience with some brief comic respite from the suffering experienced by Alec (Trevor Howard) and Laura (Celia Johnson).

It is notable that at this mid-1940s juncture in British film culture, the comic and dramatically significant moments in *Brief Encounter* are clearly demarcated and serve differing dramatic purposes – the upper classes here being associated with notions of high tragedy and psychological drama, and the working classes with instances of low humour and comic relief. For a modern audience, however, the almost painful sincerity of the upper-middle-class couple in *Brief Encounter* might lead to spectators finding the strangulated vocal sounds and uncompleted speeches emanating from Laura and Alec (as they struggle to articulate their deepest feelings within the available class and social discourses) more comically pitiful than genuinely tragic.

The film itself is aware of the incongruity of dramatising a spiritually intense and emotionally overwhelming love affair within the polite tones of English upper-class voices. This is highlighted in a scene where Alec and Laura watch a preview of a film entitled *Flames of Passion* at the Palladium cinema. The movie is introduced with adjectives in capital letters, proclaiming the film as 'STUPENDOUS! COLOSSAL! GIGANTIC! EPOCH-MAKING!' coding *Brief Encounter* as an implicitly British cinematic riposte to the more self-promoting and aggrandising tendencies associated with certain types of Hollywood cinema.

Following the hyperbole for *Flames of Passion*, an advertisement for prams in the local high street is flashed onto the screen to the amusement of the audience, suggesting that childbirth and childcare are the inevitable (and perhaps proper?) consequences of all this 'stored up' heterosexual passion.

Brief Encounter concludes with the couple's relationship remaining forever unconsummated, with the pair lacking even the chance to say a proper goodbye to each other. Alec leaves for Africa, and Laura is forced to return to her previous homely and comfortable, but essentially unexciting existence. Inwardly, they have both, perhaps, been changed forever. Laura's haunted expression is the final image of the film, testifying to her divided state of mind, and to the potential power and perceived emotional danger of true love at this point in British cinematic history. In one sense, almost nothing of lasting consequence has occurred within the film. On a psychological level, however, the two main protagonists have undertaken a painful emotional journey which leaves them with only thoughts of what might have been. The burgeoning 'flames of passion' are finally extinguished.

Post-war Britain was initially dominated by the administration of a Labour government in office from 1945 to 1951 that laid down the foundations for a welfare state, and a society based on the concept of greater opportunities for all individuals. Between 1951 and 1964, the Conservative party returned to govern Britain,[29] and certain indigenous romantic comedies from the early stages of this period dramatise the tensions implicit in this movement from a desire to affect radical social change to a more conservative view of how British society should be constructed and rebuilt after the war.

In *Genevieve* (Henry Cornelius, 1953), for instance, the characters played by John Gregson (Alan) and Dinah Sheridan (Wendy) represent aspiring upper-middle-class couples associated with the 'new Britain' connoted by the coronation of Queen Elizabeth II in 1953. Alan and Wendy are contrasted with Ambrose (Kenneth More) and Rosalind (Kay Kendall), a recently acquainted couple. Ambrose is a bachelor and something of a 'cad', whilst Rosalind is a woman aware of her sexual appeal and attractiveness to men. Tradition in the film is symbolised by the vintage car, Genevieve, which Alan desperately tries to use to defeat the competitive Ambrose. The ensuing race between the two men is also indicative of a sexual rivalry based on insecurity and fear of failure. 'Ambrose seems to think of only two things. That silly old car and the other thing', observes Rosalind. 'My husband only thinks about the car', replies Wendy.

The film ultimately affirms tradition and emotional restraint, as embodied by Genevieve and Alan respectively, with Genevieve even managing to pass the finishing post on Westminster Bridge without a driver, as if the thought of being handed over to Ambrose (in the event of him winning the bet) is too much for the vintage car to contemplate.[30] Both the comic and dramatic incidents of the narrative are generated by the clash in lifestyles, and the conflict over who will win the race. Alan is the nicer and more trustworthy of the two men, but Ambrose is freer and appears to have more fun. The implication of the ending, though, is that he too will settle down and probably marry Rosalind.

Filmed versions of plays by. Oscar Wilde, Terence Rattigan and George Bernard Shaw released during the 1950s contributed to the development of a strand of British film production which might be classified as 'drawing-room' comedies, narratives which tended to present love as a form of endless verbal sparring, taking place between characters living in colourful and luxurious surroundings.

Anthony Asquith's *The Importance of Being Earnest* (1952) played down the more subversive implications and troubled context of Oscar Wilde's play (*Earnest* had opened only eight days after Wilde was arrested for indecent conduct in February 1895, and had closed in London by the 8th of May[31]), but still depicted Wilde's characters as embarked on an unceasing series of digressions and disguises in which sincerity is a weakness, and 'truth' merely another kind of performance. Parody, irony and facetiousness are presented as ways of keeping one's private life private, even if a character's origins may turn out to be rather humble and involve such down-to-earth settings as a railway station.

The Prince and the Showgirl (Laurence Olivier, 1957, screenplay by Terence Rattigan) brings together an imperious Regent of Carpathia (Laurence Olivier) and an American musical performer, Elsie Marina (Marilyn Monroe) during the period of George V's coronation ceremony in Britain, 22 June 1911. Elsie is starring in a production of *The Coconut Girl* in the West End of London and the Regent looks to her for some fleeting romantic diversion and sexual gratification. Despite the presence of a gypsy-fiddler performing outside the Embassy drawing room, Elsie evades the Regent's attempts to seduce her, however, and he is forced to order his staff to escort her to 'a place called Brixton'. At the same time, the Regent claims that his son, King Nicolas VIII (Jeremy Spenser) is 'plotting' with 'the Kaiser's party' to 'destroy' him. Elsie, however, is largely unmoved by international affairs. 'Who cares about your Balkan revolutions?' she asks.

In a sequence very different in mood, style and tone to the farcical scenes of the Laurence Olivier character trying to seduce the 'showgirl' of the title, the depicting of the King's coronation ceremony in Westminster Abbey is presented with a sense of awe and wonder (personified by Elsie appearing mesmerised by the ceremony and its archaic rituals). The new king is never actually glimpsed during the scene, leading to a sense of myth-in-the-making, although some critics were sceptical about the relationship of this sequence to the rest of the film. For example, C.A. Lejune in the *Observer* (30 June 1957) suggested that 'one wonders just a little, about the taste of a production which combines a solemn ceremony in Westminster Abbey with the celebrated skin-tight Monroe wiggle'.[32] A *Daily Worker* (29 June 1957) review of the film claimed that the ceremonial sequence in the film revealed 'the grim fact that Britain has now become the last remnant of Ruritania in the world. The glamour and glitter of the court of St. James's, the pageantry and pomp of royal procedure have never been pilloried so blithely – with the sole object of helping the exploitation of a film in the United States and elsewhere'.[33]

The film's conclusion is open-ended, with Elsie making a positive contribution to world peace by acting as an intermediary figure between the Regent and his son (revealing that a 'general election and a motorbike' are his primary requests), but the two distinctive characters head off in separate directions at the close (as in *The Demi-Paradise* and *Brief Encounter*), and it is not clear whether they will ever meet again, even though the Regent declares, 'With such a girl anything could happen'.

Indiscreet (Stanley Donen, 1958) was also adapted from a stage play, and similarly involved two world-famous performers playing a couple embarking on a relationship within an upper-class London setting. Ingrid Bergman appears as an actress (Anna Kalman) and avid modern-art collector (Alexander Walker noted in a contemporary review that 'three dozen Picasso sketches flank the chimney piece'[34] of her living-room), who has made London her 'adopted home'.

Anna (who appears as something of a prototype for the character of Anna Scott in *Notting Hill*) is described by friends as 'beautiful, talented and famous'. At the beginning of the narrative, she is introduced to Philip Adams (Cary Grant), an American executive and member of NATO. Anna is attracted to him, but their affair is complicated by the fact that he pretends to be a married man in order to avoid serious commitment. Through this ironic scenario, the film hints at the gradually changing nature of sexual and personal relationships in late 1950s British and American society – 'How dare you make love to me, and not be a married man!' complains Anna to Cary Grant's character – but the film (like *Genevieve*) ends on a note which suggests that the errant couple are settling down ('You'll like being married', Philip tells Anna at the close).

The Millionairess (Anthony Asquith, 1960) – adapted from a play by George Bernard Shaw, and featuring Peter Sellers as an Indian doctor working in London and Sophia Loren as Epifania, a wealthy (but occasionally suicidal) Italian heiress – represented something of a culmination of this particular British cinematic tradition of 'drawing-room' comedies, focusing on couples working out their romantic difficulties against numerous backdrops and signifiers of London at various stages in its history.

In *The Millionairess*, despite Sellers' character being Indian, the film does not explore issues of race and ethnicity (Epifania makes a passing reference that Dr Kabir has the 'same colour' skin as a kipper she is given in a London fish factory). Instead, Loren's character is a personification of high-capitalism, while Dr Kabir symbolises humble and hard-working Eastern practices that seek no material reward for their labour. Kabir does not desire to return to his native India because it 'resists organisation', but equally he does not wish to accommodate himself to the impersonal and detached spiritual nature of a technologically advanced modern-day health system financed by Epifania.

The final image in the film is of Sellers' character transfixed, however, by her beauty, charm and efficiency ('I have fallen in love with your pulse' states Dr Kabir, recalling Ivan's 'revolution in my head'), whilst she is finally impressed by his sincerity, humanity and lack of concern with material considerations.

Such stylised, theatrical and star-based forms of romantic comedy were to be somewhat displaced from their prominent position within British film culture due to a number of corresponding social and cinematic developments. Alexander Walker, reviewing *Indiscreet* in the *Birmingham Post* (5 January 1958), wittily alluded to the possible audience for such a film by suggesting, 'It is a film to which you would not hesitate to take your architect, your jeweller, your home decorator, your dressmaker and your domestic staff'.[35]

The emergence of the *Carry On* series of films from 1958 onwards (which promoted a somewhat bawdy and group-based view of human relationships), and the social realist, 'new wave' novels, plays and films from around the same period were both indicative of a movement away from the concerns and settings central to such upper- and middle-class comedies as *The Prince and the Showgirl* and *Indiscreet*. The late 1950s and 1960s 'new wave' dramas explored such themes as homosexuality, mixed-race relationships, contraception, abortion and teenage pregnancy, themes which would not have fitted comfortably into the world of the 'drawing-room' comedy.

A Taste of Honey (Tony Richardson, 1961), for instance, engaged with several of these topics, and was shot on location in Salford and Blackpool, a factor which added to its sense of social vitality and verisimilitude. While fundamentally 'serious' in its representation of a relationship between a single mother and her pregnant daughter, the film also contained moments of comedy reminiscent of music hall, as mother and daughter climb out of the windows of their rented accommodation to avoid paying money which is owed, and characters frantically chase each other around kitchen tables to express their innermost emotions (when the mother's 'fancy-man' tries to intervene in one family argument, the mother (Dora Bryan) declares, 'Leave us alone, we enjoy it').

The narrative also featured a lonely gay man (Murray Melvin), who befriends and looks after the pregnant daughter (Rita Tushingham), and a black sailor (Paul Danquah), last glimpsed peeling potatoes on the deck of a ship bound for distant ports, leaving Britain without ever knowing that he is the unborn child's father. Such images suggested a broadening and complicating of representations of relationships within British cinema.

In *Only Two Can Play* (Sidney Gilliat, 1962), Peter Sellers became part of a more socially conscious form of British romantic comedy (albeit one with farcical elements), as he portrayed a Welsh librarian tempted into an adulterous affair with an exotic Norwegian woman, before realising the error of his ways and returning to his wife, family and humdrum existence (suggesting that in this particular instance, the ethos of *Brief Encounter* had not been entirely banished from British cinema). Kingsley Amis, the author of *That Uncertain Feeling* (1955) on which the screenplay was based, commented that in the film (unlike the novel) the married man 'has an attack of principle' rather than succumbs to sexual desire because (according to Amis), the British 'heroes of romantic screen comedies' didn't overtly have sexual encounters 'in those days'.[36]

The increased possibilities for romantic and sexual experimentation associated with the concept of 'Swinging London' and the advent of the 'permissive society' did, though, lead to the production of romantic comedy-dramas which acknowledged that individuals might pursue an independent and lively sexual existence outside of the confines of marriage and established relationships. Both *The Knack . . . And How to Get It* (Richard Lester, 1965) and *Alfie* (Lewis Gilbert, 1966) presented sexual and emotional relationships as existing in a state of flux, and floated the idea that finding a perfect lifetime partner was no longer the main motivation for men and women venturing out in an evening in the hope of making new acquaintances. (Stylistically, *The Knack* and *Alfie* also represented a movement away from the tradition of the well-constructed play being transformed into a film narrative.)

Neither film, however, unambiguously affirmed the advent of a more sexually liberated society. The opening sections of *Alfie* contain a comic (if somewhat ironic) introduction to the character's lifestyle, but the final parts of the narrative give way to an increasing sense of loss and potential tragedy, as a married woman is forced into a painful and illegal abortion, and Alfie, the confident storyteller and 'street-philosopher', finally begins to wonder if his life is as purposeful and controlled as he imagined it to be at the start.

The figure of an unrepentant and non-reflective 'Casanova'-style lover did, however, grace 1970s British cinema screens in the shape of the Robin Askwith character from the *Confessions of* series of films (1974–77). These sex comedies promised greater explicitness than could be displayed on television, but audiences discovered that with the exception of brief moments of sexual interaction (which were usually quickly interrupted by husbands coming home unexpectedly), the films were constructed in an episodic form similar to the dramatic structure of television situation comedies, and consequently tended to retain something of the censorship principles governing such programmes.

The 1970s, as a whole, remained something of a barren decade in terms of British romantic comedies, with indigenous film production being partly dominated by the making of family-based, situation-comedy narratives adapted from television programmes (as discussed in the previous chapter).

It was not until the release of *Gregory's Girl* (Bill Forsyth, 1980) that there was something of a revival in narratives centring upon the day-to-day idiosyncrasies and agonies of romantic relationships. John Sinclair's Gregory is mesmerised (but somewhat overwhelmed and confused) by girls, but during the course of a midsummer evening in Scotland he is manoeuvred into the presence of a suitable partner, even if she is not the original 'Girl' of his dreams. Two of Gregory's male friends are less fortunate and, at the close, are glimpsed contemplating a move to South America where they have heard that women out-number men by a ratio of eight to one!

Following the introduction of Channel 4 in 1982, and the station's willingness to offer financial support to independent film producers, there was a significant increase in the number of drama-based narratives shot on film and released in British cinemas, a number of which focused on relationships underpinned by a somewhat bitter and ironic comic perspective, as in *A Letter to Brezhnev* (Chris Bernard, 1985), *Rita, Sue and Bob Too* (Alan Clarke, 1988) and *Sammy and Rosie Get Laid* (Stephen Frears, 1989). A strand of films produced under the title of 'First Love' also explored teenage romances in their formative stages: *Experience Preferred but not Essential* (Peter Duffell, 1982) and *Those Glory Glory Days* (Philip Saville, 1983) were notable examples.

Film Four productions were generally keen to explore the experiences of characters within a clearly designated social and historical environment during a period dominated by a Conservative government from 1979 to 1997. *A Letter to Brezhnev* (1985) took the theme of a relationship between a Russian visitor to Britain and an English woman (evoking memories of *The Demi-Paradise*), and by setting the story in Liverpool the filmmakers were able to explore the possibilities for international romances to be initiated between characters from very different social systems and political backgrounds.

The film revolves around a relationship between a young Kirby woman, Elaine (Alexandra Pigg), and Peter, a Russian sailor on shore leave. In *The Demi-Paradise*, the Russian traveller was played by Laurence Olivier, and in *Brezhnev,* an English actor, Peter Firth, similarly, takes the part of a Russian character. The major difference between the two films is that in the more recent dramatisation British society is presented frankly and unflatteringly. Elaine's family home is a site of foul-mouthed conflict, and local couples appear to be existing in states of mutual antagonism, bound together only by sexual desire or habit. Consequently, the Soviet Union tends to be viewed by Elaine as a more attractive alternative to Liverpool, and so she begins a quest to be allowed to move from Kirby to the Kremlin, so to speak.

Teresa (Margi Clarke), her friend, accuses Elaine of having read too many 'Mills and Boon' novels, but latterly comes to realise that it is better to have some kind of dream than to face being reconciled to a daily routine which promises only repetitive monotony and limited outlets for creative pleasure. Elaine (like Alec in *Brief Encounter*) leaves Britain at the close for a new way of life abroad, but it is not clear whether she is in the grip of a romantic delusion which can only result in social and emotional disappointment (the British Foreign Office inform her that Peter is a married man), or whether her departure from Liverpool – and British society – is a bold and affirmative act. The humour in the film comes from the women's robust repartee and spirited approach to life, but the remaining drama is a reminder of the oppressive social situation existing in declining cities during the mid-point of Margaret Thatcher's eleven-year position as Prime Minister.

Rita, Bob and Sue Too (1988) was another Film Four production, providing a raucous, savage satire on marriage and monogamy in late-1980s Britain. The film details an affair between two young women (who have no opportunities, or apparent urge to escape from their dour surroundings), and a married man. Set in Bradford, the film's sex scenes are presented in a detached, dispassionate style, and the film emanates from an urge to endorse (if not necessarily to uncritically celebrate) the essence and world view of a certain type of British 'low brow' humour in the tradition of George Formby and the *Carry On* (1958–78) series of films.

A *Time Out* reviewer of the film accused its makers of displaying 'humour in the worst possible taste' during the freeze-frame ending, which has Bob diving onto his Union Jack bedspread, beneath which lie *both* Rita and Sue in amused anticipation of sexual pleasure.[37] This moment of narrative closure, arguably, parodies the European 'art-house' ending of *Jules et Jim* (François Truffaut, 1962) where the film's three lovers, on deciding that they cannot live with or without each other, opt instead for a lethal combination (initiated by the woman character) of suicide, murder and spiritual desolation.

Two 1980s biographical films, by depicting the doomed love affairs of dramatist Joe Orton (1933–67) and punk musician Sid Vicious (1957–79), were able to construct narratives depicting love as a phenomenon capable of moments of extreme black humour, before they too descended (within their particular contexts) into incidents of murder and suicide, and a corresponding sense of spiritual desolation and exhaustion. In *Prick Up Your Ears* (Stephen Frears, 1987), the relationship between Orton (Gary Oldman) and his romantic partner, Kenneth Halliwell (Alfred Molina) deteriorates into a parody of an emotionally traumatic heterosexual marriage, culminating in death and destruction. *Sid and Nancy* (Alex Cox, 1986), similarly, presents the relationship at the centre of its narrative as a kind of grotesque parody of motifs denoting ideals of true love and the exciting possibilities offered by Anglo-American relationships.

American Nancy (Chloe Webb) introduces British punk, Sid, to hard drugs, which serve to aid his rejection of 'straight' society and conventional behaviour, in ways far exceeding the solipsistic antics and fantasy phases enacted by such earlier 'dreamers' in British cinema as Billy Fisher and Gregory. Sid and Nancy's notions of reality are increasingly determined by the effects of the drugs they consume, and concepts of courtship, love and commitment are re-imagined from a nihilistic British punk perspective, defiantly promoting itself in opposition to the Queen's Silver Jubilee celebrations of 1977 (in stark contrast to the sense of awe expressed towards the coronation of George V in *The Prince and the Showgirl*). The film's stridently anti-romantic imagery and outlook (Sid declares that he was 'so bored once', he 'fucked a dog . . . A corgi'), led veteran film critic, Dilys Powell to declare

> If this is romantic, the cinema has suffered a revolution. But then it has. *Sid and Nancy* is a British film; we have come a long way since the days of Margaret Lockwood. No doubt we were right to move. All the same, we might have stopped short of the repulsive.[38]

On meeting Nancy's parents, and being asked about his intentions towards her (as if they were a conventional romantic couple, beneath their outlandish costumes and disaffected poses), Sid replies that they are 'going to go down the methadone clinic on Monday, and go off to Paris, and just sort of go out in a blaze of glory'. This seemingly haphazard, but actually quite formulated plan, puts Cavell's much quoted definition of the ideal filmic romantic couple (he takes his example from *It Happened One Night*, Frank Capra, 1934) into a new, specifically modern perspective: 'What this pair does together is less important than the fact that they do whatever it is together . . . that they would rather waste time together than do anything else – except that no time they are together could be wasted.'[39] In one contemporary usage of the term, all that Sid and Nancy really aspire to do is to get 'wasted' together. Prior to their demise, and realising that America may be a land for the wrong kind of opportunity, Sid announces that he is going back to London to be with his friends and 'people who care'. But Nancy persuades him not to make the journey, and the film suggests that they die out of a bungled suicide pact. The closing inscription – 'Sid and Nancy R.I.P.' – is inevitably ironic, as the film presents them resisting any possible moments of peace and reconciliation during their lifetime. Their drug-induced fantasies result in terrible and tragic incidents, and while the film records their excesses with a certain gleeful detachment, the comic outrageousness of the narrative is gradually eclipsed by a sense of a situation – and a couple – spiralling hopelessly out of control.

The Anglo-American relationship in social and cinematic terms seems to arrive at a literal and symbolic 'dead-end' by the close of *Sid and Nancy*, with a certain brand of nihilistic hedonism seen as emerging from the British 'punk' movement of the 1970s crossing over to America to meet a violent and horrific end. Efforts to revive notions of more romantically inclined Anglo-American relationships would have to take very different forms in subsequent British films.

Sid and Nancy, like several of the narratives considered in this section, did not suggest that the formation and depiction of successful romantic encounters in British feature films was a straightforward or easily achievable process. Pressures from a somewhat repressive society to conform or refrain from sexual encounters outside of marriage, responsibilities felt by lovers to other partners, troubling international situations, ideological differences between couples, and the sometimes unpropitious surroundings of the British environment, all played their part in ensuring that the course of 'true love' in many of the films discussed, invariably, did not run smoothly. The following section will discuss how a group of 1990s films engaged with these themes and subject areas in a British context from a distinctly modern and contemporary perspective.

Constructing romantic scenarios in 1990s British cinema

The beginning of the 1990s witnessed the release of two films which presented romantic and sexual passion in a disturbing manner, without the 'sensationalism' of *Sid and Nancy*, but in ways far removed from the more 'comic' and hopeful approaches which would follow later in the decade. *Close My Eyes* (Stephen Poliakoff, 1991) and *Damage* (Louis Malle, 1992) dramatised the experiences of couples embarking on transgressive, incestuous and doomed relationships.

Stephen Poliakoff's film depicted the consequences of a brother and sister developing a sexual relationship in the context of a British society entering its twelfth year of life under a Conservative government administration. Harriet Waugh, reviewing *Close My Eyes* in the *Spectator*, drew particular attention to the bleak and emotionless mood of the film, with its sense of a constricted and morally vacant society, observing that 'life' in the narrative is deadly 'serious, there are no jokes', a character 'gets Aids', and that, in her view, 'All this happens without a vestige of wit'.[40]

Nigel Andrews in the *Financial Times*, linked *Damage* with *Accident* (Joseph Losey, 1967), an earlier drama about obsessive relationships meeting a traumatic end in an upper-class English setting.[41] Both *Accident* and *Damage* were made by non-British directors, and possess titles alluding to the destructive passions being acted out within each film. The affair in *Damage* between the British Conservative Minister for the Environment (Jeremy Irons) and his son's girlfriend, Anna Barton (Juliet Binoche), a kind of French *femme fatale*, led Andrews to observe ironically that with 'tariff barriers crumbling, not even passion now bothers to stop at borders'.[42] In *Sid and Nancy* and *Damage*, passionate relationships between English men and American or French women are presented as equally destructive and careless of human life.

The Rachel Papers (Damian Harris, 1989), an adaptation of a novel by Martin Amis, represented an attempt to resurrect representations of Anglo-American male–female relationships in British cinema in a more comic, if similarly sexually explicit manner. (Charles Highway (Dexter Fletcher) declares that for his American girlfriend, Rachel (Ione Skye), 'sex was Disneyland, and I was the ride'.) The film included two American film performers in its cast (James Spader played Rachel's American boyfriend), and referenced *Alfie* in the way its central character, Charles, regularly reveals his innermost thoughts directly to the camera. Rachel eventually chooses Charles over her American boyfriend, although in the film's closing sequence, she leaves both Highway and London and returns to New York.

Truly, Madly, Deeply (Anthony Minghella, 1991) explored an intense and sombre subject (the premature death of a loved one) in a narrative and stylistic form drawing upon modes of humour, fantasy, and psychological drama. The film charts the grieving process endured by Nina (Juliet Stephenson) as she mourns the loss of her lover, Jamie (Alan Rickman, giving a particularly self-reflexive and playful performance). Judging by her relationships with a group of supportive male admirers, she appears to be coping, but meetings with a psychiatrist reveal that she is actually in an acute state of despair. Overcome by the distress of observing this situation from beyond the grave, the dead Jamie returns as a ghost to the flat and Nina's life, and the film allows the two lovers to briefly withdraw from the everyday world into a magical setting, where they can be truly alone (and *alone truly*) together.

Having imbued the opening stages of the story with an acute sense of loss and sadness, the film subsequently initiates a plot development predicated on notions of 'comic' wish-fulfilment (Jamie's return from the dead), before introducing a further level of ironic absurdity to the narrative, signified by Jamie inviting his fellow dead friends to come and live in Nina's flat and relax by watching videos in the living room (*Brief Encounter*, significantly and resonantly, is one of the films viewed by the ghosts. The closing line spoken by the deceived husband in *Brief Encounter* – 'Thank you for coming back to me' – can be seen as appropriate to the more tragic aspects of both films).

Truly, Madly, Deeply (like *Close My Eyes* and *Damage*) implies that British society in the early stages of the 1990s cannot be judged to exist in a vibrant or inspiring condition, and during a sequence set on the London embankment involving a parody of a first date, Nina declares that she hates 'what this country is doing to itself and other races'.[43]

As the film progresses, Jamie eventually comes to the conclusion that he needs to die (again), so that Nina can create a new life for herself without him. *Truly, Madly, Deeply* may present the 'after-life' as an entity beyond understanding (hence, the tragi-comic absurdities of the ghosts' behaviour), but the key line in the film's mythology is perhaps a reference to the rising of Christ from the cross uttered by the friendly Camden council pest control expert who, despite being a widower himself, declares that 'Death shall have no dominion'.[44]

Truly, Madly, Deeply was initially filmed on 16mm stock for BBC television as a Screen Two presentation, and then enlarged to 35mm after the finished product was deemed suitable for cinematic release, which meant (as Mark Shivas, the head of BBC drama during this period recalled) that 'All the contracts had to be renegotiated for its new incarnation, at a cost of several hundred thousand pounds'.[45] Anticipating the promotional and marketing policy of *Four Weddings and a Funeral*, the film was premiered in America to what Shivas described as 'decent reviews and business'.[46]

Soft Top Hard Shoulder (Stefan Schwartz, 1992) did not feature American performers, or focus on issues of love and mortality, but sought to demonstrate that British cinema was capable of producing popular films which engaged with narrative patterns and motifs associated with Hollywood cinema such as the 'road movie' and 'screwball' comedy. Revolving around Peter Capaldi's character's frantic drive from London to Scotland to be eligible for an inheritance from his Italian grandfather (Richard Wilson), the film records the geographical and emotional journey that he undertakes with Yvonne (Elaine Collins), an independent-minded Scottish woman, who, it emerges, has just run away from her own wedding.

This attempt to create an updated model for indigenous romantic comedies was criticised by Adam Mars-Jones in the *Independent*, who argued that the locations used in the 'road movie' aspects of the film (London, Morecambe and Scotland) could not be made to compete with the wide-open spaces and vistas of America, as regularly featured in Hollywood films: '*Soft Top Hard Shoulder* gets much mileage out of a British cultural dilemma that won't go away – of being haunted by imported dreams inappropriate to our habit, our temperament or simply, our climate'.[47]

Early 1990s British romantic comedies that employed American actors, or that were felt to be too obviously seeking to recreate Hollywood-type plots and situations were, thus, prey to criticisms that their approaches were misconceived or doomed to failure. The international success of *Four Weddings and a Funeral* in 1994 and *Notting Hill* in 1999, however, created opportunities for further British films to be produced which focused on relationships between characters from the United Kingdom and America.

Martha – Meet Daniel, Frank and Laurence (1998), one of the late-1990s Anglo-American romantic films to emerge from the revivification of this sub-genre in British cinema, revolved around an American woman and the three men who all fall in love with her. The much-longed-for Martha (Monica Potter) eventually judges Laurence (Joseph Fiennes) to be the most romantic and sincere of her three suitors, and, by the close of the narrative, the two of them leave London and fly to Iceland, a place chosen for its cheapness ('a ticket for anywhere for £99'), and the possibilities it offers for their love to grow, if nurtured within a less artificial and cynical environment than that offered by the 'big city'.

A subsidiary character in the film played by Ray Winstone comments that the tale told to him by the film's narrator, Laurence, is really about a group of 'self-obsessed friends' who are 'locked in a futile rivalry', and it is difficult not to see this statement as a pertinent observation about the schematic and somewhat contrived nature of the film itself. (Neither Martha nor her three admirers are quite as fascinating and desirable as they appear to imagine themselves.)

Sliding Doors (1997), after *Four Weddings and a Funeral* and *Notting Hill*, was the most successful 1990s British film to incorporate an Anglo-American alliance into its narrative. The twist in this particular film was that its American star, Gwyneth Paltrow, appeared as a British woman (Helen) who regularly employs such indigenous expressions as 'Ease up, for Christ's sake' in her speech. Paltrow was also required to perform two variations on the same character, illustrating that even love stories which turn out well in the end are haunted by the possibility that everything might have turned out differently.

In one of the contrasting scenarios in *Sliding Doors*, Gwyneth Paltrow's character misses a tube, and does not realise until the end of the narrative that her boyfriend is seeing another woman. In an alternative story (and parallel universe), she catches the tube and then catches her boyfriend in the act of being unfaithful, and meets a potential new love, James (John Hannah). This version of Helen goes on to make a new life for herself, but ends up dying in the arms of James, after being run over by a car; knowledge in this case proving to be both dangerous and fatal. Helen number one survives a fall downstairs, caused by the belated recognition that her boyfriend is unfaithful, and the film ends with a curious sense of *déjà vu* as she meets James in a lift without recognising him, hinting that the seeds of her future were contained in the tragic parallel plot (or, more disturbingly that the film's narrative can have no real meaningful or coherent conclusion).

By not making Gwyneth Paltrow's character American, audiences can appreciate her sustained and skilful impersonation of an English character, and her willingness to participate in a British movie (albeit, one largely American-funded). Mark Steyn in his review of *Sliding Doors* in the *Spectator* even went so far as to suggest that 'Gwyneth Paltrow presents a far more enchanting vision of Englishness than any other English actress I can think of; on the other hand, she seems more far more natural as an Englishwoman than she does as an American'.[48]

A British film released during the same year as *Sliding Doors*, *Love and Death on Long Island* (Richard Kwietniowski, 1997), also focused on Anglo-American relationships, detailing how an esoteric British writer, Giles De'Ath (John Hurt), becomes obsessed with a young American actor, Ronnie Bostock (Jason Priestley), whom he observes in a 'trashy' teenage-Hollywood movie, after entering the wrong auditorium in his local cinema (thus missing the English E.M. Forster 'heritage' movie he was originally seeking out). Giles becomes infatuated by the star, but not by the strand of American popular culture he represents. Moments of humour and pathos are consequently generated out of Hurt's character's attempts to establish contact with Bostock at his Long Island home, and his desire to encourage him to find work in more dignified and worthwhile parts.

Gilbert Adair's first-person novella has De'Ath declaring that Ronnie 'should not lazily fly out to Hollywood and make *Hotpants College III* as though there were no alternative . . . I would write the kind of role and the kind of film which his gifts merited'.[49] The film adaptation ends with a sense of loss and disappointment as Giles dares to 'come out' to both America and Ronnie, but ends up wondering, 'What have I done?' as Ronnie politely, but firmly, rejects his offers of love and total devotion. The final image in the film is of Giles once more being reduced to watching his idol on the cinema screen, rather than in a state of close personal proximity, an indication of a cultural and sexual gap between the two characters that cannot in the end be bridged.

Beautiful Thing (Hettie Macdonald, 1996), the other most significant gay British romantic comedy of the 1990s, was a very different kind of 'coming out' drama. Mark Steyn, reviewing *Notting Hill* in the *Spectator*, argued that he would have respected the makers of that film more if they'd 'had the guts to make a film called *Tower Hamlets* or *Broadwater Farm* especially given that . . . the differences between the Portobello Road and the Commercial Road are to the average Hollywood star . . . virtually undetectable'.[50]

The Thamesmead tower block where the story of *Beautiful Thing* unfolds was an attempt to make an unorthodox romantic comedy and 'unlikely couple' film, which could possibly have been released under the title of 'Tower Hamlets' or 'Broadwater Farm'. Hettie Macdonald and screenplay writer, Jonathan Harvey (adapting his own play), sought to produce a film, however, which focused on sexual and emotional themes rather than the social problems and employment difficulties which often dominated British films situated in such environments.

The tale begins with Jamie (Glen Berry) being bullied at school, and vainly looking to his friend, Ste (Scott Neal) for support. The film will close with them openly dancing together and embracing each other in front of the inhabitants of the housing estate: a utopian image of what relationships could be like in a perfect world and a striking illustration of the gap between ideal outcomes and everyday reality in British culture.

Humorous observations and dramatic developments in the narrative tend to stem from the characters' antagonistic and explosive confrontations with each other. Jamie's mother, Sandra (Linda Henry), complains that she works 'all the hours God sends to keep [her son] in insults', and characters within the film often make remarks and statements which allude to unpleasant and unfunny realities. When Ste announces that he is being taken to watch a boxing match with his father, Sandra quips that she thought he would have had enough of that by now (a coded reference to the beatings he receives from his father and brother). Jamie objects to her finding humour in such a distressing situation, and reminds her that it wasn't funny when *her* ex-boyfriend was beating her up. This exchange ends with Sandra slapping Jamie, and both of them rolling around on the floor in a state of extreme frustration and anger, indicating a sudden transition from 'comedy' to despair and sadness, which is emblematic of many of the films discussed in this and the previous two chapters.

Most of the characters in *Beautiful Thing* are depicted as fighting with their inner 'demons' and fears, and some take out their anger on those nearest to them, and others (particularly Sandra) try to channel their aggression towards making a better life for themselves. I would suggest that *Beautiful Thing*, significantly, does not envisage humour as an end in itself, or simply as a defence mechanism employed by characters at the end of their tethers. Instead, the film seeks to negotiate a way through all the bitter exchanges and harsh remarks and seek out some kind of better way forward.

The film does not suggest that humour can be easily deployed to shrug off the hurt caused by non-ironic homophobic abuse, as, for example, when Jamie's mother discovers that her son's school exercise books have the words 'bum-fucker', 'queer', and 'bent bastard' scrawled all over them. Cavell's notion of a magical place where love might blossom in such a context remains a distant and elusive concept (*The Gloucester* gay bar and a 'magical woods' setting are the nearest the boys come to finding a kind of sanctuary from a harsh and generally unforgiving society), but the film implies that this is no reason for gay (or heterosexual) lovers not to still dream of (and work towards) establishing such a place.

Beautiful Thing is important for the ways in which it seeks to expand the British romantic comedy format in terms of setting, sexual orientation and character construction. Equally, the film harks back to some of the themes and indices of mood identified in a number of British films discussed earlier. The mixture of broad farce, sexual desire between characters and naturalistic observation present in *Rita, Sue and Bob Too* can also be observed in an updated, raw fashion in *Beautiful Thing*, which nonetheless seeks to go beyond the northern setting and hetero-sexual groupings of Alan Clarke's film, and its corresponding sense that the characters really don't have much of a future ahead of them.

The relentless comic banter and innuendo between the characters in *Beautiful Thing* can be read as an attempt to appropriate the discourses of Oscar Wilde and Joe Orton for a contemporary working-class envi-ronment, while the unfulfilled couples of *Rich and Strange* and *Brief Encounter* might be perceived as hovering in the filmic background to the narrative. The longing for something emotionally richer and more meaningful than that offered by the film's setting can also be discerned in the ending to *A Letter to Brezhnev*, where Elaine refuses to renege on her belief that true love (and perhaps a more just and equal society) might exist somewhere over the horizon.

The case studies of *Four Weddings and a Funeral*, *Notting Hill* and *Love Actually* that follow will examine the treatment of such subjects as love, courtship, marriage, sexuality, and the effects generated by the combining of comic and dramatic modes of narration in these particular films. I shall consider the importance of place in creating a romantic atmosphere, the possibilities for Anglo-American and transnational rela-tionships to prosper in a modern age, and the ways in which these three narratives proved that forms of British cinema could successfully com-pete with Hollywood in the production of romantic comedies capable of appealing to audiences all over the world.

Case studies: *Four Weddings and a Funeral* (1994), *Notting Hill* (1999) and *Love Actually* (2003)

Four Weddings and a Funeral (1994)

Four Weddings and a Funeral (Mike Newell, 1994) was one of the most commercially successful British films of the 1990s, but the unanticipated extent of the film's popularity did lead to some dissension that the British film industry had not been better positioned to benefit from its impact. *Four Weddings* was produced on a budget of £2.9 million, with the majority of the production cost being provided by PolyGram, with addi-tional financial input from Channel 4.[51] Michael Grade, Chief Executive of Channel 4 during the period of the film's initial release, claimed that the channel would eventually receive 'around £4 million' for its initial investment.[52]

However, the Labour MP Joe Ashton, at a 1995 committee meeting discussing the present state and future of the British film industry, suggested that Channel 4 (in the wake of the huge and ongoing profits made by the film) had been 'taken to the cleaners' by their financial arrangement with PolyGram: 'It does seem there should have been some sell on rights that you weren't aware of',[53] he told Grade. Such queries led to a virulent response from Michael Kuhn, President of PolyGram Filmed Entertainment, who commented that 'Channel Four puts 2p into our films and then complains when they get £5 million back, so screw them'.[54] A fellow Labour MP, Gerald Kaufman, concluded that on the basis of the film's funding by a 'foreign-based multi-national company', it should not be perceived as a 'British film', especially as 'most of its profits' would 'end up in Eindhoven, Holland, home of Philips, the parent company of PolyGram Filmed Entertainment'.[55]

In terms of its distinguishing narrative and stylistic features, the film was notable for the ways in which its characters were placed within a tightly structured series of public occasions and situations revolving around a series of weddings. The logical progression of the narrative is to move the central characters, Carrie (Andie MacDowell) and Charles (Hugh Grant), from being observers of other characters' weddings towards taking part in their own wedding. This particular romantic couple, however, deliberately express their love for each other by declaring a commitment *not* to get married to each other, as if their accumulated experiences have taught them that weddings represent a curse, rather than a blessing. Paul Dave in a 1997 essay, 'The Bourgeois Paradigm and Heritage Cinema', highlighted the sense of social entrapment (and fear of personal failure) motivating the narrative, and suggested that the film was fixated upon the riddle of 'how to imagine a ceremony which does not turn out to be closed'.[56]

'Who is it today?' asks Charles, as a second wedding follows three months after the first (although the narrative crucially presents the weddings and the funeral in quick succession, thereby accentuating the impression that such ceremonies completely dominate and determine the lives of the film's characters). The formal structure of the narrative is partly a result of what Richard Curtis conceives of as a particularly effective method for constructing scenarios in which comic situations can be initiated and then deepened and refined: 'having thought of one thing, I just exaggerate and expand and move it around . . . [in] a very simple line of expansion and repetition',[57] he claimed in an interview.

In *Four Weddings*, Charles is presented as someone who is uneasy about displaying emotions, and he is not a character who appears to possess clear aims and objectives in life. Carrie is depicted as a liberated, cosmopolitan and sexually experienced woman. She is also someone who is prone to making self-destructive choices (after the marriage to Hamish (Corin Redgrave) quickly fails, she declares that she will never again 'marry someone three times my age'). Both characters have to be pushed to a stage where they are forced into abandoning their 'surface' demeanours and have to make a decisive break with past and present relationships and attitudes. Charles and Carrie, thus, have to fight against both their own instincts *and* the structural flow of the narrative, which keeps them apart. The film, therefore, has to work towards reaching an ironic denouement, where the declaration, 'I do not', can also, in an emotionally meaningful and positive sense, really signify 'I do' or 'I will'.

Beginnings and endings

It was nice not quite meeting you (Carrie to Charles)

An invitation card announcing the wedding of Angus and Laura to be held in Somerset, England, on 1 May, signifies the first wedding of the narrative. The seemingly unnecessary information (as far as British spectators are concerned) that Somerset is in England signals that the film is aimed at a worldwide audience who may not be aware of such details. The use of the wedding invitation motif to initiate the narrative is a means of making spectators almost feel that they, too, are being hailed by the film to attend the ceremony, and observe the series of ritualistic events to follow.

Part of the viewing pleasure for those who do respond positively to the film may lie in the 'fly-on-the-wall' documentary aspect to several stages of the first wedding where comparatively few plot developments (except the introduction of Carrie) are instigated, and instead we witness the procession of vows, speeches, mishaps, performances and idiosyncratic incidents of the wedding and subsequent party.

The first wedding-ceremony sequence draws upon comic scenarios familiar from television situation comedies, such as the joke that the best man is late *and* has forgotten the ring. The second ceremony is dominated by Rowan Atkinson's comic performance as an incompetent and tongue-tied priest, who at one stage enquires if anyone knows of a reason why the couple 'may not be johned in marriage'. This scene concludes with applause from the congregation, affirming the sketch-like nature of the sequence, which is clearly distinguished from those romantic comedy threads of the narrative that specifically seek to initiate both comic and dramatic developments.

Charles' keynote 'best man' speech at the first wedding allows the film to move from situational comedy to a form of 'stand-up' comedy, which also serves to deepen and complicate the nature of the film's attitudes to marriage and issues of emotional commitment. His talk, delivered in a style which is both guardedly playful, mocking and heartfelt, mixes references to sheep, unfaithful partners, bridegrooms who sleep with their loved one's sister *and* mother, and two-day marriages which immediately become a 'nightmare of recrimination and violence'. Unsurprisingly, in view of the horrors he alludes to for comic (rather than dramatic) purposes, Charles expresses his 'bewildered awe' and admiration for those couples who are prepared to make a commitment to marriage, and to each other, regardless of all the possible disturbing and disappointing consequences.

Charles is immediately fascinated by Carrie, who first appears wearing an enormous black hat in the style of a visitor to 'Ladies Day' at Ascot races. Upper-class English aristocrat Fiona (Kirsten Scott Thomas), perhaps sensing Carrie as a future rival for Charles' affections, dismisses Carrie as a 'slut' and an 'American' in a tone which implies that, in her view, the two categories may be mutually inclusive or complementary.

In the scenes which serve to establish a tentative relationship between Carrie and Charles, Carrie is portrayed as the more sexually confident figure, informing Charles where she is staying, seemingly as an invitation for him to spend the night with her, and then ingeniously pretending to be his wife in room twelve in order to prize him away from the bar-room bore, who (at this stage) constitutes the major obstacle (aside from Charles' own diffidence) to their first sexual encounter.

When they do succeed in having sex together in the Boatman hotel, the shots delineating the scene focus briefly on images of Charles's back and Carrie's outstretched thighs, as if the total experience of their sexual engagement with each other cannot be completely represented or comprehended on screen. Whilst engaging in sexual activity with each other, the couple ironically and irreverently wonder about what the symbolic figure of the vicar might think of their behaviour, but the film's narrative from this stage onward will come to rest upon what exactly this moment of sexual intimacy means in emotional and practical terms for Charles and Carrie.

Carrie will subsequently joke to Charles about expecting to get married after they have now slept together (implying that she is not the 'slut' of Fiona's derogatory moral judgements), and Charles will respond in kind by expressing concern that he has woken up and found himself in *Fatal Attraction* (Adrian Lyne, 1987), a film concerned with the terrible events that can occur when a man chooses not to replace his wife with his mistress. This scene of psychological and social intimacy, and comic playfulness between the couple, is abruptly concluded by Carrie's sudden announcement that she has to leave immediately for America. Charles declares that this constitutes a great tragedy (what one might term 'An American Tragedy'). The ambivalent, contradictory side of Carrie's nature is subsequently evident in her statement to Charles that 'I think we both missed a great opportunity here'. It is not exactly clear what Carrie means by this observation, although it seems to suggest that they could have (and should have?) more readily contemplated planning a future together, rather than just joking about its possibility.

Carrie's departure the day after their sexual intimacy means that this prospect cannot be discussed, however, and the next time they meet, Carrie makes another yet more startling and unsettling statement – that she is now engaged to be married to a Scottish politician, Hamish. Carrie's mobility and subsequent unpredictability is linked to her transatlantic lifestyle, which allows her to operate and function in differing locales in marked contrast to Charles, who appears more restricted to specifically British settings. Carrie's emotional and geographical elusiveness will become the central component of the story, binding together the other supplementary strands of the narrative. Carrie and Charles notably *do* sleep together again (after Carrie announces her engagement, thus introducing an adulterous element into their relationship even before Carrie is married), but on this occasion, unlike their previous tryst, the scene concludes with Charles leaving Carrie alone in bed the following day.

Such sequences allude to the changing social and moral codes and values of romantic-comic traditions, suggesting that whatever other difficulties the couple face an absence of sex is not one of their problems. The romantic-comedy structural motif of the 'wrong partner' is still significant in the narrative, though, and is represented by Hamish in Carrie's life, and the unreciprocated affection that Henrietta (Anna Chancellor) has for Charles.

Carrie and Hamish's relationship will soon become associated with images of decay and futility. Following Gareth's death at her wedding, Carrie will go on to describe her marriage in curious metaphors, informing Charles that 'March was hell', and by 'April, it was sordid'. Carrie's choice of language implies that her desire for romance has been contaminated and undermined by a misguided pursuit of wealth and privilege (Hamish is described as 'owning half of Scotland'). Carrie does embrace traditional Scottish dancing at her wedding reception, suggesting a willingness to adapt to the ways of her new cultural milieu, but ultimately she comes to a realisation that money cannot compensate for a lack of empathy and sexual compatibility with her chosen partner.

Carrie, despite her liberated, confident profile, consequently, has to be saved from her own actions by the unlikely hero figure of Charles, who is the only character able to provide her with an alternative to the domestic unhappiness caused by her marriage to the wrong person.

In this sense, the film might be conceived as operating within the moral terrain of the classic 'screwball' Hollywood comedies of the 1930s, with their implicit message that romantic happiness cannot be bought, and that personal relations are ultimately much more important than profits and percentages. Tom (James Fleet) may be the seventh richest man in England (he acknowledges the greater wealth of the Queen and Richard Branson), but the film reveals that his main hope in life is to find 'a nice, friendly girl' who is not made 'physically sick' by the sight of him, and who might subsequently be willing to share her life with him.

Gerald Kaufman complained in an article for the *Evening Standard* that 'It was impossible to understand' how the characters in *Four Weddings* 'managed to outfit themselves so expensively, since none of them seemed to have any kind of job and only one was independently rich'.[58] Such a literal reading, however, does not take into account the fact that classical Hollywood screwball comedies, similarly, tended to take the economic prosperity of their leading characters for granted, as it was precisely this freedom from financial constraints and considerations which enabled the couples in question to explore the nature of their passionate feelings for each other, within a privileged dramatic space unencumbered with everyday worries and concerns.

Hugh Grant's persona in the film of harassed but thoughtful inarticulateness, and his tendency in moments of stress to put on his old-fashioned pair of glasses, as if they might help him to see situations more clearly, brings to mind the bespectacled, philosophically inclined but unworldly character played by Cary Grant in the classic Hollywood romantic comedy *Bringing Up Baby* (Howard Hawks, 1938). In that film, Katharine Hepburn enacts a disruptive but ultimately liberating influence on the central male character.

In *Four Weddings*, the central female protagonist is explicitly presented as more sexually experienced than the male character, and we learn that Charles has only 'slept with nine people', compared with Carrie's 33 lovers. Enquiring, perhaps, on behalf of the audience, what constitutes a 'fair-run' sexually in the late twentieth century, Charles learns that Carrie had slept with six men by the age of seventeen, and that subsequent lovers included two men simultaneously, a boyfriend's father, and an English lover (number 22) who 'kept falling asleep on the job'. Carrie sums up her sexual experiences in terms of 'American experience' compared to 'British innocence', claiming that she has had fewer lovers 'than Madonna', but more than 'Princess Diana'. Charles, feeling somewhat impotent and ineffectual, in comparison, wonders what he has been doing with his life. 'Working', he concludes, although the film notably does not tell us at what.[59]

The dramatic and cultural significance of this discussion between the characters is that whereas, in certain previous traditions of Hollywood and British cinema, such unrepentant accounts of sexual activity on the part of the woman character might have led to her being ostracised or marginalised by the narrative, in *Four Weddings*, Carrie's sexual worldliness is coded as one of the potential rewards for Hugh Grant's character. In the film, only Fiona refers to Carrie as a 'slut', and that remark may be motivated by jealousy of Charles' incipient attraction to this experienced American woman.

Nevertheless, despite the relatively 'advanced' or liberated sexual moral values alluded to (if not explicitly displayed in the narrative), characters in the film find it difficult to equate word with deed, and to express their true emotions and feelings. Matthew (John Hannah) has to turn to the poetry of W.H. Auden to express his acute sense of loss at Gareth's funeral, stating that the poem, 'Funeral Blues' (1936), constitutes what he 'actually' wants 'to say'.

On the embankment in London (the setting for Nina's date with the man who will replace Jamie in her life in *Truly, Madly, Deeply*), Charles seeks to state his feelings for Carrie in an authentic and considered fashion, but he is forced to resort to a post-modernist parody of the phrase, 'I love you', by expressing himself through David Cassidy's lyrics from a Partridge family song, 'I think I love you'. In response to Charles' statement that he feels that it is important 'to have said it', Carrie perceptively asks, 'Said what exactly?' To which Charles replies, still deferring to another, 'What I just said about David Cassidy'. Carrie, herself, invokes the words of John Lennon – 'Love is the answer, and you know that for sure' – at the point where she is embarking on a self-destructive marriage to a man she does not love, and who will not appear in the narrative again.

From this perspective, Carrie and Charles' disrupted and disruptive relationship is only consolidated when they are able to equate word and deed, intention and action, even if this means drawing upon essentially negative formulations: 'You might agree not to marry me for the rest of your life', ponders Charles at the close – to which, Carrie is able to respond by saying, 'I do' in a truthful and purposeful manner, rounding off the film's probing of romantic discourses in a modern age, and allowing her to say 'I do' without having to get married.

Ironically, this final reconciliation is engineered by Charles' deaf brother, David (David Bower), who, through sign language, is able to force Charles into expressing his true feelings about loving Carrie, and not Henrietta, and thereby accepting the truth of the maxim (and perhaps conveying the film's essential message) that marriage is only justified if you love the person 'with all your heart'.

The other seemingly well-suited pair, Gareth and Matthew, who are presented as a couple at the beginning of the narrative (in contrast to Charles and Carrie, who are only emotionally united at the close) are wrenched apart by Gareth's sudden and unexpected death. Carrie's Scottish wedding ceremony, where Gareth cheerfully invokes Oscar Wilde, before dancing enthusiastically with an American woman, proves in effect to be Gareth's 'last fling'. He expires in the midst of what he has termed *Brigadoon* (Vincent Minnelli, 1954), a reference to a Hollywood musical set in the Scottish Highlands in which members of the community live for only one enchanted day each century, a utopian setting where the price of true love conversely depends upon a character's willingness to die (as in the ending of *Truly, Madly, Deeply*).

Gareth comes to be perceived as the possessor of a joyful attitude towards life, which manifests itself in his colourful waistcoats and extrovert manner (especially when compared to Matthew's more sober and understated Scottish persona). It is noticeable, however, that the highest degree of intimacy we witness between Gareth and Matthew occurs during the credits sequence at the beginning of the narrative, when Matthew wipes a speck of food from Gareth's grey beard. Just as the details of Carrie's 'sordid' marriage can be alluded to, but not actually represented in the narrative, gay sexual acts between a loving couple were also presumably considered to be antithetical to the romantic comic aspects of the film, and so were omitted or suppressed.

The most explicitly sombre elements in the narrative are the occasions recording Gareth's death and funeral. His demise leads the film to a very different setting where modes of farce, fantasy and comic narration are briefly, but significantly, banished. The location of Gareth's funeral (in striking contrast to the film's desire to locate the weddings in particular places) is *not* identified, adding to the symbolic resonance of the sequence. The film cuts from an image of Charles informing Matthew of Gareth's death as the wedding guests sing, 'For he's a jolly good fellow' at Carrie's wedding to a crane shot of a rainy day in a semi-industrial area where Gareth's funeral is taking place. Philip French in the *Observer* described the setting as one in which 'a dull suburban church' is 'over-shadowed by Thames-side factories and refineries',[60] and Anne Billson in the *Sunday Telegraph* drew attention to the unexpected break

in narrative style, genre classification and images of the nation represented by the funeral sequence: 'The once cheery characters are set
against a bleak, grey backdrop of smoking chimneys and the industrial
north. It's as though Branagh and Ivory had run slap-bang into Ken
Loach'.[61]

Paul Dave suggested that the creative inspiration for the geographical
and historical terrain implied by the funeral lay in the movement of
British cinema identified as representing a 'new wave' of socially aware
and gritty native filmmaking exemplified by such films as *Room at the
Top* (Jack Clayton, 1958) and *This Sporting Life* (Lindsay Anderson,
1963).[62] Both of these narratives notably conclude with the deaths of
leading characters. Richard Curtis revealed in an interview that what
one might term the neo-realist effect of the funeral scene in *Four Weddings* was partly achieved by 'all the people in the church', apart from
the main performers, being made up of 'extras who lived around there',
whom he described as providing 'marvellous found faces . . . on the
day'.[63]

The emotional impact of this sad occasion on the lovelorn characters
in *Four Weddings* is ultimately therapeutic in that it cures them of some
of their more habitual and regressive attitudes (Fiona, for example,
abandons her 'traditional black' clothes at Charles' wedding). The over-
riding impression of the funeral section of the narrative is that Gareth
had embarked upon a geographical and cultural journey that had
separated him from his humble origins, and enabled him to take up a
position amongst a new class of wealthy, upper-class socialites. This
emotional distance between his past and present (conjoined with the infinite void represented by his 'future') adds to the pathos of the occasion.

Gareth's parents are not shown speaking at the funeral, and this
pained silence and look of incredulity on their faces implies that they
may feel that their son had been led astray by his well-to-do friends, and
that his flamboyantly gay lifestyle, in stark contrast to the greyness of the
provincial industrial town where he is laid to rest, could possibly (in
their unexpressed view) have contributed to his premature demise.

The film is conscious of the cruel irony involved in killing off one of
its most life-affirming characters, and fleeting medium close-up shots of
selected mourners at his funeral (which include a black man, a smiling
elderly man with a hearing aid, and a couple of men possibly coded as
gay), testify to Gareth's social accessibility, and his life outside of the
close circle of friends who constitute the film's main sphere of interest.

The funeral sequence extends the film's thematic concerns about the
difficulties of finding an appropriate language to express feelings of love
and loss, and the reading of the Auden poem suggests that the sense of

despair engendered by Gareth's death may mean that there will be no real happiness to come for the central characters ('Pour away the ocean and sweep up the wood; For nothing now can ever come to any good'[64] are the final two lines of the poem).

Auden's bleak prophecy is not confirmed by the end of the narrative, however, which contrives to bring about a series of affirmative and optimistic endings. Charles and Carrie express their true feelings for each other in a torrential rainstorm, suggesting that the 'ocean' is being poured back into the universe by the couple's belated and (hopefully) permanent reconciliation, enabling them to break out of the patterns of circular and painful repetition in which they have hitherto been trapped.

The final photographic montage sequence informs us (through a series of images of the future lives of individual characters, serving as a parody of the Victorian novel tradition, which Henry James ironically termed as 'a distribution at the last of prizes, pensions, wives, babies . . . and cheerful remarks'[65]) as to what transpired *after* the story proper is completed. The sequence of pictures reveal that Henrietta went on to marry a member of the Royal Guards, Scarlet (Charlotte Coleman), who initially feared that Americans were as 'dull as shit', is pictured wedding the tall, dashing American she met at the ill-fated Scottish ceremony, and even Tom achieves his aim of finding a nice girl with whom to settle down, and live alongside in his castle with his Labrador dog.

Matthew is photographed drinking with a handsome young man in uniform, suggesting that he has succeeded in forming another kind of loving relationship. Fiona's future is the only one that apparently cannot be seriously imagined, and she is pictured alongside Prince Charles, replacing Princess Diana at the Royal wedding of 1981, a concluding joke that has taken on something of a tragic dimension following Diana's divorce from Charles and subsequent death in 1997. Charles and Carrie are pictured together holding a baby boy, but significantly, their picture is a snapshot image, and not a wedding photograph.

Charlotte O'Sullivan, whilst reviewing *Notting Hill* in *Sight and Sound*, suggested that in *Four Weddings*, 'vulgar America is in thrall to cultured, wealthy Britain', but that 'aside from such embarrassing worship, the US barely figures in it', concluding that 'Andie MacDowell's character could have been any nationality'.[66] The commercial significance of MacDowell's presence in the film is that it indicates an awareness on the part of the filmmakers of the importance of stars (as opposed to character actors) in promoting a film to international audiences.[67] The cultural significance of Carrie's American nationality, beyond allusions to her greater degree of social mobility and sexual experience compared to her English counterparts, is not explored or dramatised in any great depth by the narrative, which does tend to concentrate on Charles' English-based struggle to achieve a state of romantic fulfilment and happiness.

Carrie's American 'otherness' does imbue her character, however, with the possibility of broadening the horizons of Charles' more socially confined and somewhat claustrophobic world, with their liaison offering the possibility of a synthesis of progressive and traditional tendencies and social outlooks. In *Notting Hill*, Richard Curtis and Hugh Grant would return to this question of the possibilities existing for a relationship to blossom between an English gentleman and a modern American woman and, instead of surrounding it with a series of digressive sub-plots, would make this topic the central subject and theme of the narrative.

Notting Hill (1999)

You think I should do Henry James instead? (Anna to William)

Notting Hill, unlike *Four Weddings*, was officially categorised as a USA/UK co-production, produced on a much larger budget of £15 million, and distributed by Universal pictures.[68] Producer Duncan Kenworthy described the film as 'not a sequel' to *Four Weddings*, which he identified as concerning itself with 'big social events with none of the real life in-between', in comparison to *Notting Hill* which, in his view, focused on 'the day-to-day details of a love affair'.[69]

Richard Brooks in the *Observer* suggested that the difference between the two films was that *Four Weddings* was 'very much a film of the hesitant John Major era', whereas *Notting Hill* portrayed 'a Britain where an ordinary person's dreams can come true'.[70] John Smith, Leader of the Opposition, had died unexpectedly on 12 May 1994, the day before *Four Weddings* was released in British cinemas, and Tony Blair went on to replace him as Leader of the Labour Party, in which position he subsequently guided the party to victory in the May 1997 election.[71]

Notting Hill was, hence, conceived and produced under a Labour government. However, the film's ethos, ironically enough, tends not to be imbued with (or inspired by) notions of 'Cool Britannia'.[72] The Demos research monograph produced on behalf of the Labour government, *Britain™: Renewing our Identity* (1997), claimed that after 'an autumn of slow decline' in which 'Britain's power and influence were in retreat', the nation was 'now ready for its spring, a period of renewal and increased self-confidence'.[73] The British group of friends at the centre of *Notting Hill* display none of these qualities or feelings about themselves, and spend most of their conversations together discussing which of them constitutes the most abject failure within a circle of people who already consider themselves to be chronic under-achievers.

Notting Hill dramatises the complications and pleasures created by a romance between an unexceptional English man and an exceptional American woman. In this film, the presence of Julia Roberts ensures that the narrative is transfixed by the collision between a Hollywood super-star's exalted, if somewhat rarefied world, and the ordinary, undramatic, but possibly more comforting universe inhabited by Grant's divorced, upper-class English character. *Notting Hill*, subsequently, becomes something of a narrative about the conditions of its own production, exploring (in the process) both the influence of Hollywood filmmaking on British cinema, and the dialectical opportunities for reciprocal enrich-ment, when the two contrasting film cultures and nations are brought together by constructs of romance and mutual commercial interests in a world of high-capitalism.

William Thacker (Hugh Grant) is promoted as a possible ideal partner for Anna Scott (Julia Roberts), the superstar who picks up $15 million for a picture, but the film does equally stress that he is 35,[74] divorced, and the proprietor of a specialist bookshop which is not pros-pering financially (Anna is the only customer whom we witness buying a book in the film, and William, in his typically self-deprecatory manner, even does his utmost to persuade her that the travel book she has selected to buy is not really worth purchasing), raising the question of whether he is a sufficiently dynamic and inspiring partner for Anna Scott.

As regards representations of indigenous popular culture in the film, the British newspaper press (with its incessant desire for scandals and stories exposing the private lives of public figures) is depicted in an unflattering light, with photographers and reporters glimpsed pursuing Anna with no regard for her feelings or safety, and gleefully exploiting her uncovered nude photographs for commercial purposes (although it is implied that this may be an international rather than a solely British phenomenon: the pictures of Anna, which we tantalisingly never see, were presumably originally taken in America).

Anne Billson of the *Sunday Telegraph* noted that both *Notting Hill* and *Four Weddings* were predicated on the same episodic and repetitive structure of 'Boy meets girl, boy loses girl, boy meets girl again, boy loses girl again and so on'.[75] The impression of entrapment implied by this cir-cular narrative form (with its disturbing implication that logically the two films could go on forever) is only broken in the closing moments of each narrative, when the Hugh Grant character finally realises that he has made a bad decision, and should henceforth commit himself forever to Carrie/Anna. Thus, for the duration of most of the two scenarios,

Charles/William is a divided character, caught up in a state of anxiety brought upon by a fear that he will not be able to break out of the vicious circles impeding him in his search for a lasting romance, and a sense of definite narrative closure.

One notable difference between these two Hugh Grant/Richard Curtis films is found in the opening sequences of the films. Following shots of Anna Scott at various film premieres, *Notting Hill* opens with a voice-over narration from William, introducing the spectator to the eponymous London setting – which he describes as 'not a bad place to be' – where the story will unfold. *Four Weddings* begins with Charles oversleeping, and subsequently being late in his role as 'best man' at the first wedding, a scene which adds a comic note of urgency to the proceedings, and implies that he needs some kind of emotional 'awakening' to make the most of his life.

Notting Hill, in contrast, depicts William moving calmly and confidently through his surroundings, where he claims to 'lead a strange half-life', before his narration suddenly changes from its travelogue-style manner, and adopts a more portentous tone, as he recalls the incident which transformed his existence: 'And so it was just another hopeless Wednesday, as I set off through the market for work, little realising that this was the day which would change my life forever' (this has echoes of Laura's narration recalling the mundane setting out of which her tempestuous love affair in *Brief Encounter* emerged: 'It all started on an ordinary day, in the most ordinary place in the world').

Anna, the 'unquiet' American, is introduced in the second scene of the narrative, depicted surreptitiously entering William's travel bookshop and, consequently, his life and inner being. It is somewhat fitting that she is seeking a travel book, as she herself is on a journey from America, and a key question addressed to Anna (to which her own responses will fluctuate) is 'How long are you staying in Britain?' Whereas *Four Weddings* revolves around a series of public occasions commemorating private events, *Notting Hill* will be predicated upon Anna Scott's visits to and from Thacker's flat and bookshop, William's journeys to luxurious London hotels to 'interview' Anna, and the successful return of both of them to the 'magical setting' of the local private park; first, discreetly, by night and second by day, as a private couple in a venue to which the public have limited access.

Having met each other by chance, William and Anna subsequently bump into each other by accident on the street, when he spills orange juice on her: such an incident in the iconography of romantic comedy indicating that the couple are torn between expressing antagonistic *and* erotic feelings towards each other. For the first of two occasions, his nearby apartment, distinguished from other buildings by its blue door, offers refuge from the outside world. Anna (understandably, given the paucity of attractions unveiled by William) refuses offers of sustenance from his fridge, and the two characters begin the process of looking intently at each other, with neither expressing their underlying thoughts or emotions. Upon leaving, however, she unexpectedly kisses him on the mouth, thus introducing and initiating the possibilities of a romantic entanglement to follow (although the fact that she kisses William *when leaving* indicates, that as in *Four Weddings*, Grant's character's love of an American woman will turn out to be an emotionally painful and frustrating affair, defined more by a sense of absence than plenitude).

William and Anna are both associated with concerns about the passing of time, particularly in relation to unfulfilled ambitions and dreams. Anna initially says to William, 'You played it pretty cool here, waiting for three days to call', not knowing that his flatmate's inaction has in fact caused the delay. The male character (Matthew Modine, uncredited) in Anna's black–and–white romantic-comedy film ('Woody Anna'[76] according to the screenplay) turns to her in a Manhattan art gallery, and announces, 'In about seven seconds, I'm going to ask you to marry me': to which Anna's blonde-haired character seductively smiles, leaving William, whilst watching the film on video, to contemplate the fine line between reality and fantasy in his own life.

William is worried that he will never find the right woman, and imagines that in 'thirty years' time', he will still be an unattached bachelor, spending time on the couch of his two best friends. Anna observes that William has only been subjected to the intrusive attentions of the press for 'ten minutes', while she has endured 'ten years' of 'this garbage' in which her private life is converted into 'entertainment' for the masses: 'Our perspectives are [therefore] different', she informs him. The glimpses of Anna's science-fiction film *Helix*, which we observe William watching in the cinema, portray her (this time red-haired) character rotating and drifting in a spaceship, suggesting something of the circular, aimless motion of the meta-narrative itself at times, and connoting a 'fantastical' sense of time which may ultimately be beyond human comprehension.

The film's most visually innovative sequence denoting the passing of time depicts William embarking on a stroll through Portobello Road, telescoping a six months' journey into ninety seconds of screen time, and presented in the form of an extended tracking shot which encompasses the seasons of autumn, winter, spring and summer. This sequence captures and exaggerates the changeable nature of British weather, even within a single day, and the tendency for showers of rain to break out at any moment to possibly dampen romantic liaisons (or, conversely, to correspond to intense human passions as symbolised by Andie MacDowell's closing line in *Four Weddings*: 'Is it raining? I hadn't noticed').

This particular scene in *Notting Hill* equally denotes the cyclical inevitability of the seasons, summer revealed as coming to an end, but eventually being eagerly anticipated once again following the emergence of spring, and so on, as outlined by Northrop Frye in *Anatomy of Criticism: Four Essays* (1957).[77] A pregnant woman is glimpsed in the first sequence of William's walk, and, in the final images, she is pictured holding a young baby, suggesting the infinite renewal and enlargement of human narratives and forms of existence.

Frye associated tragedy with autumn, comedy with spring, and romance with summer. This sequence from *Notting Hill* significantly concludes with William taking off his jacket due to the heat of the sun, and depicts the woman gazing lovingly at her newly born child, an image of optimism and hope, in contrast to the sentiments of the song, 'Ain't No Sunshine When She's Gone', accompanying these seasonal transitions on the film's soundtrack. Just as *Notting Hill* combines comedy and drama, and features musical interludes and incidents of farce in a generically hybrid mixture, this particular sequence refuses to treat the seasons as separate entities, insisting instead on the interconnectedness of setting and mood, humour and romance, in the mysterious processes involved in forging human relationships and connections between the individual and wider cosmic and natural forces.

In such an ever-changing world, Anna and William are drawn to images that might offer some sense of permanence or endurance. Anna, for instance, is moved by an inscription on a bench containing a dedication from a husband to his dead wife, and concludes from this that 'some people do spend their whole lives together'. The film is structured around the more permanent places occupied by William, and the more transient and public settings (appropriate to her status as a visiting superstar), such as the Ritz and Savoy hotels and film sets, occupied by Anna, who lives in a world in which 'illusion' can be profitably marketed as entertainment.

William, subsequently, finds it difficult to know when Anna is being sincere, compared to when she is acting out or faking her emotions, just as she (on her part) is conscious of the difficulties involved in unambiguously expressing her feelings in an era of post-modern surfaces lacking in depth and solidity, within the context of a culture dominated by 'gutter-press' journalistic practices, ever eager for any opportunity to expose, embarrass or humiliate her. William is contrasted with Anna's

American film-star boyfriend (Alec Baldwin), who is presented as the opposite to Grant's clean-cut, diffident, well-spoken character. His arrival reduces William to the level of a support player, rather than a true match for the star, and Anna once again becomes a remote, almost imaginary figure, apt to turn up in images on the side of buses advertising her new film, *Helix*.

William Thacker, like most of the Western world, now has to go to the cinema to see Anna. In one scene, William is depicted, looking starstruck, watching Anna in *Helix* at the local cinema, where she appears as an astronaut floating inside a spaceship. This sense of drift pervades subsequent stretches of *Notting Hill*, where the two characters are presented as deeply divided by their existences in completely different kinds of worlds and environments. It transpires that William is the only one of his group not to know that Anna had a boyfriend. 'My whole life ruined because I don't read *Hello* magazine', he remarks in a sarcastic aside about the celebrity-infatuated culture of both Britain and America.

William's aloneness is broken by Anna's unexpected return to his flat, as she seeks refuge from the British press, which has published topless photographs of her taken several years before. 'With your papers, it's the worst place to be', she observes. William has earlier passed a news-stand with headlines referring to Anna's exposure (the *Daily Star* declares 'Watta lotta Scott', and the *Daily Mirror* 'Anna Stunna', whilst the more serious-minded *Daily Telegraph* emphasises 'Gloom over Middle East talks'). William's lack of interest in the populist culture of contemporary British society, however, means that he walks by the headlines without even noticing their existence.

In a subsequent conversation with Anna, he will reference Henry James as a possible cinematic source of inspiration, rather than the romantic comedies and science-fiction films she has been making. Such a direct suggestion could be interpreted as a clear allusion to the 'heritage' films produced within the British cinema industry, and a tacit endorsement of their value and worth. (It is notable that many of the 'heritage' films have been subjected to similar criticisms as *Notting Hill*, regarding their emphasis on upper-class characters and pictorially attractive images of Britain.)

Anna, after her consequent immersion in the British past evoked by Henry James, will return to the present, and more particularly William's travel bookshop, conferring an original and valuable painting upon him, and declaring her love. In a turn of phrase unlike any other she utters during the course of the narrative, Anna pleads that she is 'just a girl . . . asking a boy to love her'. In a film that (for all its fascination with the splendours and wonders of love) has largely downplayed excessively verbalised expressions of love and devotion, this statement stands out for its directness and winsomeness. William will subsequently declare that as an actress she would know how to deliver a line, but the film, I think, encourages an audience to take her admission at face value, and acknowledge the effort made by Anna to articulate her true feelings.

As *Four Weddings* began with a frantic effort by Charles to get to the church on time, *Notting Hill* concludes with a frantic effort by William to reach Anna before she leaves both him *and* Britain. Resorting to impersonating a film journalist once more – he offers his *Blockbuster* card as proof of his status, in a line alluding to the increased importance of video rentals and sales in the total success of a film[78] – he infiltrates the inquisitive world of popular newspaper culture, and uses the methods of its representatives to both apologise to Anna for doubting her sincerity, and ask her to reconsider her position. Anna, after asking to have a journalist's question repeated, announces that she will stay in Britain 'indefinitely'. William's friends at this point are placed in the position of observers and critics, asking such questions as 'What happened?', and subsequently declaring that the proposal scene 'was good'.

The film, like *Four Weddings*, concludes with a series of codas and images alluding to what happens in the future, after the temporal narrative is over. In *Notting Hill*, these wordless vignettes concentrate on what becomes of William and Anna, and are not presented in quite the same ironic style as the concluding moments of *Four Weddings*, which (as noted earlier) juxtaposes Fiona and Prince Charles in one of its photo-montages, suggesting that the images are not to be taken at face value, or entirely seriously. At the close of *Notting Hill*, William and Anna are pictured getting married, and then attending a premiere of (presumably) Anna's Henry James film at the Leicester Square Odeon cinema, symbolising a further fusion and strengthening of Anglo-American culture.

The couple are last glimpsed, relaxing peacefully, in the private park on the bench which symbolises a lifetime of togetherness for a particular loving couple. William is reading what appears to be *Captain Corelli's Mandolin* (which director Roger Michell was due to film next![79]), and Anna is clearly in an advanced state of pregnancy. This concluding image, therefore, is able to celebrate the triumph of romantic love over all obstacles, the combining of career and motherhood on the part of the central woman character, and the forging of a relationship between what the British advertising posters described as a love affair between 'the man in the street' and the 'most famous star in the world'.

Julia Roberts' performance as a world-famous film star enables *Notting Hill* to consider the financial rewards, lifestyle and more problematical aspects of achieving fame on such a level. Richard Dyer in his study *Stars* (1979), proposed a number of conceptual categories under which issues of stardom might be explored. These included the notion of 'star as person', 'star as image', and 'star as auteur'.[80] In reference to the category of 'star as person', one can note that Anna Scott is so wary of revealing her true feelings to anyone, because of the risk of being exploited or misinterpreted, that it is not easy for William to gain a clear sense of her 'real' personality and 'true' nature. Her star image, as constructed in the extracts from her movies, appears to signify both emotional openness and a certain aloofness. This latter feature of her persona is symbolised by the images of her face on the side of London buses, depicting Anna as a larger-than-life-figure, always on the point of disappearing from view around a corner. Anna's decision to make a movie adapted from a Henry James novel could be read as an indication of her desire to exercise a greater degree of creative control over her career, and so initiate the process of establishing herself as more of an 'auteur' figure in the Hollywood film industry.

In *Heavenly Bodies: Film Stars and Society* (1987), Richard Dyer noted that there may be both convergences and conflicts between the ways in which film studios seek to promote stars as a means of publicising their movies, and the media's desire for 'unofficial', unsanctioned exposures or revelations regarding the private lives of stars, which can be used to improve newspaper sales.[81] In *Notting Hill*, Anna Scott draws upon the media to promote her new movie through a series of individual and group interviews with representatives of the British press, but she is also the victim of unwanted publicity which she cannot control or contain, when topless photographs of her appear in the daily papers. This incident recalls the publicity generated by Marilyn Monroe's nude photographs as featured in the first (1953) edition of *Playboy* magazine. According to Richard Dyer, the cover 'Golden Dreams' photograph had been taken in 1948 and 'used for several different calendars ... However, in March 1952, the fact that this image was of an important new Hollywood star became a major news story'.[82] The photographs of Monroe contributed to the mythologising of her image and were subsequently recuperated into the realm of art photography.

There is no sense in *Notting Hill*, however, that the pictures of Anna Scott can be similarly reclaimed or redeemed in this late period of twentieth-century culture, or that the relations between stars, media organisations and studio production companies can be revitalised or revised. The failure of Anna's sincere plea to William in the privacy of his bookshop, compared to the success of their interaction in the midst of a press conference, does suggest that for major stars distinctions between private and public aspects of their lives are inevitably blurred and sometimes indivisible.

Notting Hill is a film, partly, about an American actress, such as Julia Roberts, adjusting to the slower tempo and drama-based style of a particular strand of British filmmaking, which does not utilise spectacular special effects or outlandish plot developments to achieve its narrative effects. In an essay entitled 'But do we need it?', Geoffrey Nowell-Smith commented that 'When matched against American films . . . their British counterparts come across all too often as restrictive and stifling, subservient to middle-class artistic models and . . . values', before concluding that 'the British cinema is in the invidious position of having to compete with an American cinema which . . . is by now more deeply rooted in British cultural life than is the native product'.[83]

Notting Hill reflects thoughtfully upon these kinds of claims and observations, but seeks to question and challenge such preconceptions and prejudices. In deciding to be with William 'indefinitely', Anna is also choosing to be with his circle of friends, thus implicitly accepting the British middle-class values and modes of conduct which they represent: a course of action which could be read in symbolic terms as contemporary Hollywood cinema acknowledging and supporting the very kind of drama-based British cinema which Nowell-Smith suggested in 1985 was disliked and unpopular in this country. *Notting Hill* strives to combine the strengths of popular American cinema – the generally accessible and clearly delineated stories, and seemingly infinite creation of imaginative fantasies drawing upon the talents of world-famous stars – with British cinema's ability to construct small-scale, emotionally intimate, and socially aware narratives.

Notting Hill is a reflective British-American film about the possibilities of British-American relationships, formulated around a 'What if?' scenario, where Hugh Grant can represent the character of the English gentleman at his most diffident, modest and likeable, and Julia Roberts can personify the film star goddess, who (like Madonna?) is prepared to quit America (if not its powerful entertainment industries) and settle down in Britain, while still remaining a world-famous star. *Notting Hill* similarly meditates upon the international appeal of Hugh Grant, a performer who, in his own low-key manner, is able to appear as an imaginative and attractive partner for Julia Roberts in an Anglo-American romantic comedy.

Notting Hill, though, is equally capable of suggesting that not all American films are successful with British audiences: one notes that while Hugh Grant's character is predictably awe-struck by Anna

Scott's performance in the Hollywood science-fiction movie *Helix*, the auditorium screening the movie is by no means full . . .

Love Actually (2003)

Praise the Lord! (Colin's exclamation on meeting the women of his dreams)

Love Actually is a post-1990s narrative, but in forming a sort of coda to *Four Weddings* and *Notting Hill* (and through its promotional claim to be the 'ultimate romantic comedy'), the film presents itself as a useful end-point for this chapter. Produced on a £20 million budget, and released during the weeks leading up to Christmas 2003, the film, according to a *Guardian* report, had already grossed $185 million worldwide by July 2004.[84] *Love Actually* (like *This Year's Love* (1999) and *Born Romantic* (2001), both written and directed by David Kane), focuses on the love lives of a number of different couples, allowing the film to explore contrasting examples of love, and examine different kinds of relationships.

In *Four Weddings*, we never learn what Hugh Grant's character does for a living, while in *Notting Hill*, despite running a not-especially-successful travel bookshop, he is still presented as a desirable partner for the film star, who earns millions of dollars for each film in which she appears. In *Love Actually*, Grant has been promoted to the powerful figure of an incoming Prime Minister, although in keeping with the mood and tone of the earlier films he is more concerned with the state of his love life than the state of the nation. In the 'democratic', multi-narrative format of *Love Actually*, Grant's character's senior position within the social structure does not mean, however, that his story is privileged above that of other characters, or accorded extra screen time.

The significance of the seemingly ungrammatical and enigmatic title – *Love Actually* – is explained in a voice-over by Hugh Grant's character at the beginning of the film, over footage of real-life people being reunited with friends, relatives and loved ones at Heathrow airport. In a sequence which is presented almost in the form of a party political broadcast for the 'Love Party', Prime Minister David (who has a portrait of Margaret Thatcher in his office) claims that love actually is all around our daily lives if we look closely and deeply enough.

In the guise of a wise sage (which is somewhat contrary to how David will subsequently come across in the film), he even somewhat contentiously goes on to refer to the absence of expressions of hatred in the phone and text messages sent by the victims of the 9/11 atrocity in 2001. This reference to a terrible tragedy serves to differentiate the film from other Richard Curtis movies and, perhaps, identifies *Love Actually* as a kind of belated humanist response to this traumatic historical event; love (through its connotations of peace, happiness and contentment) is posited throughout the film as a positive force for creating a sense of purpose and well-being in the world.

The film will go on to explore the romantic adventures of figures much more glamorous than those glimpsed in the 'reality-based' excerpts at the start, and by concentrating on a range of characters in search of sex, emotional warmth and expressions of love that last, *Love Actually* works at constructing a panoramic and expansive picture of courtship patterns in the setting of a modern city (what one might term 'London Actually') at the start of a new century.

Churches in *Four Weddings* were signifiers of places where people came to celebrate the finding and confirming of love and to acknowledge its inevitable end. Private parks, cinemas, hotel-rooms and restaurants functioned in *Notting Hill* as settings where romance might slowly blossom and prosper. In *Love Actually*, schools and airports, in particular, feature as places where declarations of love may be affirmed, enabled or questioned.

Speaking on *Newsnight Review* about *Love Actually*, Tom Paulin warmed to the film's representation of the nation as a kind of 'Merry England', a 'decent country [where] everybody goes to the local comprehensive' and 'class divisions don't matter'.[85] Paulin also responded positively to the choice of Portugal – which he described as an 'ancient ally of this country going back centuries' – as the nationality for the woman who restores Colin Firth's character's faith in love and womankind.[86]

Love Actually presents the formation of couples as both a localised and global phenomenon, allowing the film to depict characters who find love within the United Kingdom, as well as revealing the emotional and geographical journeys undertaken by those who venture to seek love in more distant places. The film dramatises a number of contrasting examples of love: failed, obsessive love (Mark (Andrew Lincoln) is secretly besotted with his best friend's wife (Keira Knightley)); romantic infatuation as a response to the emotional void created by a family bereavement (Sam (Thomas Sangster) dreams of being noticed by an American girl (Olivia Olson) who attends his school); love between people occupying very different social positions (the Prime Minister of Britain and his domestic assistant (Martine McCutcheon)); married love that is threatened by a third party (Karen (Emma Thompson), Harry (Alan Rickman) and Mia (Heike Makatsch)); familial love that stands in the way of a couple embarking upon a relationship (Michael (Michael Fitzgerald),

Sarah (Laura Linney), his sister, and a work-colleague, Karl (Rodrigo Santoro), to whom Sarah is attracted); companionable love, which develops after a couple has already achieved a degree of sexual intimacy (John (Martin Freeman) and Judy (Joanna Page)); love as a belatedly recognised form of emotional friendship (an ageing rock star (Bill Nighy) and his manager (Gregor Fisher)); love as sexual attraction (Mia and her desire for Harry: Colin (Kris Marshall) and the women from Wisconsin (Ivana Milicevic, January Jones and Elisha Cuthbert)); and romantic and wistful love between inhabitants of different nations (Jamie (Colin Firth) and Aurelia (Lucia Moniz)).

The film's introduction to the stand-in performers simulating sexual activity on a film set prompts recollections of the references to Anna Scott's body doubles in *Notting Hill*, and humour in the scene comes from the fact that both John and Judy are presented as having their minds elsewhere, as John is instructed to 'massage' Judy's naked breasts, while she leans against a pillar. The mundane remarks about local traffic congestion subsequently made by the couple appear incongruous in view of their physical closeness. At one level, this short sequence offers a parody of lovers who may be simply going through the motions of sexual attraction, whilst also hinting at the complex patterns of behaviour involved, more generally, in reconciling notions of friendship with sexual intimacy, a theme which the film will explore as its multiple stories unfold (Karen and Harry's marriage appears to be currently predicated around notions of companionship and nostalgia for the past, rather than intense mutual sexual desire – hence the danger posed by the calculatingly and overtly sexual Mia).

The sudden unexpected cut within the narrative from this sequence of simulated intimacy, featuring John and Judy, to the beginning of a funeral oration spoken by Daniel (Liam Neeson) for his dead wife, contrasts sexual activity (however faked or artfully constructed) with the stark reality and unavoidability of death. Daniel declares that he and his late wife, Jo, had 'a lot of time to prepare for this moment', implying that the death of Jo was anticipated, and seen as inevitable for a long period. This scene briefly casts a shadow over the other relationships detailed in the film, and illustrates that lovers have only a limited time available to them in life to find personal happiness and fulfilment.

In *Four Weddings*, the reading from a poem by W.H. Auden served to commemorate deeply felt love between partners separated prematurely, with particular regard on this occasion to love between gay men. *Love Actually*, in contrast, focuses on heterosexual love, and the playing of a Bay City Rollers hit, 'Bye Bye Baby', following Daniel's address to the mourners signals a movement from 1930s poetry to 1970s popular music within Richard Curtis's work as a means of signifying painful emotions pertaining to the themes of love and death.

An emphasis on time, and the significance of popular British culture, is also evident in a subsequent scene in which Prime Minister Grant's character lists some of the figures (past and present) who have made Britain 'great'. The speech is intended as a calculated riposte to the President of America (Billy Bob Thornton), who has tried to seduce the woman whom David, himself, secretly desires. This patriotic speech cites such timeless figures as 'Shakespeare, Dickens, Churchill and the Beatles', alongside more contemporary icons such as Sean Connery, Harry Potter and David Beckham's feet in a bid to highlight Britain's contributions to the world. At the mention of Harry Potter, some members of the cabinet and gathered assembly do start to laugh, perhaps, denoting that British audiences should not take Grant's speech too much at face value, as a sort of modern-day Shakespearean ode to notions of Britain as a 'royal throne of kings' constructed around a 'happy breed of men' inhabiting a 'little world' of 'precious stone', and so on.[87]

The fact that Connery and Beckham live and work abroad, and the Harry Potter films are financed by Hollywood suggests that the scene could be read ironically as denoting that Britain currently exists within a global economy, and consequently, there can be no real value or gain in adopting the isolated stance of a 'little Englander', either from an emotional or economic perspective.

One fascinating piece of information gleaned from the audio commentary by Richard Curtis and Hugh Grant on the DVD retail release[88] of the film is that the Prime Minister was originally to include Catherine Zeta-Jones's breasts as further examples of British greatness, but Grant demurred to include this line on the grounds that he didn't think that a British Prime Minister would make such a reference. As Grant seems to be a Prime Minister in much the same style and manner as, for instance, Will Hay is a railway station manager in *Oh Mr Porter!* (Marcel Varnel, 1937) or a police sergeant in *Ask a Policeman* (Marcel Varnel, 1939) in the majority of his scenes, this apparent reluctance to make the scene too transparently farcical or fantastical is striking, and connotes something of the tension within the narrative as a whole, perhaps, as to how seriously and sincerely (at times) we are encouraged to respond to the film, and some of the relationships formed therein. (One might note respectfully that Catherine Zeta Jones's breasts are also somewhat in exile since her move to Hollywood.)

This sequence carries echoes of the concluding press conference scene in *Notting Hill* in which a group of gathered journalists ask the Hollywood film star, Anna Scott, exactly how long she intends to stay in Britain. In *Love Actually*, the message appears to be that this most famous and powerful figure in the USA has outstayed his welcome, and has not adapted to the British way of doing things. The conflict over Natalie is also symptomatic of a wider ideological dispute inherent in this strand of the film about how far Britain should accede to American policies about the environment and the future state of the world. Curtis, at this stage of the narrative, appears to want to re-write actual developments in contemporary British politics and international relations with America (post-9/11) from a satirical and farcical perspective, with the apparent intention of entertaining the idea of a world in which Britain is not inextricably linked with American foreign policies.[89]

Another sequence within the film predicated upon a form of 'wish-fulfilment thinking' depicts the journey to Wisconsin made by Colin, a sexually frustrated British male in search of sexually accommodating and welcoming American women. This story reveals that Curtis's promotion of Anglo-American relationships, and of the delights associated with America, are not simply past features of his work.

In his essay "'Civilised' Sexual Morality and Modern Nervous Illness" (1908), Sigmund Freud claimed that

> If a man is energetic in winning the object of his love, we are confident that he will pursue his other aims with an equally unswerving energy; but if . . . he refrains from satisfying his strong sexual instincts, his behaviour will be conciliatory and resigned rather than vigorous in other spheres of life as well.[90]

In the light of such an observation, Colin's determination to avoid a life of enforced celibacy can be seen as an positive act, which might ultimately lead to him becoming more active in pursuing other goals within his life (although the film as a whole – somewhat obsessively, even by romantic comedy standards – focuses on aspects of love, rather than any work-related issues).

The sequence linking Basildon man and Wisconsin women explores the notion of instant attraction, however improbable Colin's immediate effect on the women in the bar might appear (Colin will exclaim 'Praise the Lord!' in grateful thanks for his luck, evoking memories of Spike's (Rhys Ifans) whispered appreciation – 'Thank you, God' – on finding Anna Scott in his bathtub in *Notting Hill*). In *Being and Nothingness* (1943), Sartre argued that 'Desire is an object aiming at enchantment'[91] and John Bayley in a 1960 study entitled *The Characters of Love: A Study in the Literature of Personality*, suggested that 'Taking other people's reality for granted is . . . the first requirement of love'.[92]

In this scene of seduction set in snowy Wisconsin, Colin and the three women succeed in enchanting each other, whilst taking an interest in each other's place of origin. Basildon, an unexceptional suburban town in Essex, is greeted by Jeannie (January Jones) as if it were an almost unspeakably enticing place, promising all kinds of unimaginable pleasures. To an American audience, the cheese-making state of Wisconsin might seem a less exotic place than California or New York for a British person to visit, but Colin's determination to go beyond the well-travelled path of others is rewarded beyond his wildest hopes. Concepts of difference and otherness (however mundane the 'realities' of life in Basildon or Wisconsin) are here eroticised, and invested with a sense of the 'fantastic' and the marvellous.

In *Four Weddings*, American Carrie was presented as more sexually experienced than upper-class English man, Charles, having had 33 lovers compared to his 9. In *Love Actually*, Colin's lack of success with women is spectacularly reversed, at least for one night, as he participates in his own version of the 'American dream' (the three women are listed in the credits as American dream-girl, American angel and American goddess). The sequence, for all its roots in a certain type of male wish-fulfilment fantasy, does acknowledge, too, that there are other ways of loving and interacting sexually with others than those enshrined in monogamous and exclusive couplings (Colin will return to London in the company of two other American women).

Towards the close of the narrative, two relationships are contrasted in scenes depicting one couple (Karen and Harry) drifting apart, and another couple (Aurelia and Jamie) growing closer. In a sequence set in a school hall, Karen confronts husband Harry over why he substituted an expensive necklace for a Joni Mitchell CD as a Christmas gift for her. The scene engages with such themes as the loss of trust between long-standing married couples, and the corresponding anxiety over what happens next in the relationship.

The two characters are in a state of physical proximity, but are possibly being prised apart by a third character not present in the sequence (a woman notably comes between the two of them as they discuss their problems). Harry appears rooted to the spot when confronted with his actions and prompted to spell out their significance, but it is not clear whether his unease proceeds from being found out, or from having made a terrible error in judgement.

Karen offers several possibilities as to what the necklace might signify, none of which appear to bode well for their future together. The sign 'Merry Christmas' in the background appears ironic given the characters' essential unease with each other. The open-ended conclusion to their story as a whole implies that in the 'real world' serious difficulties or incompatibilities in a relationship are not easily or quickly resolved.

Jamie and Aurelia constitute a couple who are not plagued by the prospect of sudden departures, divorce or death, but who, nonetheless, have to work hard at relating to each other. As Jamie proposes to Portuguese-born Aurelia in her native language as she works in a French restaurant, both are separated from their home territories, a factor which appears to act as a liberating feature in their relationship (Karen and Harry, in contrast, seem somewhat trapped and oppressed by their prosaic British surroundings, and the final shot of Harry in the film is of him arriving at Heathrow airport from some unexplained destination).

Jamie woos Aurelia while she is at work, serving the needs of others, and she is positioned in a spatially elevated setting within the restaurant, looking down upon her male devotee, without crucially being beyond his emotional reach. Learning to speak another's language (however falteringly) becomes a means for Jamie and Aurelia of both recreating the self, and of learning to love and live more fully and completely. When Aurelia exclaims, 'Is the question!' to Jamie's declaration, she is affirming the value of love in her own words, unlike Carrie in *Four Weddings*, who drew upon the lyrics of John Lennon ('Love is the answer') to make the same point, whilst marrying the wrong person in the process.

The applause from the restaurant customers greeting the couple's formal commitment to each other symbolises a kind of hope for future international personal relationships. During the period of the film's release in the winter of 2003, state membership of Europe was expanding, whilst in Britain the UK Independence Party and certain section of the Conservative party promoted the setting of limits to Britain's ties with and obligations to Europe.[93]

The presence of subtitles in the scene detailing Jamie's valiant attempts to propose to Aurelia in Portuguese provides a comical way of illustrating for spectators that other cinematic forms than Hollywood narratives exist which are capable of constructing compelling tales of romance. The proposal sequence equally suggests that if English is an international language, love may be an even more universal and timeless form of communication.

Love Actually, I would suggest, implicitly invites audiences to respond positively to those characters who find redemption through loving and being loved (what Sigmund Freud in his essay 'Civilisation and its Discontents' (1930) described as a means of creating 'new bonds with people' who were previously 'strangers'[94]), whilst constantly acknowledging, through its multiple stories, that the processes of finding love, overcoming feelings of failure and alienation, and sustaining balanced relationships are not necessarily easily accomplished feats. The constant cutting within the narrative between the romantic (or non-romantic) experiences of different characters serves to create an impression of love as an exciting, variable and unpredictable phenomenon.

John and Judy simulate sexual activity and yet, by the close, have become a 'real couple', not an imitation or a 'stand-in' for others. Karen and Harry stand on the edge of splitting up, a movement that signals a possible rupture between their past and future. Bereaved son Sam finds solace in the pursuit of a young black American girl, who happens to have the same name as his deceased mother, suggesting that love is part of a cyclical process involving inevitable losses and (sometimes) pleasing gains (supporting W.H. Auden's assertion in a late poem, 'The Entertainment of the Senses' (1974), that in the end 'We must love one another *and* die!'[95]).

Inter-racial relationships are present in the multi-layered narrative, even if gay relationships are notably absent from the film's portraits of modern love. The male characters, too, tend to have more exalted work positions than their female counterparts, but the former are presented as suffering from low self-esteem until redeemed by love in its many forms and guises – for example, Billy Mack states that his comeback record is 'crap', a term which is also used by David to describe the performance of members of his cabinet, whom he declares must do better next year. Jamie similarly announces that his writing is 'rubbish' and not worth the trouble of saving, but when Aurelia is prepared to dive into an unappetising lake to retrieve his novel, he realises the extent of her feelings for him, and gradually becomes less self-deprecating and more assertive.

Jamie and Colin both travel in order to find meaningful love or ecstatic pleasure, evincing a flexibility of movement, and a desire for integration with European and American citizens, which is presented as laudable and worthy. Equally, however, in its depiction of the unlikely partnership formed between Grant's Prime Minister and Wandsworth woman Natalie, the film also suggests that in this increasingly global age, love, like charity, may still sometimes begin at home.

Conclusion

I have sought to illustrate in this chapter that there are important and idiosyncratic traditions of romantic comedy existing within British film culture, traditions that have been considerably developed by Richard Curtis and other practitioners in a series of films produced during the 1990s and beyond. The thematic concerns of many of the 1990s British-made romantic comedies remain somewhat universal in that they often

revolve around concepts of chance, accident and the difficulties characters experience in fathoming their true desires. But wider, more socially
oriented issues ('the doubling of the divorce rate ... the rise of the
single parent ... gay rights movements'[96]) are still referenced, and are
important in certain cases to the overall impressions generated by the
narratives.

Patterns of continuity and advancement are always difficult to recognise and achieve in the context of British film production, partly because
of the lack of structure and central planning in the industry (the achievements of Working Title and Richard Curtis have been quite notable in
this respect), but certain narrative features and character traits can be
identified which link past and more recent films within the particular
generic category of romantic comedy.

The 'no-holds-barred' verbal exchanges of characters in *Pygmalion*
find an echo in the harsh words and views expressed in *Beautiful Thing*.
Both *Rich and Strange* and *A Letter to Brezhnev* suggest that Britain, in
particular periods of its social history, may not constitute an especially
propitious setting for fulfilling romances to flourish, leading to situations
where characters look abroad for true love and real passion (a process
continued on a grander scale, and in a more obviously comic manner in
Four Weddings, *Notting Hill* and *Love Actually*).

A series of films (often coming to symbolise the hopes and anxieties of
a particular decade in British society) sought to derive both humour and
drama out of the romantic and unromantic aspects of 1930s Britain, the
'swinging sixties', 'Thatcher's Britain' of the 1980s, and during the
1990s decade when Britain was governed by John Major from 1990 to
1997, and by Tony Blair from 1997 onwards. The popularity of *Sliding
Doors*, *Four Weddings and a Funeral* and *Notting Hill*, amongst other
films produced during the 1990s, and the continuing critical interest
created by many of the earlier films discussed, testifies that this is a
thematically rich and important aspect of British film culture.

True love, the films imply, may be both a comic and potentially tragic
business (the object of one's affection may leave, die, or fall in love with
someone else), but in the British films discussed in this chapter the
attempt to seek sensual pleasure, and empathetic states with other characters, will always be applauded, even if the narratives themselves reveal
that such aims are not necessarily easily achieved or maintained.

Notes

1 *Four Weddings and a Funeral* (Mike Newell, 1994).
2 See the section entitled 'Third Essay. Archetypal criticism: Theory of Myths'

in Northrop Frye, *Anatomy of Criticism: Four Essays* (Princeton University Press, Princeton, 1973: first published in 1957), pp. 163–223.

3 *Ibid.*, p. 170.

4 Patrick Murray, *Literary Criticism: A Glossary of Major Terms* (Longman, London, 1978), p. 26.

5 Kathleen Rowe, *The Unruly Woman: Gender and the Genres of Laughter* (University of Texas Press, Austin, 1995), p. 102.

6 *Ibid.*, p. 212.

7 *Ibid.*, p. 103.

8 Bruce Babington and Peter William Evans, *Affairs to Remember: The Hollywood Comedy of the Sexes* (Manchester University Press, Manchester, 1989), p. 18.

9 Wes. D. Gehring, 'Screwball Comedy: An Overview', *Journal of Popular Film & Television*, 13:4 (winter 1986), p. 5.

10 Stanley Cavell, *Pursuits of Happiness: The Hollywood Comedy of Remarriage* (Harvard University Press, Cambridge MA and London, 1981), p. 2.

11 *Ibid.*, p. 88.

12 Stanley Cavell, *Contesting Tears: the Hollywood Melodrama of the Unknown Woman* (University of Chicago Press, Chicago and London, 1989), pp. 116–17.

13 Brian Henderson, 'Romantic Comedy Today: Semi-Tough or Impossible?' (1978), reprinted in *Film Genre Reader*, edited by Barry Keith Grant (University of Texas Press, Austin, 1986): 'The effective prohibitions of romantic comedy are prohibitions within language … speaking the question "Why haven't we ever fucked?" [is] destructive of romantic comedy' (p. 327). *Four Weddings*, as noted, is also concerned with finding an appropriate language for love, and Charles' tentative and fumbling attempts to express his feelings are eventually recognised by Carrie as sincere and worthy, despite their fundamental inarticulateness.

14 Steve Neale, 'The Big Romance or Something Wild? Romantic Comedy Today', *Screen*, 33:3 (autumn 1992), p. 284.

15 Anne Billson's summary of the plot of *Four Weddings and a Funeral* in her review of the film in the *Sunday Telegraph* (15 May 1994).

16 Robert Murphy, 'Citylife: Urban Fairy-tales in Late 90s British Cinema', in *The British Cinema Book* (second edition), edited by Robert Murphy (British Film Institute, London, 2001).

17 *Ibid.*, p. 297.

18 Vladimir Propp, *Morphology of the Folktale*, translated by Laurence Scott (second edition, revised and edited by Louis A. Wagner, University of Texas Press, Austin and London, 1968).

19 Thomas E. Wartenberg, *Unlikely Couples: Movie Romance as Social Criticism* (Westview Press, Oxford, 1999), p. 7.

20 *Ibid.*

21 *The Importance of Being Earnest*, Oscar Wilde (1895), Act II, Scene I (filmed by Anthony Asquith, 1953).

22 Robin Wood, in *Hitchcock's Films Revisited* (Columbia University Press, New York, 1989), claims that Hitchcock used the espionage plot in *The 39 Steps* as 'a cover for the film's real concerns with gender and sexuality' (p. 275), classifying the narrative as a 'double chase' story 'combined with romantic love story' (p. 283).

23 David Sutton, *A Chorus of Raspberries: British Film Comedy 1929–1939* (University of Exeter Press, Devon, 2000), p. 208.

24 Graham Greene in a favourable review of *The Ghost Goes West* (*Spectator*, 27 December 1935) described the film as 'a humorous fantasy' in which the 'only opportunities for satire are at the expense of rich and tasteless Americans'. (The review is reprinted in Graham Greene, *The Pleasure-Dome: The Collected Film Criticism 1935–40*, edited by John Russell Taylor, Secker & Warburg, London, 1972, pp. 40–1.)

25 Wartenberg, *Unlikely Couples*, pp. 41–2.

26 *Ibid.*, pp. 42–3.

27 Campbell Dixon, review of *The Demi-Paradise*, *Daily Telegraph* (22 November 1943).

28 William Whitebait in a review of *Brief Encounter* in the *New Statesman and Nation*, 30:771 (1 December 1945), summed up the film as a 'Humdrum little romance' in which 'every moment is made alive and pathetically touching' (p. 369).

29 Brian Spittles, *Britain Since 1960: An Introduction* (Macmillan, London, 1995), and Arthur Marwick, *A History of the Modern British Isles 1914–1999, Circumstances, Events and Outcomes* (Blackwell, Oxford, 2000), provide informative and illuminating accounts of British post-war political life.

30 Christine Geraghty in *British Cinema in the Fifties: Gender, Genre and the 'New Look'* (Routledge, London, 2000) interprets the ending of Genevieve as not presenting 'the men and women moving equally towards each other, as the romantic comedy model suggests', but rather depicting the women moving into a 'more sympathetic position with their men' (p. 164).

31 Dates taken from William Tydeman (ed.), *Wilde: Comedies: A Casebook* (Macmillan, London, 1982), pp. 16–17.

32 C.A. Lejune, review of *The Prince and the Showgirl*, *Observer* (30 June 1957).

33 Unnamed author, review of *The Prince and the Showgirl*, *Daily Worker* (29 June 1957).

34 Alexander Walker, review of *Indiscreet*, *Birmingham Post* (5 January 1958), reprinted in Alexander Walker, *Double Takes: Notes and Afterthoughts on the Movies 1956–76* (Elm Tree Books, Hamish Hamilton, London, 1977), p. 14.

35 *Ibid.*

36 Kingsley Amis quoted in Roger Lewis, *The Life and Death of Peter Sellers* (Century, London, 1994), p. 544.

37 Elaine Paterson, review of *Rita, Sue and Bob Too* in the *Time Out Film*

Guide (seventh edition, edited by John Pym, Penguin Books, Harmondsworth, 1999).

38 Dilys Powell, review of *Sid and Nancy*, *Punch* (30 July 1986), p. 49.

39 Stanley Cavell, *Pursuits of Happiness*, p. 83.

40 Harriet Waugh, review of *Close My Eyes*, *Spectator* (7 September 1991), p. 37.

41 Nigel Andrews, review of *Damage*, *Financial Times* (4 February 1993).

42 *Ibid.*

43 *Truly, Madly, Deeply* and *Close My Eyes* were amongst the first post-Thatcher films, following her resignation as Prime Minister in November 1990. The basis of Nina's lament about the unattractive qualities of British cultural attitudes in the early 1990s is echoed by Andrea Stuart in an essay, 'Original Sins', published in *Marxism Today* (January 1991), which suggests that 'In the 90s, collective action' had been 'replaced by individual salvation' (p. 49).

44 The quotation alluded to in *Truly, Madly, Deeply* is from the New Testament, Romans 6: 8: 'Christ being raised from the dead dieth no more; Death hath no more dominion over him'.

45 Mark Shivas, 'Little Big Screen' in *Cinema: the Beginnings and the Future*, edited by Christopher Williams (University of Westminster Press, London, 1996), pp. 184–9.

46 *Ibid.*

47 Adam Mars-Jones, film review of *Soft Top Hard Shoulder*, *Independent* (1 January 1993).

48 Mark Steyn, review of *Sliding Doors*, *Spectator* (2 May 1998), p. 44.

49 Gilbert Adair, *Love and Death on Long Island* (Minerva Press, London, 1992: first published in 1990), p. 134.

50 Mark Steyn, review of *Notting Hill*, 'Follies of Fantasy', *Spectator* (29 May 1999).

51 Nick Roddick, 'Four Weddings and a Final Reckoning', *Sight and Sound*, 5:1 (January 1995) p. 13.

52 Michael Grade quoted in David Lister, 'C4 "taken to the cleaners" over cash for film', the *Independent* (20 January 1995), p. 5. Grade suggests in the article that 'A £4m return on a £400,000 investment is a nice little earner for anybody'.

53 Labour MP Joe Ashton, quoted in Lister, 'C4 "taken to the cleaners"'.

54 Michael Kuhn, president of PolyGram Filmed Entertainment, quoted by Mike Ellison in 'Four Weddings – and a bust-up' in the *Guardian* (23 May 1994), p. 4. This article claims that PolyGram contributed 90 per cent of the budget for the film.

55 Gerald Kaufman, 'Four Weddings and an Oscar? Let's hope not', *Evening Standard* (27 March 1995), p. 6.

56 Paul Dave, 'The Bourgeois Paradigm and Heritage Cinema', *New Left Review*, 224 (July/August 1997), p. 125.

57 See 'Richard Curtis: A Slow-motion Career', interview in *Now That's*

Funny! Conversations with Comedy Writers, by David Bradbury and Joe McGrath (Methuen, London, 1998), p. 100.

58 Kaufman, 'Four Weddings and an Oscar', p. 6.

59 Tony Parsons in an article in the *Daily Mirror* (21 July 2003) entitled 'Men can't handle a worldly woman', claims that the scene 'where Andie MacDowell tells Hugh Grant about her sexual history' is the 'most unrealistic scene in cinema history', because of the way Grant's character responds so passively to the revelations. Parsons argues that women spectators as a result 'loved' the film because 'it pretended that men find the sexual history of their partners full of charm and wonder'.

60 Philip French, review of *Four Weddings and a Funeral*, *Observer* (15 May 1994).

61 Anne Billson, review of *Four Weddings and a Funeral*, *Sunday Telegraph* (15 May 1994).

62 Paul Dave ('The Bourgeois Paradigm') notes that the 'actual location' of the funeral scenes was Deptford in London, but argues that the iconographic features 'mark them as belonging to the discursive construct of 'Northernness' (p. 120).

63 Richard Curtis interviewed in *Story and Character: Interviews with British Screenwriters*, edited by Alistair Owen (Bloomsbury, London, 2003), p. 80.

64 'Stop all the clocks, Cut off the telephone', Poem XXXIV (April 1936), *The English Auden: Poems, Essays and Dramatic Writings 1927–1939* edited by Edward Mendelson (Faber & Faber, London, 1977), p. 163. Joseph Warren Beach in *The Making of the Auden Canon* (University of Minnesota Press, Minneapolis, 1957) describes the poem (also know as 'Funeral Blues') as a 'lively composition in a vein appealing to world-weary modern readers as well as sophisticated nightclub audiences' (p. 184). The use of Auden in the funeral sequence cleverly evokes Auden's ambivalent position in British literary culture, with regard to his leaving Britain for America in 1939. Humphrey Carpenter in *W.H. Auden: A Biography* (George Allen & Unwin, London, 1981) records that Auden did return to Britain during the final period of his life, but was buried in Kirchstetten (Austria), following his death in 1973 (p. 451).

65 Henry James, 'The Art of Fiction' (1884), *Aspects of the Novel* (Harcourt Brace and World, New York, 1954), pp. 26–7.

66 Charlotte O'Sullivan, review of *Notting Hill*, *Sight and Sound*, 9:6 (June 1999), p. 50.

67 Prior to appearing in *Four Weddings*, Andie MacDowell had starred with Gerard Depardieu in *Green Card* (Peter Weir, 1990), a romantic comedy about an American woman and a French man set in New York. In 1989, she had played a woman troubled by modern sexual mores in *sex, lies and videotape* (Steven Soderbergh, 1989).

68 Information on *Notting Hill* taken from the *BFI Film and Television Handbook* (2000), p. 20, and the *BFI Film and Television Handbook* (2001), p. 41, edited by Eddie Dyja.

69 Duncan Kenworthy quoted on the official web site for the film: www.notting-hill.com.
70 Richard Brooks, 'Brit Cool Puts Hugh in the Picture', *Observer* (5 April 1998), p. 3.
71 www.labour.org.uk/historyoflabourparty provides details of the date of John Smith's death.
72 Michael Quinion in 'World Wide Words' claimed that the phrase 'Cool Britannia' 'started to appear in the British press near the end of 1996, shortly after *Newsweek* declared London to be the coolest city on the planet. Most people who live in that scruffy and under-governed metropolis didn't recognise this description . . . However, the press soon changed its mind and it has been taken up with enthusiasm' (www.worldwidewords .org/turnsofphrase/tp-cool.htm, accessed 25 February 2005).
73 Mark Leonard, *Britain™: Renewing our Identity* (Demos, London, 1997), p. 72.
74 Age of William (35) taken from the screenplay by Richard Curtis at http://home.online.no/~bhundlan/scripts/Nottinghill.htm (accessed 25 February 2005).
75 Anne Billson, review of *Notting Hill*, *Sunday Telegraph* (23 May 1999).
76 'Woody Anna' term used in the screenplay of *Notting Hill*.
77 Frye, *Anatomy of Criticism: Four Essays*, pp. 163–223.
78 The 'Blockbuster' joke in *Notting Hill* hints at the increased importance of video and DVD transactions by the close of the 1990s. According to the (2001) *BFI Film and Television Handbook*, edited by Eddie Dyja, *Notting Hill* was the fifteenth most popular rental video in Britain during 1999, and the seventh most popular retail DVD (pp. 48–9).
79 Andrew Anthony in the *Observer*, Screen section (4 April 1999), describes the concluding images of *Notting Hill* as 'insufferable' (p. 7).
80 Richard Dyer, *Stars* (British Film Institute, London, 1979), pp. 181–3.
81 Richard Dyer, *Heavenly Bodies: Film Stars and Society* (British Film Institute/Macmillan, London, 1987), p. 15.
82 *Ibid.*, p. 29.
83 Geoffrey Nowell-Smith, 'But do we need it?' in *British Cinema Now*, edited by Martyn Auty and Nick Roddick (British Film Institute, London, 1985), p. 152.
84 Staff and agencies, 'British film industry celebrates record year', *Guardian* (21 July 2004): http://film.guardian.co.uk/news/story/0,,1265910,00.htm1 (accessed 25 February 2005).
85 Tom Paulin, *Newsnight Review* (24 November 2003). Paulin was less enthusiastic about *Love Actually* by the end of the discussion, which ended with him complaining that the characters 'were all badly dressed and scruffy looking', and concluding that the film 'doesn't work really': http://news.bbc.co.uk/1/hi/programmes/newsnight/review/3234746.stm (accessed 25 February 2005).
86 *Ibid.*

87   Roger Scruton in *England: An Elegy* (Chatto and Windus, London, 2000)
     notes that these phrases used by John of Gaunt in the play *King Richard II*
     (1595) by William Shakespeare encompass references to both the 'Kings of
     England' and the 'common people' (p. 212). Grant's character, in contrast,
     refers only to celebrities in his idiosyncratic ode to Britain. Scruton claims
     that the 'English have the highest rate of divorce in Europe . . . are blatantly
     promiscuous and litter the country with their illegitimate . . . offspring' (p.
     246). *Love Actually* presents a different view of modern English courtship
     patterns.
88   Retail DVD edition of *Love Actually* released by Universal Studios, March,
     2004, featuring an audio commentary on the film by Richard Curtis, Hugh
     Grant, Thomas Sangster and Bill Nighy.
89   The *Independent on Sunday* (29 August 2004) in a front page article by
     Francis Elliot and Rupert Cornwell entitled 'Howard Fury over White
     House Ban' reported that the Conservative party leader had become 'the
     first Tory leader in modern times to have been denied a meeting with a
     Republican president', following his 'calls for Mr Blair to stand down over
     the Iraq war' and to adopt a more sceptical and less pliant attitude towards
     the President and his international policies. The scene of the (Conserva-
     tive?) British Prime minister in *Love Actually* confronting the President is
     clearly tapping into real-life concerns and issues (however seemingly
     unlikely or preposterous the narrative motivations for Grant's character's
     conduct might be).
90   Sigmund Freud, "'Civilised' Sexual Morality and Modern Nervous Illness"
     (1908) in the Pelican Freud Library Volume 12: *Civilisation, Society and
     Religion: Group Psychology, Civilisation and its Discontents and Other
     Works*, edited by Albert Dickson (Penguin, Harmondsworth, 1985), p. 50.
91   Jean Paul Sartre, *Being and Nothingness: An Essay on Phenomenological
     Ontology*, translated by Hazel Barnes (Methuen & Co, London, 1957: first
     published in 1943), p. 394.
92   John Bayley, *The Characters of Love: A Study in the Literature of Person-
     ality* (Constable Books, London, 1960), p. 273.
93   The political affiliations of David, the Prime Minister in *Love Actually*, are
     not identified, although the presence of a portrait of Margaret Thatcher in
     his study implies that he is a Conservative Prime Minister, who, in some
     kind of alternative universe, has replaced Tony Blair in office. Apart from
     his patriotic speech and scepticism about America, his character is rather
     apolitical, and more concerned with pursuing his own domestic policy (that
     is, pursuing Natalie to her home in Wandsworth) than running the country.
     The political background to the film is that in June 2001 Labour succeeded
     in winning the British General Election by a majority of 167 seats, and
     William Hague subsequently resigned as leader of the Conservative party.
     Michael Heseltine MP, speaking on the BBC news, criticised the Conserva-
     tive party for having presented to the electorate what he described as 'an
     image of a right-wing xenophobic party', and claimed that Mr Hague had

failed 'to take account of social changes such the rise of multi-culturalism, gay rights and increased breakdown of marriage'. Mr Heseltine also warned against a faction within the party, whom he felt were 'determined to move on to a "Europe out" basis': http://news.bbc.co.uk/vote2001/hi/english/newsid_1377000/1377309.stm (accessed 25 February 2005).

94   Sigmund Freud, 'Civilisation and its Discontents' (1930), in *Civilisation and its Discontents and Other Works*, p. 292.

95   W.H. Auden, 'The Entertainment of the Senses', in *Thank You Fog: Last Poems by W.H. Auden* (Faber & Faber, London, 1974), p. 49.

96   Brian Henderson, 'Romantic Comedy Today: Semi-Tough or Impossible?', *Film Genre Reader*, p. 327.

Conclusion

My study has examined the significant and innovative role played by three distinctive generic forms in British cinema during the decade of the 1990s. The films discussed, considered and explored such wide-ranging topics as the plight of men rendered redundant by the British economy, the contrasting emotional and intellectual values of first-, second- and third-generation immigrants to Britain, and the hopes and fears of associated individuals seeking love and personal fulfilment in their private lives.

In *The Fantastic: A Structural Approach to a Literary Genre*, Tzvetan Todorov points out that 'works need not coincide with categories', and that 'a work can . . . manifest more than one category, more than one genre'.[1] The three generic strands I have focused upon share a common interest in issues of identity, and a person's relationship to his or her family, place of residence and position in society, and are also linked by their shared tendency to seek out instances of humour, farce and irony in the various narrative scenarios as they unfold. Several of the key films analysed in the case studies possess a self-reflexive quality which enables characters within particular narratives to consider the consequences of their actions, and their options for the future.

Thus, the miners in *Brassed Off* consistently discuss the issues regarding their economic plight. In *East is East*, the authoritarian father and his disobedient children are engaged in an ongoing debate, which turns into an aggressive struggle about the criteria for determining how they should live their lives. Hugh Grant's characters in *Four Weddings, Notting Hill* and *Love Actually* constantly meditate on what they need to do in order to feel that their life is more complete and worthwhile (in each case, the answer lies in meeting, and then sustaining a relationship with, the right woman).

Humour is often forged out of dialectical situations in which there is a sender of a joke and a receiver, a teller of and target for the comedy, and subsequently, in the films above, the presence of a comic element within the narratives serves to animate the dramatic conflicts and ideological disagreements, enabling important concerns to be explored in a vivid and unpredictable process of cultural exchange and interaction. In such dramatic frameworks, comedy, like melodrama, becomes a means of bringing tensions and conflicts to the surface, enabling characters to stand up openly for the codes of conduct and values which are precious to them (as in *Brassed Off*, *My Son the Fanatic* and *East is East*).

The heightened characterisations common to both comic and melodramatic treatments of social and personal themes allow for the formation of characters such as Charles in *Four Weddings*, Anna in *Notting Hill*, Danny in *Brassed Off* and George in *East is East*, figures who, in the narrative landscape of their particular films, are both ordinary *and* extraordinary in certain vital respects. Spectators follow their 'final' positions within the respective narratives with interest because these characters come to symbolise much more than themselves as they become embroiled in larger-than-life situations in which issues of love, power, the relationship between the past and the present, and the universal and the everyday are imaginatively opened up and dramatised.

The stylistic elements of the films, at crucial moments within the narratives, offer subtle judgements on the behaviour and attitudes of individual characters. When the camera perceptibly moves towards the character of Danny in *Brassed Off*, as he eloquently points out to the band the importance of their honouring and continuing the efforts of their predecessors, an elegiac mood of sadness and respect is engendered, and we, as viewers, are brought emotionally nearer to an understanding of the kinds of cultural tradition which Danny personifies so concretely and vitally. Danny is at the emotional centre of both his family and the local community by the end of the film's story, even if other characters have not always appreciated his 'conduct'.

When, in a contrasting scene from *East is East*, the camera pulls away from witnessing George's hideous acts of domestic violence any further, the implication is that George has brought shame upon himself, and that it would be an imposition on his victims (and possibly too distressing for audiences) for the camera to linger any longer at the scene of the crime. George Khan in *East is East* is presented as both a conservative and somewhat revolutionary figure, a zealot-like character who is prepared to destroy his own home in order to build a newer, more spiritual base. It is important in the film, however, that George is not just an entirely comic or cruel figure, and the narrative as a whole does not suggest that he is a totally reprehensible character, or that his beliefs are completely misguided. He cannot be contained within the family, by the close, given his refusal to admit defeat or to moderate his demands, and yet it is not clear that he has anywhere else to go.

East is East and *Brassed Off* never fall into the trap of suggesting that anything or everything can be considered humorous if viewed from a certain perspective. Laughter does though (in many of the past and present films I have examined) often serve a purpose of puncturing pretensions on the part of characters who may have an inflated impression of themselves. George, for example, pumps up his precious barber's chair to create a sense of himself as an important and influential figure, but, by the end of the narrative, the 'resistance activities' of his recalcitrant family have humiliated him, and reduced the level of his status and position of authority.

A concern with language can also be seen as linking the various examples of communal, ethnic and romantic comedy-drama in 1990s British cinema. A particular dispute in *Brassed Off* centres upon the question of whether the character of Andy can be classified as a 'scab', or a 'stupid fucker'. Carrie in *Four Weddings* tells Charles she liked hearing him say what he said on the Embankment, even if she is not quite certain exactly what he said or implied, given the indirect nature of his discourse. *East is East* culminates with the two outsider figures of George and Earnest, man and boy, briefly managing to make contact with each other through a shared cultural greeting, at a time when communication appears to have broken down between all the other characters.

In *The Melodramatic Imagination: Balzac, Henry James, Melodrama, and the Mode of Excess*, Peter Brooks defines melodrama as a 'form for secularised times', and suggests that 'melodrama may be born of the very anxiety created by the guilt experienced when the allegiance and ordering that pertained to a sacred system of things no longer obtain'.[2] As noted, many of the 1990s narratives explore ethical and political questions in situations in which there are no easy answers to problems, or magical solutions close at hand.

In the communal cycle of films, as exemplified by *Brassed Off* and *The Full Monty*, a stable system of employment, and clear prospects for the future, no longer exist for the characters, and the communities of which they are a part. In the ethnic comedy-dramas, characters that are entirely sure about what is right and wrong are (in turn) contrasted with figures who are deeply confused about what to believe in any longer. In the romantic comedies, individuals are often torn between how to reconcile sexual desires (which may be in a permanent state of flux), with underlying urges to settle down and live a more orderly and family-based existence.

I have sought to demonstrate that important links can be made between films produced within very distinct periods of British film history, and that British cinema has often returned to concerns around issues of community, and cultural, sexual and national identity, and treated these subjects in imaginative and thoughtful ways.

The commercial success and critical interest generated by *Bhaji on the Beach* (1994), *Four Weddings and a Funeral* (1994) and *Brassed Off* (1996) may initially have been unexpected, but these films encouraged writers, directors and producers in Britain to continue and extend the stories, situations and themes of these films where possible. *Bhaji on the Beach* sought to expand the nature and depth of representations of Asian communities in British cinema, whilst *Four Weddings* reflected upon the position of marriage, and the role of romantic ritual in modern Western culture. *Brassed Off* drew attention to cinematically neglected areas of northern working-class culture and society, whilst paying homage to earlier traditions of British cinema.

It is too early to assess whether the generic forms initiated by these particular films will continue to play an important role in British film production and resonate with cinema audiences. It is in the nature of generic cycles that there will be periods of expansion and retrenchment, cinematic peaks and lows. Two post-1990s films, *Lucky Break* (Peter Cattaneo, 2001), a communal comedy, set in a men's prison, and featuring musical-comedy sequences, and *Crush* (John McKay, 2002), a romantic comedy-drama starring Andie MacDowell, both performed disappointingly at the UK box office, suggesting that the appeal for audiences of comedic narratives focusing on small, localised communities, and romantic comedies staring familiar American performers in British settings, was possibly waning.[3]

British films offering a comic-dramatic account of the emotional ebbs and flows of regional communities were less evident in recent British cinema, a development which in many ways was anticipated by the mood of resignation prevalent in *Brassed Off* (1996), and the 'for one night only' tone of *The Full Monty* (1997). *Purely Belter* (Mark Herman, 2000) did, however, return to the problems of economically depressed and socially troubled areas of the north, but concentrated on dramatising the effects of these harsh conditions on a second generation of unemployed males, rather than focusing on the lives of the communities as a whole. This tendency to privilege the formative experiences of young adults could also be discerned in three other comedy dramas released in 2002: *Bend It Like Beckham* (Gurinder Chadha), *Anita and Me* (Metin Huseyin) and *About a Boy* (Chris and Paul Weitz).

Gurinder Chadha and Meera Syal had done much to initiate the 1990s cycle of ethnic comedy-dramas with their work on *Bhaji on the Beach* (1994), and therefore it was fitting that the new century saw them produce belated follow-up films: *Bend It Like Beckham* (directed by Chadha) and *Anita and Me* (scripted by Syal). The near ten-year gap between their first and second British films tended to suggest, however, that the place of the ethnic comedy-drama within contemporary British film culture was by no means assured or secure, and that the genre was dependent on new writers and directors being allowed the opportunity to make films within this area, if it was to flourish and become a truly established feature of British film production and culture.

Chadha's *Bend It Like Beckham* was a determinedly populist narrative aimed at breaking out of the art-house circuit and appealing to a multiplex generation of cinema audiences. The director was quoted as saying that she was 'tired of issue films' that continually presented aspects of 'race and culture as a problem', and, therefore, she had set out to 'make a feel-good comedy'.[4] *Bhaji on the Beach* had initially opened on only five screens in Britain, while in April 2002 Gurinder Chadha was able to proudly announce in the *Eastern Eye* Asian newspaper that *Bend It Like Beckham* was the 'Number One film across the UK'.[5] Such an extension in exposure and interest was, she declared, an indication of how the United Kingdom had 'changed enormously' in the eight-year period separating the two films.[6]

Bend It Like Beckham does not seek to dramatise or make explicit the kind of social changes which Chadha may have perceived as taking place in British society between the years 1994 and 2002, but instead engages with the theme of young teenagers being allowed to follow their own instinctual urges, rather than having parental or communal aspirations foisted upon them (*East is East* and *Billy Elliot* also explore this subject). *Bhaji on the Beach* had sought to reveal the motivations and fears of characters through an ongoing series of dialogues between central figures, and (apart from the dream sequences) was filmed largely in the televisual style of a drama shot on film in the early 1990s.

Bend It Like Beckham, in contrast, contained a number of sequences shot in the style of a modern 'popular music' video, constructed out of fast and frequent editing, and regular changes of setting. This more recent film also seemed unabashed about working its way towards what might be interpreted as a 'Hollywood-type', life-affirming resolution (the two main characters are actually depicted leaving for America at the close).

The result was a fluently composed, accessible film, full of admiration for the 'impossible dreams' of its young characters. It could be argued that the lack of depth and range in some of the film's characterisations and dramatic situations (along with the accompanying restlessness of the film's editing style) were necessary features of a film about football aimed at an international audience.

Bend It Like Beckham can, in fact, be interestingly compared to *Mike Bassett England Manager* (Steve Barron, 2002), a comedy which parodies the provincial thinking and social inadequacies of English football and culture, as particularly personified by white managers and players. This film both laughs at – and despairs of – the dire state of the national game when placed in a wider context, and presents the fortunes of the England football team as a catalogue of failures, interspersed with moments of social disgrace.

Bend It Like Beckham, contrastingly, affirms the potential of the game to encourage sporting and cultural ambition across divides of race and gender, even if, like certain other British ethnic comedy-dramas from the 1990s, a dream of leaving Britain and making a fresh start in a new country is nurtured. The film confidently parallels the aspirations of its British-Asian heroine with the achievements of a white, English footballing hero, suggesting that Britain can now, perhaps, be perceived as a more integrated and unified community in the form of an 'extended family'. Ironically, in view of these symbolic connotations, the two female football fanatics (as noted) head for America at the close, and Beckham, himself, left Britain for Real Madrid to pursue his own 'footballing dreams' in the summer of 2003.

In both *Bend It Like Beckham* and *Anita and Me* (Meera Syal's adaptation of her novel about an Asian girl growing up in the Midlands during the 1970s), a racist remark or action by one of the (female) characters is not presented as funny, or as an example of comic banter which need not be taken too seriously. Racist observations in these two films result in the flow of the narrative being interrupted, and the victims of the remarks feeling saddened and hurt.

The racist epithets of *Love Thy Neighbour* may appear less frequently in 1990s (and subsequent) ethnic comedy-dramas, but when such moments do occur in a modern context the narrative tends to be temporarily suspended in order to highlight the heinous nature of the racist behaviour and attitudes, whereas in *Till Death Us Do Part* and *Love Thy Neighbour* such language was part of the discourse of the narratives, and central to the entertainment experience which they offered. In *Bend It Like Beckham* and *Anita and Me*, racist remarks are met with the narratives themselves entering a 'time-out' situation where audiences are given a moment to register and recognise the pain caused by such outbursts.

Hugh Grant and Colin Firth continued to be important figures in the genre of British romantic comedies aimed at international audiences. Firth appeared in a remake of *The Importance of Being Earnest* (Oliver Parker, 2002), and a curious, but enjoyably low-key comedy set in Vermont, *Hope Springs* (Mark Herman, 2003), in which he plays an artist forced to choose between his former British love (Minnie Driver), or his new-found American girlfriend (Heather Graham). It was interesting that director Herman had now moved from the British concerns of *Brassed Off* to make a romantically comic film (particularly one set in America), and that the film, itself, should be so preoccupied with the ultimate need for Firth's character to choose the American woman as his romantic partner over her British rival.

Hugh Grant and Colin Firth appeared as rivals for the eponymous Bridget (Renée Zellweger) in *Bridget Jones' Diary* (Sharon McGuire, 2001), implying that her character was mistaken in imagining that she was unattractive, or destined to be unloved. Grant played a publisher with a great deal of energy and drive, who was also a confident seducer of women (the antithesis of his Charles, William and David roles).

His role in *About a Boy* (Chris and Paul Weitz, 2002), however, drew upon some of the incipient melancholy and resignation of his character in these defining parts, casting him as Will, a 'blank' featureless thirty-something male, whose life consists of voluntary unemployment, and 'units of time' spent shopping, listening to music, and watching *Countdown*, the afternoon television quiz programme on Channel 4 (in *The Full Monty*, the male characters long for something to do to erase the boredom caused by unemployment).

In *About a Boy*, as the title suggests, the deepest and most important relationship is not between Grant's character and his various girlfriends, but between Will and a boy, Marcus (Nicholas Hoult), whom he accidentally befriends, suggesting an attempt by the American filmmakers (the Weitz brothers) to broaden the scope of the contemporary British romantic comedy genre. In keeping with this implicit intention, the final images of *About a Boy* concentrate not on the formation of a romantic couple (although liaisons have been established), but depict a kind of extended family, or loosely constructed mini-community, celebrating Christmas together.

About a Boy concludes with a close-up, freeze-framed shot of Marcus over a voice-over commentary in which he pointedly states his belief that couples are not necessarily the answer to everything: 'You need more than that, you need back-up', he explains. This observation emerges

from his own experience of family break-ups, but may also be inter
preted as an indication that, in this latter-day example of British romantic comedy, the genre can be read as implicitly drawing upon some of
the social dimensions and emphasis on common values promoted in the
communal comedy films discussed earlier, whose own post-1990s future
in British film production schedules was open to question.

In January 2000, a new organisation known as the UK Film Council
was introduced by the Labour government with a mandate to promote
'film activity in the nations and regions', support 'innovative filmmaking' and encourage 'cultural diversity and social inclusiveness'.[7] The
Chief Executive of the council, John Woodward, stated that he did not
believe the British film industry in 2001 possessed the 'resources or the
scale to compete' with American cinema, and in support of that viewpoint, he perceived the history of British cinema as being 'about offering
an alternative to Hollywood'.[8]

The Film Council appeared more significant in its role of helping to
determine the future of British cinema than might otherwise have been
the case during this period, following the announcement that Film Four
would begin downscaling its film production activities from July 2000
onwards.[9] Film Four's revised intention was that a less ambitious and
extensive strategy of investment in British and world cinema would be
pursued, with the film-production section of the company being placed
under the auspices of the Channel 4 drama department.[10]

Film Four had played an important role in facilitating the making of
Four Weddings and a Funeral, *Brassed Off* and *East is East*. The com-
pany's announcement of their more modest cinematic ambitions in future
British filmmaking coincided with its involvement in the production of
Birthday Girl (Jez Butterworth, 2002), an audacious transnational roman-
tic comedy-thriller, which begins as a low-key, 'unlikely couple' comedy
about loneliness and emotional states of exile as experienced by an
English bank clerk, John (Ben Chaplin), and his Russian mail-order bride,
Nadia (Nicole Kidman), but ends with acts of violent betrayal taking
place, within the context of an unstable and threatening world landscape.

In the video he produces for a dating agency, John hopes for a girl who
is 'intelligent, kind, pretty', and lists among his interests, 'running, reading' and watching 'films – if they're any good'. Into his dull suburban
life, comes an attractive but troubled and duplicitous Russian woman
(played by a major Hollywood star). Nadia, it transpires, exploits her
sexual appeal to men desperate for female companionship, in order to
blackmail and rob them of their possessions and money.

Birthday Girl moves between scenes of wry social observation (John
attempts to have Nadia sent back to Russia when he learns that she

doesn't speak English; Nadia responds by revealing that she has discovered the bondage videos and magazines in John's bedroom, suggesting that he contains another side to his clean-living bank-clerk persona), which eventually spiral into a vicious fight for survival between the characters of John, Nadia and her accomplices.

John's life in Britain appears so predictable and ordinary, however, that a new and uncertain life with Nadia in Russia appears preferable to his likely future in the United Kingdom. In an updating of *The 39 Steps* (Alfred Hitchcock, 1935), Nadia and John become emotionally closer as they seek to survive hostile situations in which John becomes 'a fugitive from justice', and no one (including Nadia) can be trusted. There is no equivalent of the Mr Memory character in Hitchcock's film to offer them a code denoting the possibility of salvation and rescue. The final shot of the couple, as John leaves for Russia on a false passport with Nadia, is modestly optimistic, which the film implies is the most that can be hoped for in the case of such an 'unlikely couple' existing within a climate of increasing international tensions and conflicts.

Birthday Girl illustrated that Film Four was still capable of being connected with imaginative and unpredictable films, and that British cinema continued to offer challenging parts to actresses who had become famous through appearing in Hollywood films. *Birthday Girl*, in many respects, was continuing the tradition of rousing and provocative filmmaking promoted by films such as *Brassed Off* (1996), *East is East* (1999) and *Beautiful Thing* (1996), none of which had shied away from engaging with what one might term the comedy of cruelty, hardship and outrage.

During the period 1990 to 2003, the generically flexible and robust narrative forms of communal comedy, ethnic comedy-drama and romantic comedy had all aimed at revivifying and regenerating contemporary British film culture, whilst drawing creative inspiration from previous traditions of British cinema.

When Tom (James Fleet) is asked how his best man's speech is coming along in *Four Weddings and a Funeral*, he replies that he anticipates it will result in 'tears and laughter', thus, providing 'something for everyone'. It succeeds in these intentions, but not in quite the ways he had imagined, the humour proving too harsh and outspoken for some members of the audience, and too near the truth for others. The speech, with its reference to the bridegroom's ex-girlfriends as 'complete dogs', whom he nonetheless welcomes 'here this evening', causes both comic pleasure for the *Four Weddings* circle of friends, and discomfort for the bridegroom and his father. As a symbol for much of the work undertaken by the films I have examined, this incident can stand as a worthy and fitting monument.

In *Brief Encounter* (1945), Laura recalls her spirit being uplifted by
the barrel organ playing 'Let The Great Big World Keep Turning' on the
street corner. In *Human All Too Human: A Book for Free Spirits* (1878),
Friedrich Nietzsche defined the 'comic' as occupying a momentary transition in human perception from a state of 'fear' to one of 'short-lived
exuberance', and concluded that, on balance, there was more of the
'comic than of the tragic in the world'.[11]

One of the achievements of the British comedy-dramas discussed in
this book is that while they reveal an awareness of tragic elements in
British and Western culture they also seek to celebrate the continuing
existence of the 'comic', with its attendant qualities of spirit, resilience
and a belief that mankind will persevere and carry on until the very end.
It is to be hoped that this rich tradition in British film culture will continue and prosper in future decades.

Notes

1 Tzvetan Todorov, *The Fantastic: A Structural Approach to a Literary
   Genre*, translated by Richard Howard (Cornell University Press, Ithaca NY,
   1975), p. 22.

2 Peter Brooks, *The Melodramatic Imagination: Balzac, Henry James, Melodrama, and the Mode of Excess* (Columbia University Press, New York,
   1984), p. 200.

3 Alexander Walker, reviewing *Crush* in the *Evening Standard* (6 June 2002),
   wondered 'How does Film Four allow [such a film] to reach production,
   never mind exhibition?' Walker concluded that 'A shake-up there is long
   overdue'.

4 Gurinder Chadha quoted in the *Asian Age* article by Rithika Siddhartha
   (18 April 2002), p. 20.

5 Article by Chadha in the *Eastern Eye* (19 April 2002), p. 6.

6 *Ibid.*

7 Film Council objectives as stated in the *Annual Film Council Review*
   2001/2002, p. 9.

8 John Woodward quoted in an article, 'In Bed with the Film Council', *Sight
   and Sound*, 11:1 (January 2001), p. 16.

9 Geoffrey Macnab in an essay 'That Shrinking Feeling' in *Sight and Sound*,
   12:10 (October 2002), reported that 'Film Four had enjoyed no substantial
   hit since *East is East* in 1999' (pp. 18–20).

10 Adam Minns writing in *Screen International* (14–20 June 2002) stated that
   executives were considering 'folding Paul Webster's loss-making film operation back into the main channel', and returning Film Four back to its
   1980s 'remit' (pp. 11–4). Referring to the changed conditions of British film
   production in 2003, Peter Bradshaw concluded his review of *Love Actually*
   in the *Guardian* (21 November 2003) by claiming that 'The career of this

uniquely clever and talented man [Richard Curtis] is practically all that we have left from the 1990s wave of hope for a native film-industry to rival Hollywood'. Bradshaw felt, however, that *Love Actually* represented the culmination of a style of filmmaking, rather than a new beginning: 'this kind of comedy has just hit the wall'.

11 Friedrich Nietzsche, *Human All Too Human: A Book for Free Spirits*, translated by Marion Faber with Stephen Lehmann (University of Nebraska Press, Lincoln and London, 1984), Aphorism no.169, p. 115 (first published in Germany, 1878).

Filmography

Case study films in chronological order

Four Weddings and a Funeral (1994), certificate 15, 117 minutes, distributed by Rank, PolyGram Filmed Entertainment/Channel 4 Films/a Working Title production, directed by Mike Newell, screenplay by Richard Curtis. Cast: Hugh Grant (Charles), Andie MacDowell (Carrie), Kristin Scott Thomas (Fiona), James Fleet (Tom), Simon Callow (Gareth), John Hannah (Matthew), Corin Redgrave (Hamish), David Bower (David).

Brassed Off (1996), certificate 15, 107 minutes, distributed by Film Four, produced by Channel 4 Television Corporation/Miramax Film Corporation/Prominent Features Ltd, written and directed by Mark Herman. Cast: Pete Postlethwaite (Danny), Tara Fitzgerald (Gloria), Ewan McGregor (Andy), Jim Carter (Harry), Philip Jackson (Jim), Peter Martin (Ernie), Stephen Moore (Mackenzie).

The Full Monty (1997), certificate 15, 91 minutes, distributed by Twentieth Century Fox, Twentieth Century Fox Searchlight, a Redwave Films production, developed by Channel 4 Television Corporation, screenplay by Simon Beaufoy, directed by Peter Cattaneo. Cast: Robert Carlyle (Gaz), Tom Wilkinson (Gerald), Mark Addy (Dave), Emily Woof (Mandy), Steve Huison (Lomper), Hugo Speer (Guy), Bruce Jones (Reg).

East is East (1999), certificate 15, 96 minutes, distributed by Film Four, an Assassin Films production for Film Four in association with the BBC, directed by Damien O'Donnell, screenplay by Ayub Khan-Din. Cast: Om Puri (George Khan), Linda Bassett (Ella Khan), Jordan Routledge (Sajid), Archie Panjabi (Meenah), Chris Bisson (Saleem), Jimi Mistry (Tariq), Ian Aspinall (Nazir).

Notting Hill (1999), certificate 15, 123 minutes, distributed by Universal, PolyGram Filmed Entertainment in association with Working Title Films, directed by Roger Michell, screenplay by Richard Curtis. Cast: Julia Roberts (Anna), Hugh Grant (William), Hugh Bonneville (Bernie), Emma Chambers (Honey), Rhys Ifans (Spike), Gina McKee (Bella).

Love Actually (2003), certificate 15, distributed by Universal, DNA films in association with Studio Canal and Working Title, directed and written by Richard Curtis. Cast: Alan Rickman (Harry), Bill Nighy (Billy Mack), Colin Firth (Jamie), Emma Thompson (Karen), Hugh Grant (David, the Prime Minister), Laura Linney (Sarah), Liam Neeson (Daniel), Martine McCutcheon (Natalie), Andrew Lincoln (Mark), Heike Makatsch (Mia), Keira Knightly (Juliet), Kris Marshall (Colin Frissell), Lucia Moniz (Aurelia), Martin Freeman (John), Thomas Sangster (Sam), Joanna Page (Judy).

Selected filmography

About a Boy (Chris and Paul Weitz, 2002)
Accident (Joseph Losey, 1967)
Alf Garnett Saga, The (Bob Kellett, 1972)
Alfie (Lewis Gilbert, 1966)
Anita and Me (Metin Huseyin, 2002)
Ask a Policeman (Marcel Varnel, 1939)
Beautiful Thing (Hettie Macdonald, 1996)
Bend It Like Beckham (Gurinder Chadha, 2002)
Bhaji on the Beach (Gurinder Chadha, 1994)
Billy Elliot (Stephen Daldry, 2000)
Billy Liar (John Schlesinger, 1963)
Birthday Girl (Jez Butterworth, 2002)
Born Romantic (David Kane, 2002)
Bridget Jones' Diary (Sharon McGuire, 2001)
Brief Encounter (David Lean, 1945)
Brigadoon (Vincent Minnelli, 1954)
Bringing up Baby (Howard Hawks, 1938)
Carry on Sergeant (Gerald Thomas, 1958)
Close My Eyes (Stephen Poliakoff, 1991)
Come on George (Anthony Kimmins, 1939)
Confessions of a Window Cleaner (Val Guest, 1974)
Crush (John McKay, 2001)
Damage (Louis Malle, 1992)
Demi-Paradise, The (Anthony Asquith, 1943)
Distant Voices, Still Lives (Terence Davies, 1988)
Divorce of Lady X, The (Tim Whelan, 1937)
Educating Rita (Lewis Gilbert, 1983)
Englishman Who Went Up a Hill But Came Down a Mountain, The (Chris Monger, 1995)
Fatal Attraction (Adrian Lyne, 1987)
Fever Pitch (David Evans, 1997)
Flashdance (Adrian Lyne, 1983)
Genevieve (Henry Cornelius, 1953)
Ghost Goes West, The (Rene Clair, 1935)
Gregory's Girl (Bill Forsyth, 1980)

Gregory's Two Girls (Bill Forsyth, 1999)
Hindle Wakes (Victor Saville, 1931)
Hobson's Choice (David Lean, 1953)
I'm All Right Jack (John Boulting, 1959)
Importance of Being Earnest, The (Anthony Asquith, 1952)
Indiscreet (Stanley Donen, 1958)
In the Bleak Midwinter (Kenneth Branagh, 1995)
It Always Rains on Sunday (Robert Hamer, 1947)
Kind Hearts and Coronets (Robert Hamer, 1949)
Kind of Loving, A (John Schlesinger, 1962)
Lady Vanishes, The (Alfred Hitchcock, 1938)
Lavender Hill Mob, The (Charles Crichton, 1951)
Leon the Pig Farmer (Vadim Jean and Gary Sinyor, 1992)
Letter to Brezhnev, A (Chris Bernard, 1985)
Love and Death on Long Island (Richard Kwietniowski, 1998)
Love Thy Neighbour (John Robins, 1973)
Lucky Break (Peter Cattaneo, 2001)
Man in the White Suit, The (Alexander Mackendrick, 1951)
Martha: Meet Frank, Daniel and Laurence (Nick Hamm, 1998)
Matter of Life and Death, A (Michael Powell and Emeric Pressburger, 1946)
Mike Bassett England Manager (Steve Barron, 2002)
Millionairess, The (Anthony Asquith, 1960)
My Beautiful Laundrette (Stephen Frears, 1995)
My Name is Joe (Ken Loach, 1998)
My Son the Fanatic (Udayan Prasad, 1998)
Navigators, The (Ken Loach, 2001)
No Limit (Monty Banks, 1935)
Oh Mr Porter! (Marcel Varnel, 1939)
Only Two Can Play (Sidney Gilliat, 1962)
Orphans (Peter Mullan, 1999)
Passport to Pimlico (Henry Cornelius, 1949)
Poor Cow (Ken Loach, 1967)
Pretty Woman (Gary Marshall, 1989)
Prick Up Your Ears (Stephen Frears, 1987)
Prince and the Showgirl, The (Laurence Olivier, 1957)
Purely Belter (Mark Herman, 2000)
Pygmalion (Anthony Asquith and Leslie Howard, 1938)
Rachel Papers, The (Damian Harris, 1989)
Raining Stones (Ken Loach, 1993)
Rich and Strange (Alfred Hitchcock, 1931)
Riff-Raff (Ken Loach, 1991)
Rita, Sue and Bob Too (Alan Clarke, 1987)
Room at the Top (Jack Clayton, 1958)
Sammy and Rosie Get Laid (Stephen Frears, 1989)
Sapphire (Basil Dearden, 1959)

Secrets & Lies (Mike Leigh, 1996)
Shipyard Sally (Monty Banks, 1939)
Sid and Nancy (Alex Cox, 1986)
Sing As We Go (Basil Dean, 1934)
Sliding Doors (Peter Howitt, 1997)
Soft Top Hard Shoulder (Stefan Schwartz, 1992)
Straw Dogs (Sam Peckinpah, 1972)
Taste of Honey, A (Tony Richardson, 1961)
The 39 Steps (Alfred Hitchcock, 1935)
This Sporting Life (Lindsay Anderson, 1963)
This Year's Love (David Kane, 1999)
Till Death Us Do Part (Norman Cohen, 1969)
Titfield Thunderbolt, The (Charles Crichton, 1953)
Train of Events (Basil Dearden, Charles Crichton, Sidney Cole, 1949)
Truly, Madly, Deeply (Anthony Minghella, 1991)
Up 'n' Under (John Godber, 1998)
Waking Ned (Kirk Jones, 1999)
Whisky Galore (Alexander Mackendrick, 1949)
Wild West (David Attwood, 1992)

Bibliography

Books

Adair, Gilbert, *Love and Death on Long Island* (Minerva Press, London, 1992: first published in 1990).

Aldgate, Anthony and Jeffrey Richards, *Best of British: Cinema and Society from 1930 to the Present* (New Edition, I.B. Tauris, London and New York, 1999).

Altman, Rick, *Film/Genre* (BFI Publishing, London, 1999).

Alvarado, Manuel and John Thompson, *The Media Reader* (British Film Institute, London, 1990).

Anderson, Benedict, *Imagined Communities: Reflections on the Origin and Spread of Nationalism* (second edition, Verso, London, 1991: first published in 1979).

Anderson, Perry, *English Questions* (Verso, London, 1992).

Auden, W. H., *Thank You Fog: Last Poems* (Faber and Faber, London, 1974).

Auden, W. H., *The English Auden: Poems, Essays and Dramatic Writings 1927–1939* (edited by Edward Mendelson, Faber and Faber, London, 1977).

Auty, Martyn and Nick Roddick, *British Cinema Now* (BFI Publishing, London, 1985).

Babington, Bruce and Peter William Evans, *Affairs to Remember: The Hollywood Comedy of the Sexes* (Manchester University Press, Manchester, 1989).

Bakhtin, Mikhail, *The Dialogic Imagination: Four Essays*, edited by Michael Holquist, and translated by Caryl Emerson and Michael Holquist (University of Texas Press, Austin, 1981).

Barr, Charles, *Ealing Studios* (third edition, Cameron & Hollis, Moffat, 1998: first published in 1977).

Barthes, Roland, *A Lover's Discourse: Fragments* (translated by Richard Howard, Penguin Books, London, 1990: first published in France, 1977).

Beach, Joseph Warren, *The Making of the Auden Canon* (University of Minnesota Press, Minneapolis, 1957).

Bhabha, Homi K., *The Location of Culture* (Routledge, London, 1994).

Blanchard, Simon and David Morley, *What's This Channel Fo(u)r?: An Alternative Report* (Comedia Publishing Group, London, 1982).

Bordwell, David and Kristin Thompson, *Film History: An Introduction* (McGraw Hill, New York/London, 1994).

Bradbury, David and Joe McGrath, *Now That's Funny! Conversations with Comedy Writers* (Methuen, London, 1998).

Briggs, Adam and Paul Cobley, *The Media: An Introduction* (Longman, Harlow, 1998).

Brooks, Peter, *The Melodramatic Imagination: Balzac, Henry James, Melodrama and the Mode of Excess* (Columbia University Press, New York, 1984: first published in 1976).

Brown, Philip and Richard Sparks, *Beyond Thatcherism* (Open University Press, Milton Keynes/Philadelphia, 1989).

Carpenter, Humphrey, *W.H. Auden: A Biography* (George Allen & Unwin, London, 1981).

Catteral, Peter, *The Making of Channel Four* (Frank Cass Publishers, London/Portland, 1999).

Caughie, John, *Television Drama: Realism, Modernism and British Culture* (Oxford University Press, Oxford, 2000).

Cavell, Stanley, *Contesting Tears: The Hollywood Melodrama of the Unknown Woman* (University of Chicago Press, Chicago/London, 1989).

Cavell, Stanley, *Pursuits of Happiness: The Hollywood Comedy of Remarriage* (Harvard University Press, Cambridge MA and London, 2000: first published in 1981).

Collier Hillstrom, Laurie, *International Directory of Directors* (St James' Press, Detroit, 1997).

Critchley, Simon, *On Humour* (Routledge, London, 2002).

Curran, James and Vincent Porter, *British Cinema History* (Weidenfeld & Nicolson, London, 1983).

Daniels, Therese and Jane Gerson, *The Colour Black: Black Images in British Television* (BFI Publishing, London, 1989).

Davies, Christie, *Ethnic Humour Around the World: A Comparative Analysis* (Indiana University Press, Bloomington and Indianapolis, 1996: first published in 1990).

Dixon, Wheeler Winston (ed.), *Re-Viewing British Cinema 1900–1992* (State University of New York Press, New York, 1994).

Durgnat, Raymond, *A Mirror for England: British Movies from Austerity to Affluence* (Faber & Faber, London, 1970).

Dyer, Richard, *Stars* (British Film Institute, London, 1979).

Dyer, Richard, *Heavenly Bodies: Film Stars and Society* (British Film Institute/Macmillan, London, 1987).

Dyja, Eddie (ed.), *BFI Film and Television Handbook*(s) 1996–2003 (BFI Publishing, London).

Eliot, T.S., *A Choice of Kipling's Verse* (Faber & Faber, London, 1941).

English, James F., *Comic Transactions: Literature, Humour, and the Politics of Community in Twentieth Century Britain* (Cornell University Press, Ithaca NY and London, 1994).

Freud, Sigmund, *Jokes and Their Relationship to the Unconscious*, edited by

James Strachey and Angela Richards (Penguin Books, Harmondsworth, 1981: first published in 1905).

Friedman, Lester (ed.), *British Cinema and Thatcherism* (UCL Press Limited, London, 1993).

Frye, Northrop, *Anatomy of Criticism: Four Essays* (Princeton University Press, Princeton, 1973: first published in 1957).

Fuller, Graham (ed.), *Loach on Loach* (Faber & Faber, London, 1998).

Geraghty, Christine, *British Cinema in the Fifties: Gender, Genre and the 'New Look'* (Routledge, London, 2000).

Gilroy, Paul, *Between Camps: Race, Identity and Nationalism at the End of the Colour Line* (Allen Lane, the Penguin Press, London, 2000).

Godber, John, *Up 'n' Under* (Amber Lane Press, Oxford, 1985).

Green, Martin, *A Mirror for Anglo-Saxons* (Longmans, London, 1961: first published in 1957).

Greene, Graham, *The Pleasure-Dome: The Collected Film Criticism 1935–40*, edited by John Russell Taylor (Secker & Warburg, London, 1972).

Hayward, Susan, *Key Concepts in Cinema Studies* (Routledge, London, 1996).

Higson, Andrew, *Waving the Flag: Constructing a National Cinema in Britain* (Oxford University Press, Oxford, 1995).

Higson, Andrew, *Dissolving Views: Key Writings on British Cinema* (Cassell, London, 1996).

Hill, John, *Sex, Class and Realism: British Cinema 1956–1963* (BFI Publishing, London, 1986).

Hill, John, *British Cinema in the 1980s* (Clarendon Press, Oxford, 1999).

Hill, John and Pamela Church Gibson, *The Oxford Guide to Film Studies* (Oxford University Press, Oxford, 1998).

Hillier, Jim, *Cahiers du Cinema, Volume 1: The 1950s: Neo-realism, Hollywood, New Wave* (Routledge & Kegan Paul, in association with the British Film Institute, London, 1985).

Hobsbawm, Eric, *Age of Extremes: The Short Twentieth Century 1914–1991* (Michael Joseph, London, 1994).

Hunt, Leon, *British Low Culture: From Safari Suits to Sexploitation* (Routledge, London, 1998).

Inglis, Fred, *Raymond Williams* (Routledge, London, 1995).

Jacobson, Howard, *Seriously Funny: From the Ridiculous to the Sublime* (Viking, London, 1997).

James, Henry, *Aspects of the Novel* (Harcourt Brace and World, New York, 1954).

James, Henry, *The Art of the Novel: Critical Prefaces*, introduced by R.P. Blackmur (The Scribner Library, New York/London, 1962).

Jameson, Fredric, *The Political Unconscious: Narrative as a Socially Symbolic Act* (Methuen, London, 1983).

Kael, Pauline, *I Lost it at the Movies* (Jonathan Cape, London, 1966).

Karnick, Kristine Brunovska and Henry Jenkins (eds), *Classical Hollywood Comedy* (AFI Film Readers, Routledge, London, 1995).

Kerr, Walter, *Tragedy & Comedy* (Da Capo Press, New York, 1985: first published 1967).

Khan-Din, Ayub, *East is East* (Film Four Books/Macmillan Publishers, London, 1999).

King, Geoff, *Film Comedy* (Wallflower Press, London, 2002).

Kristeva, Julia, *Strangers to Ourselves*, translated by Leon. S. Roudiez (Columbia University Press, New York, 1991).

Kureishi, Hanif, *My Beautiful Laundrette and The Rainbow Sign* (Faber & Faber, London, 1986).

Landy, Marcia, *British Genres: Cinema and Society 1930–1960* (Princeton University Press, Princeton, 1991).

Leafe, David (ed.), *BFI Film and Television Handbook*(s) 1990–93 (BFI Publishing, London).

Leonard, Mark, *Britain*TM*: Renewing Our Identity* (Demos, London, 1997).

Lewis, Roger, *The Life and Death of Peter Sellers* (Century, London, 1994).

Lewisohn, Mark, *Radio Times Guide to TV Comedy* (second updated edition, BBC Books, London, 2003: first published in 1998).

Malik, Sarita, *Representing Black Britain: Black and Asian Images on Television* (Sage Publishers, London, 2002).

Mast, Gerald, *The Comic Mind: Comedy and the Movies* (second edition, University of Chicago Press, London, 1979: first published in 1973).

Marwick, Arthur, *A History of the Modern British Isles 1914–1999, Circumstances, Events and Outcomes* (Blackwell, Oxford, 2000).

Marx, Karl, *The Eighteenth Brumaire of Louis Bonaparte* (Progress Publishers, Moscow, 1967).

Monk, Claire and Amy Sargeant, *British Historical Cinema* (Routledge, London, 2002).

Moore-Gilbert, Bart (ed.), *The Arts in the 1970s: Cultural Closure* (Routledge, London, 1994).

Murphy, Robert, *Sixties British Cinema* (British Film Institute, London, 1992).

Murphy, Robert (ed.), *The British Cinema Book* (second revised edition, BFI Publishing, London, 2001: first published in 1997).

Murphy, Robert (ed.), *British Cinema of the 90s* (British Film Institute, London, 2000).

Murphy, Robert, *British Cinema and the Second World War* (Continuum, London, 2000).

Murray, Patrick, *Literary Criticism: A Glossary of Major Terms* (Longman, London, 1978).

Neale, Steve, *Genre* (British Film Institute, London, 1980).

Neale, Steve, *Genre and Hollywood* (Routledge, London/New York, 2000).

Neale, Steve (ed.), *Genre and Contemporary Hollywood* (BFI Publishing, London, 2002).

Neale, Steve and Frank Krutnick, *Popular Film and Television Comedy* (Routledge, London, 1990).

Nelmes, Jill (ed.), *An Introduction to Film Studies* (second edition, Routledge, London, 1999).

Nietzsche, Friedrich, *The Birth of Tragedy: Out of the Spirit of Music*, translated by Shaun Whiteside and edited by Michael Tanner (Penguin, London,

1993: first published in 1872)

Nietzsche, Friedrich, *Human All Too Human: A Book for Free Spirits*, translated by Marion Faber, with Stephen Lehmann (University of Nebraska Press edition, Lincoln and London, 1984: first published in Germany, 1878).

O'Farrell, John *Things Can Only Get Better: 18 Miserable Years in the Life of a Labour Supporter, 1979-1997* (Black Swan, London, 1998).

Owen, Alistair, *Story and Character: Interviews with British Screenwriters* (Bloomsbury, London, 2003).

Petrie, Duncan, *Creativity and Constraint in the British Film Industry* (Macmillan, London, 1991).

Pines, Jim (ed.), *Black and White in Colour: Black People in British Television Since 1936* (British Film Institute, London, 1992).

Powell, Enoch, *Still to Decide* (edited by John Wood, Elliot Right Way Books, Kingswood, Surrey, 1972).

Propp, Vladimir, *Morphology of the Folktale*, translated by Laurence Scott (second edition, revised and edited by Louis A. Wagner, University of Texas Press, Austin and London, 1968).

Pym, John, *Film on Four 1982/1991: A Survey* (BFI Publishing, London, 1992).

Pym, John, *Time Out Film Guide 1999 Seventh Edition* (Penguin Books, London, 1999).

Richards, Jeffrey, *Films and British National Identity: From Dickens to Dad's Army* (Manchester University Press, Manchester, 1997).

Rivkin, Julie and Michael Ryan, *Literary Theory: An Introduction* (Blackwell, Oxford, 1998).

Rowe, Kathleen, *The Unruly Woman: Gender and the Genres of Laughter* (University of Texas Press, Austin, 1995).

Rushdie, Salman, *Imaginary Homelands: Essays and Criticism 1981–1991* (Granta Books in association with Penguin, London, 1991).

Said, Edward, *Orientalism: Western Conceptions of the Orient* (second edition with new 'Afterword', Penguin, London, 1995: first published in 1978).

Sartre, Jean Paul, *Being and Nothingness: An Essay on Phenomenological Ontology*, translated by Hazel Barnes (Methuen & Co, London, 1957: first published in France, 1943).

Scruton, Roger, *England: An Elegy* (Chatto and Windus, London, 2000).

Sebock, Thomas and Erickson, Marcia (eds), *Carnival* (Mouton Publishers, Berlin, 1884).

Shaw, George Bernard, *Pygmalion: A Romance in Five Parts* (Penguin Books, London, 1953: first published in 1916).

Smith, Murray, *Engaging Characters: Fiction, Emotion and the Cinema* (Clarendon Press, Oxford, 1995).

Smith, Murray, *Trainspotting: BFI Modern Classics* (BFI Publishing, London, 2002).

Speight, Johnny, *If There Weren't Any Blacks You'd Have to Invent Them* (Oberon Books, London, 1998).

Spicer, Andrew, *Typical Men: The Representation of Masculinity in Popular British Cinema* (I.B. Tauris, London, 2001).

Spittles, Brian, *Britain Since 1960: An Introduction* (Macmillan, London, 1995).

Stam, Robert, *Film Theory: An Introduction* (Blackwell, Oxford, 2000).

Steiner, George, *The Death of Tragedy* (Faber & Faber, London, 1961).

Street, Sarah, *British National Cinema* (Routledge, London, 1997).

Street, Sarah, *Transatlantic Crossings: British Feature Films in the United States* (Continuum, London and New York, 2002).

Sutton, David, *A Chorus of Raspberries: British Film Comedy 1929–39* (Exeter University Press, Exeter, 2000).

Sypher, Wylie (ed.), *'Comedy: An Essay on Comedy' by George Meredith and 'Laughter' by Henri Bergson* (Johns Hopkins University Press, Baltimore/London, 1980: first published in 1956).

Thomas, Nick (ed.), *BFI Film and Television Handbook 1995* (BFI Publishing, London, 1995).

Thomson, David, *The New Biographical Dictionary of Film* (Little, Brown/Time Warner Books, London, 2002).

Todorov, Tzvetan, *The Fantastic: A Structural Approach to a Literary Genre*, translated by Richard Howard (Cornell University Press, Ithaca NY, 1975).

Tydeman, William (ed), *Wilde: Comedies: A Casebook* (Macmillan, London, 1982).

Wagg, Stephen (ed.), *Because I tell a Joke or Two: Comedy, Politics and Sexual Difference* (Routledge, London, 1998).

Walker, Alexander, *Double Takes: Notes and Afterthoughts on the Movies 1956–76* (Elm Tree Books, Hamish Hamilton, London, 1977).

Walker, Alexander, *Icons in the Fire: the Decline and Fall of Almost Everybody in the British Film Industry 1984–2000* (Orion, London, 2004).

Wambu, Onyekachi and Arnold, Kevin, *A Fuller Picture: The Commercial Impact of Six British films with Black Themes in the 1990s* (British Film Institute/*Black Film Bulletin*, London, 1999).

Wartenberg, Thomas, *Unlikely Couples: Movie Romance as Social Criticism* (Westview Press, Oxford, 1999).

Williams, Christopher (ed.), *Cinema: The Beginnings and the Future* (University of Westminster Press, London, 1996).

Williams, Raymond, *The Country and the City* (Chatto and Windus, London, 1973).

Williams, Raymond, *Resources of Hope: Culture, Democracy, Socialism*, edited by Robin Gable (Verso, London/New York, 1989).

Wolpert, Stanley, *A New History of India* (third edition, Oxford University Press, Oxford, 1989: first published in 1977).

Wood, Robin, *Hitchcock's Films Revisited* (Columbia University Press, New York, 1989).

Journal articles and chapters in collections

Barr, Charles, 'Opening up the Drama Archives', *The Listener*, 96:2484 (18 November 1976).

Barr, Charles, 'Projecting Britain and the British Character: Ealing Studios': Part 1, *Screen*, 15:1 (spring 1974); Part 2, *Screen*, 15:2 (summer 1974).

Christie, Ian, 'As Others See Us: British Film-making and Europe in the 90s' in *British Cinema of the 90s*, edited by Robert Murphy (British Film Institute, London, 2000).

Combs, Richard, 'New British Cinema: A Prospect and Six Views', *Film Comment*, 31:6 (November/December 1995).

Dacre, Richard, 'Traditions of British Comedy' in *The British Cinema Book* (second edition), edited by Robert Murphy (BFI Publishing, London, 2001).

Dave, Paul, 'The Bourgeois Paradigm and Heritage Cinema', *New Left Review*, 224 (July/August, 1997).

Dyer, Richard, 'Entertainment and Utopia', *Movie*, 24 (spring 1977).

Ellis, John, 'Made in Ealing', *Screen*, 16:1 (spring 1975).

Elsaesser, Thomas, 'Tales of Sound and Fury: Observations on the Family Melodrama' (1972) in *Movies and Methods Volume II*, edited by Bill Nichols (University of California Press, Berkeley, 1985).

Hall, Stuart, 'The Whites of their Eyes: Racist Ideologies and the Media' (1981) reprinted in *The Media Reader* edited by Manuel Alvarado and John. O. Thompson (BFI Publishing, London, 1990).

Hall, Stuart, 'Brave New World', *Marxism Today*, 32:10 (October 1988).

Henderson, Brian, 'Romantic Comedy Today: Semi-Tough or Impossible?' (1978) reprinted in *Film Genre Reader*, edited by Barry Keith Grant (University of Texas Press, Austin, 1986).

Higson, Andrew, 'National Identity and the Media' in *The Media: An Introduction*, edited by Adam Briggs and Paul Cobley (Longman, Harlow, 1998).

Higson, Andrew, 'A Diversity of Film Practices: Renewing British Cinema in the 1970s' in *The Arts in the 1970s: Cultural Closure?*, edited by Bart Moore-Gilbert (Routledge, London, 1994).

Hill, John, 'Failure and Utopianism: Representations of the Working Class in British Cinema of the 1990s' in *British Cinema of the 90s*, edited by Robert Murphy (British Film Institute, London, 2000).

Landy, Marcia, 'The Other Side of Paradise: British Cinema from an American Perspective' in *British Cinema, Past and Present*, edited by Andrew Higson and Justine Ashby (Routledge, London, 2000).

Malik, Sarita, 'Beyond "The Cinema of Duty"? The Pleasures of Hybridity: Black British Film of the 1980s and 1990s' in *Dissolving Views: Key Writings on British Cinema*, edited by Andrew Higson (Cassell, London, 1996).

Malik, Sarita, 'Money, Macpherson and Mind-set: The Competing Cultural and Commercial Demands on Black and Asian British Films in the 1990s' in the *Journal of Popular British Cinema*, number 5, 'New British Cinema', edited by Julian Petley and Duncan Petrie (Flicks Books, Trowbridge, 2002).

McFarlane, Brian, 'The More Things Change . . . British Cinema in the 90s' in

The British Cinema Book, edited by Robert Murphy (second edition, BFI Publishing, London, 2001).

Medhurst, Andy, 'Introduction to Laughing Matters: Situation Comedies' in *The Colour Black: Black Images in British Television*, edited by Therese Daniels and Jane Gerson (BFI Publishing, London, 1989).

Monk, Claire, 'Men in the 90s' in *British Cinema of the 90s*, edited by Robert Murphy (British Film Institute, London, 2000).

Monk, Claire, 'Underbelly UK: The 1990s Underclass Film, Masculinity and the Ideologies of 'New' Britain' in *British Cinema, Past and Present*, edited by Justine Ashby and Andrew Higson (Routledge, London, 2000).

Monk, Claire, 'Projecting a New Britain', *Cineaste*, 26:4 (2001).

Murphy, Robert, 'Citylife: Urban Fairytales in Late 90s British Cinema' in *The British Cinema Book*, edited by Robert Murphy (second edition, BFI Publishing, London, 2001).

Murphy, Robert, 'Another false dawn? The Film Consortium and the Franchise Scheme' in the *Journal of Popular British Cinema*, number 5, edited by Julian Petley and Duncan Petrie (Flicks Books, Trowbridge, 2002).

Neale, Steve, 'The Big Romance or Something Wild? Romantic Comedy Today', *Screen*, 33:3 (autumn 1992).

Nowell-Smith, Geoffrey, 'But do we need it?' in *British Cinema Now*, edited by Martin Auty and Nick Roddick (BFI Publishing, London, 1985).

Orwell, George, 'The Art of Donald McGill' (1941), in *Decline of the English Murder and Other Essays* (Penguin Books in association with Martin Secker & Warburg, Middlesex, 1980).

Porter, Laraine, 'Tarts, Tampons and Tyrants: Women and Representation in British Comedy', in *Because I tell a Joke or Two: Comedy, Politics and Sexual Difference*, edited by Stephen Wagg (Routledge, London/New York, 1998).

Porter, Vincent, 'Between Structure and History: Genre in Popular British Cinema' in the *Journal of Popular British Cinema*, number 1, 'Genre and British Cinema', edited by Alan Burton and Julian Petley (Flicks Books, Trowbridge, 1998).

Porter, Vincent, 'The Hegemonic Turn: Film Comedies in 1950s Britain' in the *Journal of Popular British Cinema*, number 4, 'British Film Culture and Criticism' (Flicks Books, Trowbridge, 2001).

Sawnhey, Cary Rajinder, 'Another Kind of British: An Exploration of British Asian Films', *Cineaste*, 26:4 (fall 2001).

Shivas, Mark, 'Little Big Screen' in *Cinema: The Beginnings and the Future* edited by Christopher Williams (University of Westminster Press, London, 1996).

Simpson, Philip, 'Directions to Ealing', *Screen Education*, 24 (autumn 1977).

Street, Sarah, 'Popular British Cinema?' in the *Journal of Popular British Cinema*, number 1, 'Genre and British Cinema', edited by Alan Burton and Julian Petley (Flicks Books, Trowbridge, 1998).

Sweeney, Gael, 'The Man in the Pink Shirt: Hugh Grant and the Dilemma of British Masculinity', *CineACTION*, 55 (22 March 2001).

Thomson, David, 'Listen to Britain', *Film Comment*, 22:2 (March/April, 1986).

Index

Page numbers in *italics* refer to illustrations.